The Films of Ingmar Bergman

The Films of Ingmar Bergman

Illusions of Light and Darkness

Laura Hubner
University of Winchester

First published 2007 by
PALGRAVE MACMILLAN
Houndmills, Basingstoke, Hampshire RG21 6XS and
175 Fifth Avenue, New York, N.Y. 10010
Companies and representatives throughout the world

PALGRAVE MACMILLAN is the global academic imprint of the Palgrave Macmillan division of St. Martin's Press, LLC and of Palgrave Macmillan Ltd. Macmillan® is a registered trademark in the United States, United Kingdom and other countries. Palgrave is a registered trademark in the European Union and other countries.

ISBN-13: 978-0-230-00724-6   hardback
ISBN-10: 0-230-00724-4   hardback

This book is printed on paper suitable for recycling and made from fully managed and sustained forest sources.

A catalogue record for this book is available from the British Library.

A catalogue record for this book is available from the Library of Congress.

10   9   8   7   6   5   4   3   2   1
16   15   14   13   12   11   10   09   08   07

Printed and bound in Great Britain by
Antony Rowe Ltd, Chippenham and Eastbourne

Contents

Acknowledgements

I would like to thank Jim Hillier, who taught me how to think about Bergman, and the Department of Film, Theatre and Television at the University of Reading for their help and support, especially Alison Butler, Lib Taylor and Douglas Pye. Thanks are also due to Charles Barr for his professional and constructive guidance.

I am also very grateful to my colleagues at the University of Winchester, in particular Inga Bryden, Leighton Grist, Shaun Kimber and Paul Manning for their valuable encouragement throughout the writing of this book. My thanks also go to Jesse Kalin for his insightful and detailed observations on the manuscript as well as to my editors at Palgrave, Jill Lake, Melanie Blair, and the staff of Macmillan India for their assistance over the course of writing this book. Thanks in addition to Maaret Koskinen and Erik Hedling for their helpful feedback on a draft proposal for this study.

I would also like to thank Owen Evans for his useful commentary on parts of this book, Philip Stokes for the discussions about Schopenhauer and truth, Derek Jones for supplying me with the documentaries, Jon Wengström at Svenska Filminstitutet, Edoff Lotta at Svensk Filmindustri and the staff at the British Film Institute archives. Last, and by no means least, I thank Paul Bavister for his priceless support, help, consideration and confidence.

1
Introduction

Illusion is a subject that permeates Ingmar Bergman's work, from his early films' preoccupations with art and life, through to his later films' deconstruction of truth and reality as fixities. The apex of the shift occurs during the 1950s and 1960s. At this time, fictional representation itself came under investigation in Bergman's films, resembling strikingly similar investigations elsewhere in European and North American cinema during the 1960s, where the infinite possibility of layers of illusion projecting illusion – often under the general heading of debates about reflexivity – intrigued directors and audiences. These preoccupations sparked off a greater fluidity in Bergman's films, marking the death of fixed notions of identity and existence and the evolution of a mergence between dream and reality, outer and inner, mask and person, suggesting a multiplicity of lives, selves and realities.

This study explores different kinds of 'illusion', at both thematic and formal levels, in films directed by Bergman, suggesting that there is a gradual shift from concentrating on dichotomies between falsity and truth to looking at life and film as a set of constructs. At a moment of crisis in Bergman's *The Hour of the Wolf* (1966) Johan Borg declares with a look of horror on his face, 'The glass is shattered, but what do the splinters reflect?'[1] The shattering of the illusion/reality dichotomy can be disturbing. I put to test the theory that *Fanny and Alexander* (1982) 'resolves' these disturbances by returning to them, exploring masquerade and multiplicity.

Central to this study is a close attention to film form and stylistic developments, as it posits the dual thesis that thematic substitutions of multiple truths and realities for truth are mirrored materially by stylistic and formal substitutions that render one truth unreachable. This is not to say that a multiplicity of roles necessarily implies no truth, but rather that a projection of 'selves' as opposed to 'a self' undercuts the concept of truth as essential, fixed or natural and casts doubt on locating any one (finite) level of reality. The multiple roles of the mask as cover, barrier, actualization of a self or selves and empty shell evident throughout Bergman's film-making career are explored via a range of classical, modernist, existential and postmodernist mask discourses. An interest in the cultural significance of film form and the intimate, complex, often contradictory and ambivalent relationships between Bergman's films and key areas such as gender, art, modernism and postmodernism helps to reflect on the various ways in which Bergman's films have been viewed.

Clearly, the cinema lends itself to observations about illusion, and the processes involved when watching this illusory medium have been discussed throughout the history of film theory. However, this aspect of film-making has fascinated Bergman in the extreme, critically and artistically, as the titles of his autobiography, *The Magic Lantern*,[2] and his later commentary on his films, *Images*,[3] suggest. It has been a source of constant delight to Bergman that for much of the time that a film is running, the screen is completely dark.[4] He has spoken about his fascination with film projection, rooted in his childhood; the projectionist at the Castle Cinema at his grandmother's home town of Uppsala was 'someone who went up to heaven every evening'.[5] He talks at length about his toy theatre and projector, and how at quite a young age he managed to obtain scraps of celluloid and make up narratives by scratching and manipulating them.[6] These personal preoccupations with cinema's capacity to trick spectators infiltrate Bergman's films. It is striking and very apt that the opening and closing images of two documentaries produced about Bergman, *Ingmar Bergman – The Magic Lantern*[7] and *Ingmar Bergman – The Director*,[8] should depict the lighting of a projector lamp with a match and the turning of the film reel. In addition to Bergman's extreme awareness of cinema's technical illusions, illusory elements also form an integral part of his narratives. Visions and illusions (apparitions, dreams, mental delusions and ghosts) are often conveyed as part of an everyday reality.[9]

Lloyd Michaels's introduction to *Ingmar Bergman's 'Persona'*[10] entitled 'Bergman and the Necessary Illusion' has been pivotal in helping to establish the role of illusion in Bergman's films and how this role has shifted over the course of Bergman's film-making career. For Michaels, 'the necessary illusion' means something very specific. Many of Bergman's films are considered to be dark or of a serious nature, but a considerable number of them contain significant moments of happiness, illusory sequences or dreams. Michaels suggests that with *Persona*, 'to the tyranny of lies, Bergman responds with the necessity of illusions.'[11] He argues that like many of Bergman's other films, while searching for truth, *Persona* also paradoxically values dream and fantasy, or celebrates the importance of illusory (because brief) moments of ideal happiness. Thus, the necessary illusion to Michaels encapsulates the idea that harsh 'reality' is made bearable by these illusions. He points to the wild strawberry picnic in *The Seventh Seal* (1956), the *'deus ex machina'* ending of *The Face* (1958), when the magician is called to perform before royalty, and the dream/flashback of the three sisters on the swing at the close of *Cries and Whispers* (1971):

> Bergman reminds us of the illusory element in all moments of heightened perception, community, transcendence, and happiness as he simultaneously suggests that the solace, affirmation, and joy contained in these images is something more than merely a sentimental religious faith or an existential joke. By such illusions, he seems to say, do we all manage to live.[12]

Moving on from this, it is worth considering how this notion of 'the necessary illusion' might take on a different meaning when seen in light of the argument that fixed, distinguishable concepts of truth and illusion or reality and illusion begin to crumble or merge in Bergman's work. The suggestion, pursued in this book, that the films push towards the concept of multiple truths and realities must inevitably also transform the meaning of the term 'the necessary illusion'. In other words, once an understanding of the term 'illusion' crumbles along with the binary oppositions that seemed to define it, such as falsity and truth or reality and unreality, the meaning of the phrase 'the necessary illusion' also changes. There does seem to be a shift in Bergman's films towards subjectivity, where everything is illusion projecting a multiplicity of truths and realities; hence, illusion is not only necessary, it is inevitable.

To analyse 'illusion' in any depth, it is important to acknowledge its multi-faceted nature. Broadly speaking, the two key areas of 'truth' and 'reality' are addressed throughout the book as crucial oppositions of the term 'illusion'. While different definitions of the term 'illusion' are interrelated and sometimes difficult to disentangle from each other, the book breaks them into five main areas. Each of these are analysed in terms of how they relate to their binary oppositions: the mask against true identity (Chapter 2); the fantasy of escape against real life or compromise (Chapter 3); religious faith against life or human love (Chapter 4); cinematic illusion against truth (Chapter 5); and dream against reality, considering both film as dream and dream within film (Chapter 6). By breaking the definitions down in this way, it is possible to look at how these binary oppositions shatter or begin to merge in the films discussed. This helps to reveal a pattern of transition through Bergman's film-making career without imposing an uncompromisingly rigid, chronological order. Each new chapter registers both a new take on 'illusion' and a new film, or group of films, and each is devoted to exploring precisely how different aspects of these kinds of illusion relate intricately to vital areas such as gender identity, stylistic form and modernist and postmodernist criticism. The seventh and final chapter concludes the analysis by considering the concept of 'the necessary illusion' in light of explorations of illusion in previous chapters.

The process of putting together this book has necessarily involved selecting certain films for examination, making no attempt to discuss all of Bergman's work. The films chosen seem to focus issues in particularly forceful ways, but the omission or marginalization of other films does not necessarily imply that they cannot equally be considered or that they are not relevant to the discussion. Where possible, attempts are made to acknowledge a wider scope, for example, where points relate to a number of Bergman's films or to a much broader cultural or filmic context.

Chapter 2 explores questions of identity by looking at preoccupations with the mask in Bergman's films. The mask is a fitting motif to begin with, with its inherent paradox, that while valuable for projecting and illuminating 'truths', it is also a 'dead' emblem of falsity and artifice. The mask is used, particularly in Bergman's earlier films, as a means to explore elemental dichotomies, such as truth and falsity, life and death, 'real' life and art/artifice. Furthermore, many of Bergman's films reveal an interest in the mask's metamorphosis from ritual and the theatre to everyday role-playing and performance.

The chapter focuses on *Summer Interlude* (1950) as a film centrally concerned with Marie's discovery of her true identity and the restoration of a 'healthy' balance, or compromise, between the fixed poles of her art and her life. Since Marie is a ballerina, performance is overtly displayed, as it is in many other Bergman films, so that the theatre becomes an extended metaphor for everyday mask-wearing. *Summer Interlude* is examined in light of psychological mask discourses to suggest that the mask functions here as a means to explore relatively fixed notions of truth and falsity.

Summer Interlude has a systematic structure, interweaving ballet theatre sequences with scenes of Marie's life, via an intricate pattern of motifs and flashbacks that push towards a final resolution, in sharp contrast to Bergman's later, more open, films. The film's rigid illusionist form, along with its predilection to 'work' within binaries of truth and falsity, make it a model film, helping to initiate discussion that can be carried to other Bergman films, where these formulations are either extended or challenged. The ramifications of the film's resolution, involving the cyclical reinstatement of the status quo, suggest that gender is less contested here than in Bergman's later films. *Summer Interlude*'s vision of identity within this binary structure is thus seen as fundamental when considering the shifting relationship between illusion and truth throughout Bergman's film-making career.

Chapter 3 suggests that *Summer with Monika* (1952) explores questions of identity and gender with less rigid assumptions about illusion, reality and truth than *Summer Interlude*. *Summer with Monika* depicts the escape of two teenage lovers, Monika and Harry, from the oppressive port of Stockholm to the natural landscape and apparent lawlessness of the archipelago. On the surface, the film echoes many of Bergman's 1940s films, in the sense that it is about a young couple's flight from society's restrictive conventions. As in the earlier films, the couple's escape proves an illusory, but necessary stage in the rite of passage to mature adulthood. Harry, like the male of the couple in the 1940s films, progresses from youthful illusion to return to conventional society. This return *seems* to suggest that the escape is only valuable as a *dis*illusioning experience.

However, there is evidence to suggest that *Summer with Monika* is more challenging and ambivalent than this. Although it does seem to conform to the conventional system of a journey towards self-discovery from the male point of view, its boundless enthusiasm for the escape itself makes it strikingly unique from the outset. Rather than seeing Monika as simply a catalyst for Harry's personal development, there is a suggestion that in the heavy claustrophobia of her home and in the dreamlike quality of the archipelago lie an extensive interest in Monika's point of view, making her a strong figure for identification. However, the representation of Monika is complex, as she serves to be both a figure for identification and an erotic 'other'.

While female protagonists are prominent in other Bergman films of the early 1950s, such as *Summer Interlude*, *Waiting Women* (1952, before *Summer with Monika*) and *Journey into Autumn*[13] (1954/5), it is only really with Monika's refusal to conform that the need for a compromise begins to be challenged. *Summer with Monika* is explored as a celebration of illusion rather than as just a reinstatement of the status quo. Here, the escape is shown in full, rather than just in the flashback mode common to many of Bergman's previous films, and the representation of this other world opens up the possibility of playing out different roles, suggesting that identity is socially constructed. Tensions remain between the film's resistance to the cyclical inevitability of compromise and the film's fidelity to conventional representations of the female as natural.

The fourth chapter suggests that shifts similar to those between *Summer Interlude* and *Summer with Monika* can be traced in Bergman's late 1950s and early 1960s films, specifically in relation to questions of religious faith. While remaining important throughout Bergman's career, questions of religious faith formed the main focus during this period, roughly coinciding with the time when Bergman's films were becoming known outside Sweden.

Strongly critical of orthodox religion and the illusory shell of conventional religious ritual, Bergman films of the late 1950s, such as *The Seventh Seal* (1956), search for an interior true faith or Truth. This recalls the dichotomies evident in *Summer Interlude*, in the sense that there is a quest to unveil a raw, original source of truth beneath religious convention – the 'false' outer layer (mask) of ritual. Brief moments, such as the wild strawberry sequence in *The Seventh Seal*, for example, represent a humanist communion that can be read as a *sign* of truth or a truthful way of being.

With *Through a Glass Darkly* (1960), the first of the three films later to be termed the trilogy, notions of humanism and religious truth begin to crumble. There is a shift from a focus on God to a focus on human characters. *The Silence* (1962), the last film of the trilogy, ends the quest for religious truth, and there is a further questioning of words and images as meaningful signifiers or symbols. Formally, compared with the showy confidence of the allegorical 1950s films, the trilogy 'chamber films' are less elaborate and more sparse, with reduced symbolism, emphasizing human characters over religious or philosophical preoccupations and the randomness of events over a systematic tapestry of themes and motifs. It was as though there was a stylistic quest for a more 'real' or truthful mode of representation.

Chapter 4 is thus divided into two parts, exploring first the thematic and then the stylistic developments in Bergman's films, to ascertain the relationship between the two and to consider how thematic functions of style might be discussed in terms of illusion and reality. The movement away from religious preoccupations towards the semiotics of communication and signification within fictional narrative anticipates the problems of legibility that permeate *Persona* (1965).

Chapter 5 leads on from these developments to consider *Persona* as a film that raises the question of how to relate fictional narrative. *Persona* depicts the actress Elisabet, who stops speaking mid-performance and whose silence continues as she leaves hospital with her nurse, Alma, to convalesce on an island where they share an intense and emotional time together. Discussion on the mask thus acts as a useful basis for discussion of *Persona*, distinguished from *Summer Interlude* in its awareness of itself as illusion projecting illusions. Elisabet seems to drop the *mask* of speech, but here truth and illusion are no longer so fixed, and the constructs of gender and identity are much more central to the film's thinking about illusion.

The thematic and stylistic shifts outlined in the trilogy are also vital for an understanding of *Persona*'s thinking about illusion, in its further depiction of subjectivity or questioning of coherency in relation to perceptions of the world. This involves the cinema's shifting role in relation to emerging media technologies that have adopted the responsibilities of representing 'real' human suffering. *Persona* tackles the illegibility of appearances head on, by investigating the mask, the face and filmic representation itself. Key issues surrounding performance are discussed in relation to the sequence in which Alma runs after Elisabet begging forgiveness, bearing in mind our emotional attachment at this stage of the film, and the sequence's subtle parallels with the melodramatic radio play earlier.

The chapter ends with an analysis of the final sequences of the film. Critics have frequently imposed a sense of closure onto *Persona*'s ending, often relying too rigorously on the screenplay, attempting to make sense of images that are not fully coherent. The images in themselves offer very little coherence in terms of a definitive narrative structure, or a resolution, suggesting that, in line with the film as a whole, the ending foregrounds the unreliability of interpreting from appearances.

The first five chapters explore developments in thinking about different strands of illusion, essentially enmeshed in boundaries of truth and reality. There is an increasing fluidity up until *Persona* gradually evolving from Bergman's earliest films, though not in any rigid or logical sense, as certain assumptions about the term 'illusion' are called into question. Key concepts begin to disintegrate: identity and the notion of a true core; gender as fixed or natural; distinguishable fantasy and real worlds; religious truth or a truthful way of being; the fixed significance of a word or an image; fictional representation and traditional form. These developments are discussed in relation to more general developments towards forms of cinematic 'modernism' during this time throughout Europe and North America.

Persona's concerns with the layers of images and words with no clues to a central truth or meaning are to a certain extent modernist concerns. Of the films discussed, the films made after *Persona* have been chosen on the basis that they exemplify, strongly and vividly, directions taken once the 'glass is shattered', when conventional notions of identity and gender are shunned, accommodating an awareness of fluidity and societal constructs. While the choice of films is certainly not arbitrary, similar elements apply in other later Bergman films that are not discussed in depth here. For instance, *A Passion* (1968) particularly embodies in its formal and stylistic disintegration the developments discussed in Chapters 5 and 6. Other films, such as *The Shame* (1968) and *Autumn Sonata* (1978), have a thematic interest in dream similar to the films discussed in Chapter 6, but are stylistically more illusionist, like *The Touch* (US/Sweden, 1970) and the television series *Scenes from a Marriage* (1973).

Chapter 6 takes *The Hour of the Wolf* as a film that is looking for direction after *Persona's* concerns with how cinema as mask can penetrate infinite layers of masks. It can be argued that *The Hour of the Wolf* is able to move on to convey a person's descent into madness, gradually controlled by demons, without *Persona's* extreme forms of reflexivity. *The Hour of the Wolf* meanders subjectively between disjointed, indefinable dreams and realities.

This chapter investigates the formal function of dreams in Bergman's films, against the yardstick of conventional temporal–spatial and cause–effect relationships. To enforce the argument that there is a tendency towards greater fluidity between dream and reality in Bergman's later work, three films are analysed that exemplify these shifts: *Wild Strawberries* (1957), *The Hour of the Wolf* and *Cries and Whispers* (1972). These are taken to be key films in their attempts to bend certain conventions and transgress generic boundaries. While the aim to integrate the external and internal worlds is apparent in *Wild Strawberries*, it is only later (with *The Hour of the Wolf*) that a more formal disintegration is evident.

The concluding chapter draws together the different strands of illusion to explore the richly textured tapestry of *Fanny and Alexander* (1982). The analysis centres on a reconsideration of the film's tone, disputing common perceptions of the film as a straightforward return to humanism. The chapter contains close analysis of various sequences, as it revisits the film in light of preceding Bergman films. This retrospective vantage point also enables a brief chance to consider how *Saraband*, released in 2003 as Bergman's 'last feature', might influence perceptions of *Fanny and Alexander* and even Bergman as 'auteur' into the future.

Fanny and Alexander addresses the theme of illusion directly, and as such usefully concludes the book, in the sense that embedded within the formulaic structure of the film is an awareness of modernism. The upper-middle-class extended Ekdahl family bask in their illusory securities within their labyrinthine apartment, their lives intricately linked with the theatre situated directly across the street. The film can be seen as a celebration of illusion, to a certain extent expressed in Emilie's final return to the Ekdahl family, after her bleak marriage to the Lutheran Bishop, who clings to notions of truth and a life devoid of luxuries. However, there is also discomfort with the adult male Ekdahls and their tendency to luxuriate in their illusions. The nauseous edge to the fairy-tale is examined more closely, along with the superficiality of the characters and the overindulgent set.

Fanny and Alexander explores the visionary world of the children, Fanny and Alexander, presenting an interconnectedness between visions and everyday reality. In turn, ghost visions, dreams, fairytales and telepathic occurrences point towards the inexplicable. However, stylistically, compared with films like *Persona*, *The Hour of the Wolf* or *Cries and Whispers*, *Fanny and Alexander* appears transparent and non-reflexive, complying on the whole with classical continuity. While illusion is certainly pivotal to an understanding of the film, its relationship with this concept is complex.

The chapter explores the extent to which these visionary sequences tie in with the film's overall philosophy of multiple layers of reality, leading on from ideas raised in Chapter 5, considering diverse stylistic components such as signposting of visions, subjectivity and point of view. It proceeds to look at the mask, drawing on earlier developments, arguing that thematically the notion of a true self is contested in favour of multiplicity, of a number of 'selves' equally as real as each other.

By way of revisiting the film's tone, key terms such as 'humanism' come under some scrutiny. Integral to this re-vision of *Fanny and Alexander* is a study of how the Epilogue 'works' in connection with the rest of the film. It also entails a reconsideration of the representation of gender and identity, which can be seen to comply with postmodernist concepts of fluidity and multiplicity. The final sequences are triggered by the grand post-christening meal, where Gustav Adolf formally celebrates the naming of the two baby girls, inviting them into the Ekdahl family. There are strong indications in the filming of this sequence that the truth of gender is being undercut. This corresponds with a view taken against female subjection throughout the film. Furthermore, this reading suggests that although there is no self-discovery at the end of the film, the women obtain some degree of freedom in the final few sequences.

Chronological arrangement of chapters can suggest, often justifiably, an authorial development, linking the films by recurring themes and motifs. This was a popular format in the abundance of literature published in the

US in the 1970s and 1980s, for example, which frequently used Bergman's films as a means to explore Bergman's, or even the critic's own, spiritual developments. However, there are attempts here to steer away from suggesting any rigid 'auteurist' development, and despite the fact that the structure of this book roughly correlates with the chronology of Bergman's career, another structure, based around thematic and stylistic issues, overlays the chronology.

This is not to say that chronology is not important; indeed sometimes it is fundamental. For instance, the specific take on *Fanny and Alexander* necessitates an analysis that draws not only on a wide range of films but also on key concepts raised in preceding chapters. Similarly, it would be difficult to approach *Persona* as intended without having reviewed the significant thematic and stylistic developments occurring immediately before it in the trilogy.

To some extent, this is an authorial study, accommodating the idea of Bergman choosing to work as an individual, turning down offers to work in Hollywood in an attempt to remain independent, writing his own screenplays, working on familiar territories and with familiar actors, artists and technicians. However, consistent attempts are made to try to place Bergman's work within wider concerns and perspectives. One obvious perspective is the Swedish cultural and artistic influence on Bergman's creative output. These areas often overlap. For instance, in relation to the theatrical influences on Bergman's films, authorial perspectives, such as Bergman's role as theatre director, combine with cultural concerns, such as the tremendous influence by Scandinavian dramatists August Strindberg and Henrik Ibsen on Bergman's films.

Another perspective is the phenomenon of Bergman as 'foreign' or 'art film' director, particularly during the 1950s and 1960s, when distinctions between mainstream and art cinema were being formulated explicitly. Arthur Knight's comments in 1965 demonstrate the way that definitions of film as art and the 'art film' had become linked with individuality and independence:

> Art is not manufactured by committees. Art comes from an individual who has something to say that he must express, and who works out what is for him the most forceful or affecting manner of expressing it. And this, specifically, is the quality that people respond to in European pictures – the reason why we hear so often that foreign films are 'more artistic' than our own. There is in them the urgency of individual expression, an independence of vision, the coherence of a single-minded statement.[14]

There is the further implication here that it was also the films' foreign-ness (the language, the English subtitles) that made them stand out in Britain and North America as artistic and different from those of the Hollywood studio system. Thus, responses in contemporaneous British and North American newspaper and magazine articles, where distinct waves of enthusiasm and disgust about foreign or art films were all the more extreme,[15] help to fuel discussions about films Bergman made dur-ing the period of the late 1950s and early 1960s.[16] Newspaper articles are particularly important to the study of the stylistic developments from *Wild Strawberries* to the trilogy.[17] As David Thomson summarizes, 'In England and America it [*The Seventh Seal*] made Bergman the central figure in the growth of art-house cinema . . . Inevitably he suffered from being so suddenly revealed to a volatile world . . . By about 1961 Bergman held the unenviable position of a discredited innovator in a fashion-conscious world.'[18]

Another perspective is the parallel between transitions explored in Bergman's films and developments in Western film-making more gener-ally. This attempt to place Bergman's work in the context of European art cinema from the 1950s to the 1980s conforms to a certain extent with debates about modernism in film (in the 1960s and 1970s) and debates about postmodernism that succeeded them.[19] Throughout the book, other kinds of theoretical constructs, such as those that have arisen out of feminist critical practice, are also applied.

Developments in Bergman's films from fixities of truth and reality towards multiple truths and realities are related to issues concerning iden-tity and gender, an important area considering the centrality of women in Bergman's films. For instance, there is a significant compatibility between the undercutting of the truth of gender and more recent femi-nist discourses on subjectivity, multiplicity of identity and performativ-ity. Where this is most strikingly the case, in films such as *Summer with Monika*, *Persona* and *Fanny and Alexander*, for example, this compatibility is acknowledged, while trying not to overlook the fact that the films gene-rally predate many of these discourses. Thus, these kinds of theoretical constructs are treated as secondary to, rather than in any way forcing or framing, the main argument.

On a personal note, it was on viewing *It Rains on Our Love* (1946), broadcast late on television, that I began to formulate ideas about Bergman and illusion. My knowledge of Bergman's work was very limited at that time, mainly to films made during the late 1950s, but it seemed to me then that *It Rains on Our Love* made a fitting companion to *The Seventh Seal*. Together, the two films formed a whole. While *The Seventh Seal* was ostensibly dark with light moments, *It Rains on Our Love* radiated happiness, with occasional dampeners to this illusion. Both films advocated 'the necessary illusion': fantasies, dreams and illusory moments of happiness are necessary to endure life's darker realities.

It was in this context that my interest in Bergman and illusion began. But then I saw *Persona*. And as I continued to view the rest of Bergman's films the focus of the study shifted, as did the films of interest. *Persona* focused my attention on the constructs of film and film narrative, and later films seemed to point out that inherent in the term 'illusion' itself was a fixed dichotomous relationship; a falsity must imply a truth, an art – a reality. This suggested a fundamental shift of focus in Bergman's films from the necessary illusion to a multiplicity of illusions.

2
The Mask and Identity: *Summer Interlude*'s Legacy

A mask can provide a fundamental form of disguise, protection or empowerment, appearing also in association with transitional phases, with rituals marking annual or seasonal change or transformational events, such as birth, death and rites of passage. As A. David Napier deduces, masks communicate 'what is paradoxical about appearances and perceptions in the context of a changing viewpoint'.[1] The role of the mask in ancient Greek theatre was, according to John Mack, to deploy 'well-established characteristics whose significance was readily interpreted by all as a particular generalised human condition',[2] assisting rather than 'masking' (concealing) portrayal. Indeed, the Greeks called the actors themselves 'masks' as a way of referencing character type, a tradition that was later adopted by the sixteenth- and seventeenth- century popular form of Italian improvised drama known as *commedia dell'arte*.

While the dividing line between ancient rite and ancient theatre is a disputable one,[3] Ian Jenkins argues that 'at Athens the cult of Dionysos provided the ritual context out of which the classical theatre of the great tragedians and comic playwrights evolved', pointing to the use in the sixth century BC of a chorus of masked dancers impersonating satyrs and later, when drama developed speaking parts for actors, the continued use of a chorus of about ten in every performance.[4] It is possible that something remained from the essence of the ritual as a ceremony for death, regeneration and recovery in the cathartic nature of tragedy and the theatre's role more generally.[5]

In conventional illusionist Western theatre, the mask (whether as physical mask or actor's 'role') encourages the audience's suspension of disbelief. In more reflexive theatre, however, an acknowledged gap between

13

character and actor is important, as is outlined in Bertolt Brecht's theoretical project, summarized by Elin Diamond as: 'Demystifying representation, showing how and when the object of pleasure is made, releasing
the spectator from imaginary and illusory identifications.'[6] Works by
playwrights such as Luigi Pirandello and Luigi Chiarelli, on the other
hand, investigate the paradoxes of a fixed notion of identity and the
multiplicity of social roles in relation to diverse, ironic distinctions
between mask and face. While the use of masks is not so overt in
Western theatre today,[7] the dressing room remains an important location for psychological transformation, both into and out of 'character'.

Summer Interlude (1950)[8] employs the mask thematically and structurally to promote a 'healthy' balance between truth and illusion. The
mask functions in the film as a means to explore relatively fixed concepts of truth and falsity, in line with classical, psychological mask discourse, rather than more recent postmodernist discourses that challenge
the concept of an authentic 'real' or a 'true' identity. That is not to
assume any direct link or influence between classical, psychological discourses and the film, but to suggest that the two are working with similar
thought processes, and that outlining some of these will open up a pro-
ductive way of analysing the mask's functions in a number of Bergman's
films.

The psychologist Gordon Allport has traced the root of the word 'personality' from the classical Latin 'persona' to the antecedent phrase
'pers onare' ('to sound through') which was linked with the mouthpiece
used in theatre to project the voice. 'Persona' came to mean the noun
'mask' worn by Greek actors, but could also refer either to one who plays
a part or to the character.[9] The term 'persona' eventually indicated the
dichotomy between appearance (the mask) and the actor (the person).[10]

Mask as metaphor in psychology, art and literature has traditionally
been used to symbolize the idea that a person has superficial and fundamental characteristics. Key psychologists, such as Andras Angyal,
R.D. Laing, Henry Stack Sullivan and Allport have emphasized the contrast between the actor (inner person) and the observables (mask), between the private person and the outward signs of public behaviour.[11]
While these discourses all allude to an authentic 'inner', it is possible of
course to question the further implicit assumption that the inner person
is more genuine. In 1935, Carl Jung expressed his disbelief in studying
appearances: 'Fundamentally the persona is nothing real: it is a compromise between the individual and society as to what a man should
appear to be.'[12] Despite the element of falsity, Jung asserts that it is often
beneficial to use a mask as a front, unless people believe that they are

what they pretend to be: 'Whoever builds up too good a persona for himself naturally has to pay for it with irritability.'[13] Similarly for Laing, '"A man without a mask" is very rare'[14]; a mask is only problematic if it becomes, as Christopher Monte expounds, 'a necessity without convenience', divorcing the now stagnant 'true inner self' from the world.[15]

While Jung and Laing suggest that mask-wearing can be beneficial, so long as it remains consciously 'convenient', Abraham H. Maslow asserts that a truly healthy personality is one who discards the mask as far as possible, 'dropping our efforts to influence, to impress, to please, to be loveable, to win applause'.[16] In all these cases, concepts of a 'true' or 'authentic' inner remain fixed in a dichotomous relationship with the outer illusory mask, a position that postmodernists would refute.

Theatrical settings and stories are frequently used in Bergman's films as metaphors for the human condition, and in his films of the 1940s and 1950s they tend to signal a person's falsity. For example, in *Sawdust and Tinsel* (1953), Frans's green room is a confusion of masks and mirrors representing his deceitfulness. On stage, he plays the melodramatic seducer in elaborate costume and make-up,[17] but the artifice of the stage pursues Frans into his private life so that he is unable to feel 'true' emotion. *Summer Interlude* treats the theatrical mask and the psychological mask as specifically separate, though interrelated, categories. Marie's absorption in the ballet world, for instance, reflects her over-reliance on her projected mask. The ballet world's heavily made-up faces, tight costumes and synthetic sets represent a masking off from corporeal actuality (Marie: 'At the theatre, we dance and act the fool . . . while over there Henrik rots away'). The paradox of classical ballet, represented here by *Swan Lake*, is that while it is a performance of movement and physicality, it is extremely conventionalized and rigidly choreographed.

Maslow's discussion of the mask suggests that problems may arise if the player's dependence on (pleasing) an audience lasts beyond the boundaries of the make-believe world. In *Summer Interlude*, there are signs that Marie's personal identity has been overridden by her star status. When there is a collective panic to find (the older) Marie for the rehearsal, there is a sense that her colleagues are worried about the whereabouts of their *prima ballerina* rather than about Marie as a person. David's words, 'You keep me at a distance . . . you seek out the false-nosed idiots . . . What could I mean to someone like you?' indicate that Marie's immersion in this fantasy has detached her from her private (true) self and from (real) life. The ballet has become, as in R.D. Laing's formulation, necessary without convenience, suggesting metaphorically that Marie believes, in Jung's terms, that she is her mask.

The theatrical and psychological masks are interconnected within a particularly rigid pattern of motifs, so that Marie's masking off from pain is expressed via the donning of the theatrical mask, demanding that the ballet be represented as false. The depiction of the rehearsal in progress, for instance, draws attention to this falsity. Key technicians and practitioners are revealed to expose the underlying mechanisms of production that help to construct this artifice: the man oiling his hands to work the curtain, Peter setting the lamp or attending to the electrical appliances off-stage and the lit conductor turning the pages. When the curtain goes up, there is a dissolve to the opening of *Swan Lake*, seemingly bathed in sunlight, with dancers who appear to glide on water. This illusion is suddenly lost in darkness owing to a short-circuit, and the rehearsal is postponed until the evening. The framing of the illusion with such obvious pointers to its constructedness highlights the audience's desire to be taken in by the deception. The mask in itself is not false; it is the audience's belief in it (however short-lived) that makes it a lie. Attention to the apparatus generates the idea of the theatre as constructed (rather than false), but there is no real intimation in the film to the further implication that identity itself could be constructed.

Summer Interlude's narrative is compact and controlled, with events of the film's present occurring virtually within a 24-hour framework, echoing the dramatic unities of time, space and action in ancient Greek drama. The present is set very specifically in autumn, emphasized by the dissolve from the opening summer shots to fallen leaves, dark skies and the gothic ominousness of the ballet and opera theatre. This marks the end of the 'illusion' of summer, providing a nod towards Marie's stage of development; according to her colleague, she is 28 years old and children are calling her aunt. There is a sense both that this is just another ordinary working day, and that this is a very special moment in time: the close-up of the calendar showing the date and time of the rehearsal is illuminated by a stream of light; the package containing Henrik's diary arrives; there is a 'strange smell'; there is something wrong with Marie and there is the technical hitch cutting the rehearsal short. This merging of ordinariness with the exceptional runs through into the flashbacks, where particular events and dates are recalled in Marie's voice-over: '13 years ago . . . spring performance . . . a day like no other. . .'.

While Henrik's diary inspires Marie's memories, the words of the voice-overs are her own. The scenes set in the present are structured so that Marie passes a daylong contemplation of her identity. This involves the boat crossing to the archipelago where her summer interlude with Henrik 13 years before had happened. The times spent there and on the boat journey home are intercut with flashbacks of the past, including Henrik's death from a diving accident. That evening, after the rehearsal, Marie confronts the ballet master, who is dressed as a clown. This, and Marie's handing over of Henrik's diary to David, an exposure of her private self, combine to make way for the following night's performance, where she chooses a 'healthy' relationship with the mask.

One of the most obvious aspects of role-playing in the film is the coexistence of both an older and a younger Marie.[18] The distinction of roles is made all the more explicit by the constants in Marie's life: the familiar locations and settings, the continued presence of the ballet theatre (and *Swan Lake*) and the obligatory male lover. David and then Henrik in the flashback are both introduced trying to penetrate the ballet theatre walls, guarded by the theatre manager, to see Marie. Both lovers seem to be conjured up by Marie when she is yawning. In her current life this is due to Marie's exhaustion from late nights and ballet practice, while in the flashback it is due to lazy dozing on the fishing boat. Significantly, it is the sound of Henrik's body hitting the water as he dives that interrupts her yawning. The flashback technique thus enables retrospective emphasis on certain details, stemming from the older Marie, such as the construction of the happy-go-lucky younger Marie, and the intrusion on this identity by the harrowing significance of the dive. In such a way, the idea of two roles is strengthened, as is the concept of not only a then and now, but a then in the context of now, and a Marie that the present-day Marie thinks she was then. While there is thus a clear sense of different 'roles' (at least two in the case of Marie) being played out and explored in the film, the concept of a 'self' or 'true' identity to be lost or discovered is nevertheless retained.

It is significant that Marie's initial donning of the psychological mask occurs during adolescence. In the 1970s Henry Stack Sullivan identified the teenage or adolescent years as a time when a person may experiment with various 'selves', though it is also at this time and onwards, he asserts that it may become easier to develop 'specialised accommodation',[19] an interest in one particular field. Allport also takes adolescence to be a crucial stage in the development of the mask, a time when we may vacillate between child and adult attitudes. He suggests that problems of adolescence eventually become focused around one central issue, the last emerging aspects of selfhood, discovering finally, 'I am the proprietor of my life.'[20] This transition, though something realized at adolescence, also needs to be reaffirmed at various intervals. For this 'discovery of selfhood' a mask is discovered to fit. If too much reliance is placed on the mask, problems occur when the adult person changes without either changing the mask or renewing (faith in) it. *Summer Interlude* seems to be driven by similar psychological impulses: in addition to the trauma of Henrik's sudden death, Marie is at a period in her life that marks the development from the vacillation between childhood and adulthood to the adoption of more 'specialised accommodation'. At such a moment of self-discovery, Henrik's death prompts Marie's inner self to stagnate and the mask to freeze, recalling Laing's warning against mask-wearing as a 'necessity without convenience'.

The lingering of the present in the memory of the past is suggested in the structure and the use of the flashback form. In conventional fashion, the three flashbacks lead off from a close-up of Marie, and seem to be reflections of the ways that Marie is confronting and coming to terms with her past in her search for identity. But the absorption of Marie's identity by the ballet theatre is accentuated through the flashbacks' direct transitions into a dance sequence each time rather than into an immediate confrontation with Marie's past life. The memories themselves are shown to be masked. This is not to say that the flashbacks are Marie's memories (as will be discussed shortly, events happen in the flashbacks that Marie could not possibly have witnessed) or that they convey solely her mental point of view. Nevertheless, the recollections seem to appear only at times when the older Marie is capable of confronting them, and they lead directly to the eventual resolution of the narrative (Marie's resolution).

The sequences of the first meeting with Henrik on the archipelago and the subsequent sharing of the wild strawberry patch are preceded by a brief return to the older Marie sitting, eyes closed, in the cold cabin, as though a pause is necessary for Marie to prepare herself for this next episode. This scene then begins with the young Marie springing out of bed in the same cabin, now bathed in sunlight (drawing attention to the contrast between then and now), putting on her swimming costume and dancing with the fishing rod as if it were a prop in a cabaret act. Her relationship to dancing is here significantly shown to be a 'healthy' part of her life, with no need for an audience. The following aerial shot set to sad, expectant music suggests the presence of the retrospective older Marie, foreseeing the meeting with Henrik and the subsequent tragedy that makes her vulnerable to pain.

The mask, the diary and the dressing room

The three dressing room sequences (before the afternoon rehearsal, after the afternoon rehearsal and after the evening rehearsal) represent key transitional moments in the film, intricately linked with Marie's grow-ing openness to the diary. As Marie opens the diary during the first dressing room sequence, there is a cut to a close-up of her heavily made-up face,[21] an allusion to the player's mask. She drops the diary. In the second dressing room scene, Marie allows herself a glance across the diary pages, until the ghostlike vision of Henrik appears. Her sudden snapping shut of the book mirrors the earlier scene. There is a cut to an extreme close-up of Marie's right eye, eyebrow pencilled heavily, as she flicks her eyelid up to open her eye wider. In the final dressing room scene, the pages of the book are, significantly, wide open, and a vision of her younger self appears, suggesting a confrontation with her iden-tity. This is followed by the start of the de-masking process, as she takes off her false eyelashes. At the end of this scene, Marie hands the diary over to David, revealing a final de-masking, a sharing of her private self with a new lover. Taking these cues, the handing over of the diary sig-nifies the unveiling of previously masked pain.

However, the symbolism surrounding the diary and its handing over has been diversely interpreted, with analysts such as Frank Gado infer-ring underlying moral preoccupations at the core of Marie's actions:

> Marie's concern over being debased, and thus unworthy of David can only refer to her liaison with Erland – about which the diary can have nothing to relate . . . Nor is it likely that Marie, who is over thirty,[22] thinks David would expect her to be a virgin, but if that were the case, he would not have to read the diary – she could just tell him.[23]

This kind of attention to Marie's sexual experiences and to the male fig-ures as central protagonists is telling in terms of audience expectations about gender roles and sexual identity. However, because no clues are provided to suggest that Marie is either 'debased' or 'unworthy' of David, but rather that she has up until this point been unable to open up to him, it would seem that the film's central concern is with Marie's identity. The last sequences of the film concentrate on Marie's personal de-masking. In this perspective, it is not important whether David him-self changes, nor is the effect that the diary has on *him* important. The identities of Henrik and Erland are also relatively unimportant. Nevertheless, if it is the case that such a formulation must be under-stood for the sequence (and the film as a whole) to 'work', then the film's 'success' is thus reliant upon a specific reading of what the diary signifies in relation to the mask/truth dichotomy. The fact that the diary needs to be construed as the window to Marie's true self for it to 'work' as a motif suggests that the motif itself can be seen as rather staged and formulaic.

The diary also appears on the table next to Uncle Erland in the flashback when Henrik dies in hospital. We know that this is not the younger Marie's point of view, since the older Marie has only just discovered that it was her uncle who sent the diary to her. The placing of the uncle so obviously beside it at the moment of Henrik's death suggests that this flashback is subject to the older Marie's mental point of view and her retrospective association of the diary with painful memories.

Art as death

Other motifs used in the initial dressing room sequence continue to function throughout the film. For instance, the bell that interrupts the camera's forward tracking for a privileged moment of empathy, after the diary is dropped, is the same as the bell that beckons the dancers to the stage for rehearsal. It is also a pre-echo for the alarm which raises the curtain for the actual start of the rehearsal, and for the boat's bell that calls all passengers aboard for the journey to the archipelago. In the initial dressing room sequence there is a sense that Marie must answer to the ballet bell, no matter what is happening in her private life. It is also symbolic. Thoughts triggered by the diary are too painful to contemplate, and the bell signifies psychological alarm. The cut to the silhouetted stream of chorus dancers, running to the bell before the beam of light across the off-stage landing, expresses a blind following of orders. Marie is one of the masked masses carried along by the collective psyche, to the illusory protection of the dance floor. The dancers lack personal identities, and are presented as if running to a form of death.

This sequence can be matched with a later scene in which David walks off after an argument and a familiar set of motifs is employed (the diary is dropped and a bell rings, this time from the boat). These references to Marie's blind response to the bell earlier make her decision to board the boat less active, detracting from the idea that she is consciously retracing the past. She is still following orders. Her journey to the archipelago is like a visit to the underworld, enhanced by the trance-like state she adopts. At the cross-roads she meets 'Death', who it later transpires is Henrik's ancient aunt with the moustache,[24] and is led to the 'summerhouse' where her recollections of the past will renew her vitality. The deployment of the mask in conjunction with death and rebirth recalls masked rituals associated with transitional modes. Marie needs to be led to the underworld by Death, to retrace her past and to face the final de-masking in the dressing room that evening, in order to recognize the distinction between the mask that has become fixed and the 'true' person.

Ballet is presented at some points of the film as a dead form, invoking late-Romantic distinctions between art and life. When Marie shows Henrik her ballet practising room, the lifeless aspect of her work is glimpsed. As the door is opened there is a cut to a black area of floor, spot lit in the left corner, in which, like a vanitas of Marie's working life, two ballet shoes are placed with the artistic array of shoe laces, a record and a record sleeve. The ballet shoes are foregrounded here, as they are in the montage of shots in the final dressing room sequence, as emblems of the ballet world, like the mask of theatre, or the skull and crossbones of death.[25]

After Henrik's death following a diving accident, Marie dons the mask psychologically. To the extent that she becomes absorbed in the illusory protection of her work, she loses touch with what might be termed the truth beneath the mask. Bergman describes this loss as a kind of death: 'And when the boy died, she died too.'[26] In this sense, the lifelessness of her art represents a spiritual death; in Jung's formulation, Marie becomes the mask she is wearing, ego and mask become one. When Henrik dies, Marie follows her uncle's advice: 'I'll show you how to build a wall Marie.' Building a wall is not an unusual phenomenon in the film. In addition to Erland, the ballet master, Marie's ballet colleague and the theatre manager have all closed themselves off. This makes Marie's transformation at the end all the more poignant. She has achieved something special rather than normal.

The uncle's role in mirroring Marie's spiritual death is crucial. After Henrik's death, Erland's exploitation of his niece's vulnerability is depicted subjectively in the corridor sequence after the nurse covers Henrik's face with the white sheet, representing a masking off from death as well as life, and matching the symbolism of the white sheets covering the furniture when Marie returns to Erland's house, not in use during winter. There is a very slow dissolve from the hospital room to the corridor sequence, so that Henrik's face is superimposed over Marie as she slowly progresses through the hospital. As she walks on, the vision dissolves completely and the uncle follows behind. His shadow soars up domineeringly behind and above Marie's relatively small body. As she walks towards the camera to the sound of footsteps, the uncle's shadow appears expressionistically in each window on the facing wall, large and threatening. The scene dissolves into a particularly exhausting ballet rehearsal with the ballet master stamping out the rhythm. This sequence of events conveys the uncle's power over the niece, as well as the relationship between Henrik's death, the influence of the uncle and Marie's absorption into her ballet.

The uncle's spiritual death is conveyed during the evening lounge scene, when he plays the piano morosely, clinging to the idea of Marie's likeness to her (dead) mother, also a dancer, as he might to a corpse or stone replica:[27]

> Your mother Marie . . . sometimes danced for me in the moonlight on such nights . . . the moon lit this room . . . and I played . . . she used to sit there . . . and I played . . . and I looked at her face and I wondered whether I was imagining it all.

The close-up on Marie's face during these words suggests Erland's vision of his dead love, but also anticipates the ghosts that are to haunt Marie after Henrik's death. Framed within the flashback, Erland's morbidity ('The flowers in the window boxes have faded and died') appears to be subject to the viewpoint of the older Marie, emphasized by the close-up on Henrik at the uncle's words: 'But then we were alive.' As Marie and Henrik ascend the stairway to the ballet practice room, shot from an extreme high angle, Marie's voice-over and the shadows of the banisters and their bodies on the white walls add a ghostly vision against the sound of the wind outside. The close connection between Erland and the older Marie is further signified when the words of Marie's voice-over ('The music, the moonlight, the silence, the excitement . . .') echo her uncle's words ('The surroundings, the piano, the floor, the unreal moonlight').

In turn, the fat stage manager symbolizes all that has gone stale within the theatre, seeing only the commercial elements of his enterprise and its female commodities. He objectifies Marie, discussing the size of her legs and the business of her private life, attempting to extinguish any hope of a life for her outside the theatre. He tries to take the packet containing Henrik's diary to Marie himself. When David says that he wants to see Marie for private reasons, the stage manager replies smugly, 'Nothing private on dress rehearsal days.' The strange smell, observed by the postman and Karl, a friend and colleague of Marie, represents the peculiarity of the day's events, but goes unnoticed by the stage manager, signifying his insensitivity: 'Forty years I've been here. You can't tell me anything about the theatre.' The sharp contrast between the stage manager and Karl is communicated visually in two simple shots. The first shot depicts the stage manager shutting the curtain of his small office from right to left, masking himself off from the rest of the theatre. This is followed by a cut to a shot of Karl facing towards the camera, opening the curtain to the private world of Marie's dressing room from left to right, ensuring that the important package – the catalyst for the day's events – arrives safely in Marie's hands.

It is significant that the stage manager should shut the curtain on the outside world. Over the course of the film, both Aunt Elizabeth and the older Marie will pull down the blind. Aunt Elizabeth does so to conceal from Uncle Erland the young lovers' excitement as they run down the lane to the water. This can also be seen as a subjective vision from the perspective of the older Marie, who sees for the first time her aunt's switching-off mechanisms. The older Marie, now herself called 'aunt', pulls down the blind of the cabin, masking herself from pain.[28]

Beneath the mask

The final dressing room sequence seems to relate to the psychological viewpoint, summarized by Karen Horney and Erich Fromm, that the way to an understanding of 'being' is through penetration of appearances to inner reality.[29] At the beginning of this sequence, during a privileged period alone with Marie, a montage of static shots collates items that relate to Marie and the mask: a close-up of the right side of Marie's face, a shot of a dripping tap (time is running out), a close-up of Marie's whole face, a Degas-style figurine of a dancer, ballet shoes and a mirror image of Marie's heavily made-up face. The film-making process is more stylized here, foregrounding perhaps the masks of cinema, compared with the long takes of the wild strawberry patch scene, for instance.

Marie's look into the mirror signifies the start of the de-masking process. It is cut short by a shot of Marie looking down to the diary and the superimposed vision of the younger Marie on its pages, suggesting perhaps a 'truer' previous self, as part of the search for identity. It could be argued that the paradox of the 'truer' vision or illusion begins to shatter fixed notions of an authentic inner, and it is possible that this moment begins to touch on the concept of a number of 'selves', as well as multiple 'roles'. However, the cut to the extreme close-up of Marie in the reflection removing the false eyelashes seems to deny this reading, suggesting a continuation along the theme of the mask's falsity.

Marie's solitude is interrupted by the sound of the ballet master lurking in the shadows, dressed as 'Coppélius the Clown' (he says that he has been trying make-up for the ballet performance of *Coppélia*).[30] Sitting opposite each other, each before a mirror, Marie and the ballet master point out each other's inability to drop the mask. Marie states: 'You sit there in your clown's costume, unable to tear it off,' while agreeing with the ballet master that her dress and make-up are welded to her. The camera is positioned behind Marie, looking in the mirror, while to the left of the mirror is the ballet master, looking at Marie. In Bergman's films, being directed to look into a mirror by another character generally connotes the sense of being guided to look at the true face, or aspects of a character that are considered to be true. As the clown remarks:

> Just once we see our life unadorned. All our protecting walls crumble. We stand naked and cold, we see our true selves . . . but only once.

Significantly the dance master never looks at his *own* reflection. On the one hand, he is Mephistopheles, tempting Marie to stay at the theatre at the expense of losing her soul: 'You dance, that's your formula, keep to it, Marie, or you'll perish.'[31] Like Coppélius, he is completely absorbed in his art, drawing attention to the immortality of ballet as an art in contrast to the decaying qualities of nature. The story of *Coppélia* also marvels at the ideal, embodied in the clockwork doll, compared with the loss of the ideal in 'real'-life women.[32] On the other hand, the clown points out ballet's transience; Marie has been coming to the theatre for 20 years and in 8 years she will be out.

In order to bring about Marie's de-masking, the ballet master must paradoxically don a mask (bestowing power). Furthermore, he is disguised, not only as Coppélius, but as 'Coppélius the Clown'. Coppélius is not a clown in the traditional story, but a lonely old man, who builds clockwork toys, thus indicating several layers of disguise here. While clowns can sometimes evoke the carnivalesque spirit of transgression, the use of the clown here seems to refer to the Shakespearian clown or fool who is able via extreme disguise to cut through social masks and highlight hidden truths. As ballet master, he is the conjurer who casts the illusions; as a clown, he can play quite a different role.[33]

Marie's transformation is expressed visually when, during the premiere performance the following night, she comes back to the wings to embrace David in the final scene. The camera focuses on the ballet shoes – (dead) emblems of her work – which elegantly form a tiptoe position as she reaches up to kiss him. This leads into the transition to the make-believe world, as she completes the performance, open for the new relationship balanced with her work; as Robin Wood puts it, 'The reconciliation of life and art is beautifully suggested in the shot of her feet as she goes up on her points to kiss him.'[34] Ideologically, the film seems to suggest that the illusion of the mask is beneficial and valuable as long as its falsity is recognized. In relation to Jung's and Laing's theses, Marie has achieved maturity, involving carefully balanced compromise.

David's previous suggestion ('Why not give up this job and get married?') demands sacrifice, and would mean that Marie would lose the outward expression of her private creativity. However, the complete absorption into the ballet means death, because Marie's 'true' private self and 'real' love and life are shut out. The emergence of the unconscious beneath the mask is expressed through the series of motifs after the clown has left: Marie's 'Go Henrik' to David, her handing over of the diary and the final removal of the stage paints.

De-masking becomes a familiar motif in a number of Bergman's films after *Summer Interlude*. One of the most striking sequences to portray this de-masking visually is the flashback in *Sawdust and Tinsel* (1953)[35] where Frost the clown goes down to the beach to carry back his naked wife. Frost's humiliation and jealousy parallel the later predicament of the protagonist circus manager, Albert, who also suffers humiliation caused by a straying lover. As Frost carries his wife, the heat of the glaring sun causes the paint to drip off his clown's face, denoting a melting through to the real man. Depicted in the style of a 1920s silent melodrama, the sequence has a nightmarish quality. The camera cuts from face to face, and there are extreme close-ups of mouths, silently gesticulating laughter and shouting. There are some similarities with E.A. Dupont's silent movie *Variety* (1925), starring Emil Jannings,[36] but *Variety* does not use light in the same way as *Sawdust and Tinsel*,[37] where the threatening whiteness of glaring sunshine[38] is intensified by editing.[39] Such heliophobia is also expressed in later Bergman films such as *Wild Strawberries* (1957) and *The Hour of the Wolf* (1966). While Frost plays the paradoxical role of clown through the rest of the film, at this point there is conversely a sense of seeing through to the 'everyman', the unmasked figure of the Christian Mystery plays. Peter Cowie evocatively describes the sequence:

> Grotesque in his glittering costume and chalky make up he resembles some baroque martyr as he staggers ever pitifully over sharp rocks . . . At last he collapses like Christ on the way to Calvary, Alma clinging to him in shame.[40]

Parallels with religious imagery link Frost's experiences with Christianity's symbols of death and rebirth.[41] As with *Summer Interlude*, the mask can be used to emphasize the significance of the unmasked, or de-masked, figure. Thus, the melting of the mask highlights a moment of truth. The heavy disguise, followed by the melting, refers symbolically to the falsifying nature of the mask and its traditional associations with evil and immorality.[42]

Summer Interlude's use of the mask to denote transitional modes of death and rebirth extends into Bergman's later work. *The Rite* (1967), for example, draws on the mask's connections with ancient rituals of sacrifice, purgation and renewal. A trio of actors called 'Les Riens' ('The Nothings') are interrogated by the judge official Abramsson for an 'obscene act' they have been performing. *The Rite* mirrors Bergman's earlier film *The Face* (1958) in the way it highlights the question of power invoked by the mask.[43] At the end of *The Rite*, the trio perform their 'obscene' act, the rite based on one of the ancient rituals of Dionysus,[44] whereupon the judge dies from what is later diagnosed as a heart attack.

Abramsson has committed the rape of a woman known as Thea (lover and wife of the other two performers) and is bound to die. Symbolically, the rape is also a crime against the Dionysian god of renewal and the arts,[45] accentuated by the god's mask 'Thea' wears. The purpose is also to overpower the opponent of the god of arts, completely absorbed in the mask of his profession, and there is a need for purgation. Bergman refers to this performance as the elevation rite, driving away the face of the god, and sees ancient Greek theatre as 'inextricably tied to religious ritual'.[46] As he adds, it can also be found in the Catholic mass, when the priest raises the chalice (the raising of the host in the Eucharist).[47] In a similar way, the Dionysian seasonal sacrifices[48] were marked by the symbols of death, regeneration and recovery.[49]

The donning of bird beak masks, probably suggesting the rite's Egyptian origins, reflects the ambivalence of transcendence, as suggested in Thea's earlier poem about Sebastian (a poem Bergman claims he created as a pastiche of August Strindberg)[50] about the 'half bird, half man' and 'its heavy limbs' binding the body 'as it turns toward the sky'. As Paisley Livingston interprets it, the poem considers the 'impossible aspiration of a soul bound to the inferno of the body'.[51]

Similarly, in *The Face* the ailing actor longs for a knife to scrape out all impurity so that his spirit can soar out of its meaningless body. Later, Vogler leaves Spegel's corpse to be dissected instead of his own, permitting 'another's spirit to fly free'. The desire for dissection defines not only the face but also the body itself as mask, marking out the whole outer layer of the human body as a falsity, with the face an empty shell rather than a key to personality. Somewhere beneath lurks a truth which might be interpreted as the soul.

Summer Interlude and *The Face* begin to raise issues around the idea that the face itself is a mask. These issues are explored in Bergman's later films, such as *A Passion* (1968) and *Persona* (1965), which will be discussed later in relation to its reflexive style. Relatively classical mask discourse has been applied here to highlight the patterns and motifs operating in *Summer Interlude* and initiate some discussion on the way that later films may be approached. *Summer Interlude* draws on various functions of the mask, paradoxically as falsity masking truth and as an expression of truth, an empowering device, appropriate to transitional phases. The film intricately links the psychological and theatrical masks, drawing on possible links with rituals of transformation, suggesting that the process of death and regeneration is in some way achievable in the visionary rituals of theatre.

Summer Interlude centres on Marie's discovery of her true identity, rather than on any differentiation between Henrik and David. Indeed, switching the emphasis to the male figures, as Cowie does, shifts the focus:

> The end of *Summer Interlude* is only seemingly happy: Marie has failed in life; she merely gives in to David in resignation. She realises that it is better to have an inferior replacement for Henrik than nothing at all – or the repulsive caresses of her Uncle Erland.[52]

If the identity of the male figures is not the central concern, then it is not important whether David changes or whether he is a fit replacement for Henrik. Such an interest in an active female protagonist certainly registers the film's potential to be extremely liberating for the time. However, there is scarcely enough screen time devoted to Marie's current relationship with David to support the notion that this is a positive choice for Marie. Similarly, it is not clear to what extent Marie escapes from the patriarchal clutches of the domineering stage manager and wry dance 'master'. In respect of the strategy of the mask itself, the donning of the clown's mask to dissolve Marie's mask can also be seen as overly staged. In addition, certain motifs, such as the diary, have also proved to be problematic in terms of registering signification and meaning. The systematic pattern of motifs within such a tightly organized structure deadens the film's energy, with the result that it glosses over issues of identity that do not conform to fixed binaries of art and life or truth and falsity. As Jonas Sima suggests, the film's 'framework is certainly banal'.[53] Bergman concurs, describing the film as a 'construction' with motifs and themes that increasingly mean less to him as time goes by.[54] Motifs and symbols, so important to Bergman's 1950s films, do seem to be abandoned in Bergman's more pared down 'chamber films' of the 1960s and his stylistically more fluid films thereafter.

The systematic use of *Swan Lake* is arguably also forced, an obvious 'construction', but with a function that is fairly opaque, with its precarious reflection of Marie's life. *Swan Lake* is a tragedy, with origins in fairytale, of two lovers who end their lives in mutual suicide, because they are unable to break the barrier between their two worlds. Odette, princess of swans, is bound to the lake and Prince Siegfried is earthbound.[55] To a certain extent, art mirrors life; Marie is a person by day and a 'prima ballerina' by night. The timelessness of art is indicated by the repeated representation of *Swan Lake* throughout the film. Indeed, exactly the same part of *Swan Lake* (the final death of the lovers) is shown before Marie meets Henrik and when David comes to the wings at the end. The death by drowning resembles Henrik's death from a diving accident. Here, the parallels between the ballet and life come to a halt. It is not a tragedy for Marie. It seems that at the end of *Summer Interlude* the spell on Marie is broken, though not by David's offer of marriage. It is broken by her acceptance of a balance between the two worlds she inhabits, that of her art (the mask, the ballet) and her 'real' life (her 'true' self). She recognizes the value of the mask and is not deceived by its illusions.

However, it might be more positive to see Marie progressing onto something new. The concept of an existing 'truth' to be uncovered during Marie's journey gives the film an oppressive circularity. The film holds fast to fixed binaries, but if there can be two 'selves' (true/false), why not many? Any suggestion of diverse 'roles' is undermined by the female entrapment within these binary structures, which revolve around conventional constructs such as emotional life (inner self) versus working life (mask), love (natural, life) versus ballet theatre (unnatural, death). One side must either be defeated by the other or a 'healthy' balance (i.e. compromise) must be established between the two. It is only via the patriarchally controlled ballet that Marie seems able to approach life, implying that the ending is not new but circular, completing the performance rather than beginning anew. This suggests a compromise within conventional norms and a reestablishment of the status quo.

Summer Interlude can be seen as a model film, working with certain formulations that are extended, challenged or disputed in later Bergman films. The relationship between the theatrical and psychological mask 'works' in *Summer Interlude* via an intricately structured system of motifs that continues into later Bergman films, such as *The Seventh Seal* (1956), *The Face* (1958) and *The Rite* (1967). However, *Summer Interlude*'s binary oppositions, of false mask against true identity, contrast with the very different mind-set seeping into other Bergman films, where notions of 'truth' (and 'reality') are less fixed, for example, in *Fanny and Alexander* (1981/2) which can be analysed in light of postmodernist concepts of multiplicity and masquerade. The frequency and importance of extreme close-ups on faces throughout Bergman's film-making career raises questions concerning both the face as window to the soul – allowing access to truth – and the paradox that faces are in a sense 'unreadable'. While this paradox is acknowledged in *Summer Interlude*, it is not until Bergman's later work (*Persona*, 1965, and *A Passion*, 1968, are obvious examples) that the possibility of unveiling truth is queried more fully. Further implications are that the concept of a core identity is less contested in *Summer Interlude* than in *Summer with Monika* (1952), which explores questions of identity and gender with less rigid assumptions about illusion, reality and truth, challenging the cyclical inevitability of compromise and the reinstatement of patriarchal authority.

3
Female Defiance: Dreams of Another World in *Summer with Monika* and the Early Films

Summer with Monika (1952) is challengingly ambivalent. It bears a strong resemblance to Bergman's 1940s films[1] that value escape as a necessary requirement for the young – as a rule, male – protagonist to gain self-awareness and express defiance against an older, more staid society. However, defiance is short-lived in these films and while escape is important it is as a *dis*illusioning experience that it gains weight. The films end in compromise and a return to conventional society. The ending of *Summer with Monika* seems to suggest a similar resolution, with Harry attaining mature adulthood, returning to face up to his responsibilities and accept traditional codes of behaviour. But Monika refuses to conform; her defiance wrestles with the overt message of the film's ending. It is precisely in this respect that *Summer with Monika* is ambivalent, and it is worth teasing out this ambivalence.

The film ends with Harry, cheated on and abandoned by Monika. Left holding the baby, Harry looks into a mirror on the outside wall of his previous workplace. Two brief scenes from their summer on the archipelago shown earlier in the film appear as flashbacks in the mirror's reflection: Monika running naked across the rocks and Monika sunbathing as the boat pulls off into the sunlit horizon. Harry returns to consciousness as a bell chimes, condensing the previous summer to an illusion. The wording over the mirror 'Forsberg's Glass and Porcelain' recalls Harry's previous workplace when he first met Monika, implying that their summer was a necessary illusion, for Harry to attain maturity and establish a more rewarding career in engineering.[2]

What is even more striking about this sequence, with the benefit of later feminist theory, is its unusual employment of the male gaze. As Harry looks into the mirror, the background fades to black and the camera tracks in to close-up, readjusting as Harry shifts from looking at the baby's reflection to his own, so that his reflection now looks directly at the camera. Psychoanalytically, the use of the mirror might suggest a growth for Harry into a further stage of mature adulthood, a sign that he now recognizes himself as an individual.[3] Certainly, as discussed in relation to *Summer Interlude*, looking in the mirror in early Bergman films generally connotes looking at the true face. The shot also signifies that Harry should be seen as the subject of identification, since his reflection looks directly into the camera. The flashbacks are also concerned with looking. When Monika jumps up and runs off over the rocks, Harry turns his head to look at her, bringing to mind Laura Mulvey's assessment of the female in classical Hollywood film-making, 'displayed for the gaze and enjoyment of men'.[4] The camera pans to the right following Monika as she walks, creating a sense of voyeurism, closely aligned with Harry's gaze within the imagined diegesis. A dissolve joins this brief flashback with the next via the repeated shot of Harry's reflection looking. His face superimposes the image, positioning the dissolving Monika in the centre of his face as it comes into focus. His eyes move to the left as his face dissolves, as if looking towards Monika sunbathing on the front of the boat. The final dissolve back to Harry's reflection leaves the boat now in the far off distance, still just apparent in the right eye of Harry's reflection, reducing Monika and the memory of the escape to an illusion observed by the now mature male protagonist.

However, there are several aspects which might counterbalance this interpretation of Monika as object. Not only does the escape gain more substance in the film than this fragmentary minute-long flashback accounts for, but even within this sequence there are issues about identification and the male gaze. The mirror itself problematizes the cueing of the male gaze. Perhaps most obviously, it can act as a reflexive device, foregrounding the act of looking and male voyeurism, making clear links between Harry's gaze at the mirror surface and the spectator watching the film. But there are also intriguing similarities between this short sequence and other moments in the film. For instance, this is the same mirror that Monika looks in near the beginning of the film to tidy her hair before work, with the same non-diegetic music playing. In addition, the background fades to black, framing the mask-like face, refers back to the café sequence shortly before this where the same device is used when Monika stares straight at the camera. It is a more direct look than Harry's reflected look suggesting that identification might not lie entirely with the male.

It is possible to trace this identification with Monika from the start of the film, specifically in terms of gender, sexuality and class. Harry is the only son of a lower-middle-class man who is constantly ill as a result of his wife's death, when Harry was only eight years old. When Harry invites Monika to eat at his house while his father is at a boating-club meeting, she is impressed with the 'nice place' and goes about examining ornaments from the mantelpiece. Harry's position as a junior assistant in a china and glass warehouse not only aligns him with these 'nice' orna-ments but also serves to foreground his clumsiness, a trait that will con-trast with Monika's practical means of survival on the archipelago, but also a characteristic that he will necessarily grow out of as he matures.

In contrast, Monika's home life in a tenement flat is filmed in a sin-gle, claustrophobic long take. Physically abused by her drunken father, Monika sleeps in the one main room, with at least three young brothers and sisters. Leaning back to smoke, she interrupts her mother's baby feed-ing in a bed behind hers. That Monika's mother is still rearing children, and struggling to survive in this tiny flat, has a bearing on Monika's frus-trations later when, having left the archipelago, she and Harry live in a similar flat with their own new baby. Although not filmed from Monika's literal viewpoint, this attention to Monika's home life does manage to convey a sharing of the space Monika occupies and an empathy with her 'mental position' or attitude, according to Douglas Pye's concept of point of view and the movies.[5] Coupled with the long take, this emphasizes her frustration, allowing an insight into her motivations for revolt.

Exterior shots around Monika's home consist of women shouting, from tiny windows, at children playing hopscotch in cramped courtyards, viewed through low, damp archways. The slightly 'tinny' sounds of the voices and of the street musicians setting up add to the studio feel of these scenes (intentionally or otherwise), contrasting greatly with the outdoor shots during the journey out and the time spent away from the congested city. In a romantic moment, Monika stops to listen to the street musicians serenading, but from a balcony upstairs her young brother shouts 'Mucky Monika' and she marches off, hurling abuse back.

Monika suffers harassment as the only girl working in a wholesale greengrocer's. The surprise of one worker when Monika says that she has a 'steady bloke' and of another when she rejects him suggests that she has been sexually involved with a few of them. One of Harry's work colleagues also refers to her as a 'that slut' at the greengrocer's. Monika shows herself to be strong enough to deal with this harassment, and is as much protagonist as Harry in these early scenes – in fact we see her home life apart from Harry, whereas we only see his *with* Monika. These factors begin to shift the emphasis of the film's title.

Monika's motivations for escape are crucial. The film significantly highlights Monika's working-class roots, suggesting that her escape is more vital than Harry's is, but less goal orientated. Her defiance is more active – she actively leaves her job, she actively leaves home – and more desperate, since the alternative seems to be either financial dependence on a man (with a suggestion of prostitution) or poverty and a repetition of her mother's role.

A closer look at the narrative devices that form the foundation for Bergman's 1940s and early 1950s films will help to highlight striking similarities and differences in *Summer with Monika*. In *Frenzy* (1944), a film for which Bergman wrote the script and was assistant director to Alf Sjöberg, Jan-Erik becomes involved with an alcoholic working-class girl called Bertha who, it transpires, is being victimized by Jan-Erik's persecutor at school, the sadistic schoolmaster, Caligula. When Bertha dies of a heart attack, Caligula sets up a conspiracy to expel Jan-Erik, who then faces a confrontation with his father. After the headmaster's visit and commiserating offer of money, Jan-Erik's revolt ends in resolution; his involvement with Bertha is reduced to a necessary step towards adulthood. Like Monika, Bertha is a working-class girl, abused physically and mentally by the sadistic male, but here the concerns lie with the middle-class male's personal development and disillusionment, much less ambivalently than is the case in *Summer with Monika*.

It Rains on Our Love (1946)[6] was directed by Bergman who, with Herbert Grevenius, also wrote the screenplay, adapted from Oscar Braathen's play *Bra Mennesker*: 'Good (in the sense of "decent") People'. *It Rains on Our Love* portrays two misfits, David and Maggi, who meet at a train station, spend the night together and escape to the countryside to start a new life. Maggi is pregnant by a stranger, having been abused by her manager when she was a dancer, with suggestions that she fell into prostitution. David has been in prison for two years. They are both poor; Maggi cannot afford the train fare to her desired destination and they have to stay in a cheap hostel run by the Salvation Army. In the pouring rain, they walk along the railway tracks towards the countryside, accompanied by a stray dog (reminiscent of Marcel Carné's *Le Quai des Brumes*, 1938) and seek shelter in a summerhouse, which becomes their home. Like Harry and Monika, Maggi and David are finally forced out of the countryside by their 'decent' neighbours, to return to the town.

It is, however, David's isolation that is stressed throughout the film. For example, after the opening aerial shot of the abstract array of umbrella-owners stepping on to the bus, a single umbrella is left behind, held by the narrator (the 'Man with an Umbrella') who throughout the film symbolizes David's inner conscience. These opening shots are mirrored by the aerial shot of David when he first appears at the water fountain taking a drink. As people rush by him, running for the train, he is left spinning in the vortex, trying to pick up his falling apples. Despite the more symbolic style of *It Rains on Our Love*, David is nevertheless represented – like Jan-Erik in *Frenzy* – as an individual to be identified with, in the process of revolt and regeneration.

A *Ship Bound for India* (1947),[7] written and directed by Bergman, adapted from the play by Martin Söderhjelm, is again concerned with life's limitations if there is no escape or subsequent self-discovery. The film focuses on Johannes, who has been brought up in an unloving family on a boat stuck in the mud, spurned by his father for being a 'cripple' – he has a slightly hunched back. Although such frustrations doubtless exist in the original play, they are emphasized in the film by the mise-en-scène, which reduces the internal layout of the boat to geometrical patterns of portholes, wall edges, doorways and stairways. When Johannes returns after a seven-year trip, having finally escaped, he is straight-backed; as a local woman remarks to him, it was not his back that was deformed, but his 'soul.'

Sally, on the other hand, has fallen into prostitution under the harsh patriarchal conditions at the theatre where she works. She explains to Johannes that at her lowest point she could only hope to meet a 'sugar daddy', initially attaching herself to Captain Blom (Johannes's father). The film also explores the claustrophobia and frustration of Johannes's parents, especially that of his father. In the small cabin the parents share, they reflect on 25 years of marriage. Blom tells his wife of his plans to escape with Sally, and his wife tells him in a tone of resignation and exhaustion how her life has gradually lost its value. Blom's plans to escape are necessary illusions, complementing his escapist lifestyle. He is an immature and abusive father and husband, presumably because he has never escaped properly. Johannes experiences similar frustrations to his father, which is why it is crucial that Johannes escapes with Sally, suggesting changing times in the new generation. With the benefit of a seven-year escape, he has the energy to free her, thus fulfilling the active male figure of identification.

A *Ship Bound for India* reveals the main thrust of many of Bergman's films during this time: the revolt of the son against the father, with a

Freudian reinstatement of authority in the father's image, once he has been overthrown. As Marilyn Johns Blackwell suggests, 'What is interesting in Bergman's case is that the revolt is aligned with an allegiance to the female, to the authority of her values and sensibilities.'[8] However, in reinstating the father finally, the female role is rendered redundant.

Common to *Frenzy*, *It Rains on Our Love* and *A Ship Bound for India* is the binary role of the female protagonist as victim/prostitute, pushed to the edge of society, functioning as an agent for the male protagonist's rite of passage. However, from the late 1940s onwards, the representation of the female seems to become less fixed. For instance, while *Port of Call* (Bergman, 1948)[9] is reliant on similar narrative threads, and the stereotype of the female as victim still applies, the social predicaments of the female protagonist (Berit) are stressed more than in the preceding films, so that she is more of a character to identify with. Part of the difference between *Port of Call* and the earlier films lies in its more consistent style, strongly influenced by Italian post-war neo-realism, and specifically the work of Roberto Rossellini.[10] Bergman, agreeing that 1947 was the year the neo-realists made their 'breakthrough', asserts that *Port of Call* 'is in the spirit of Rossellini throughout' and that the semi-documentary style suited *Port of Call*: 'Rossellini's films were a revelation – all that extreme simplicity and poverty, that greyness.'[11]

Port of Call makes use of what Geoffrey Nowell-Smith terms a 'popular setting' with a 'realistic treatment'. While it does not attempt to convey 'historical actuality' or 'political commitment',[12] often associated with the movement, it does pay some attention to socio-political concerns of unemployment, poverty and social injustice, and to the individual, relating a contemporary story with believable characters. Stig Björkman observes this distinction, in discussion with Bergman:

> But one thing which really is characteristic of *Port of Call* compared with your other early films is that the people in it are less romantically conceived. *Port of Call*'s chief characters have much more inner maturity and awareness.[13]

More precisely, it is the chief *female* character that has more maturity and is 'less romantically conceived' than in previous Bergman films. Indeed, the sequence that shifts the emphasis onto Berit's boyfriend, Gösta, jars in relation to the rest of the film. This occurs after Berit reveals her past as an impoverished, dependent female with no direction, and Gösta goes through the process of getting over the shock, which involves a visit from a prostitute during his drinking session, until he sees the light, shirks the prostitute and rushes outside to look at the clouds call-ing Berit's name. Significantly, this was the only part of the film written by Bergman, which he later thinks 'clashes with the rest of the film' and is 'bad anyway' conflicting with the maturity of the characters in the rest of the script; 'It's really a miserable piece of work, thoroughly stylised and semi-literary, utterly out of tune with the rest of the film.'[14]

Significantly, this particular sequence echoes the one in *It Rains on Our Love*, where David, after hearing about Maggi's former lifestyle and that she is pregnant by a stranger, visits a café, becomes drunk and is inter-rogated by the narrator. It is the male protagonist's discovery of matu-rity through escape from the confines of society that forms the pivot for the film, along with acceptance of the low life that the working-class female has fallen victim to. Thus, in these early films, the woman rep-resents a form of escape from the beaten track, potentially dangerous,[15] but necessary if the male is to mature and learn from the experience in the correct way. The fact that the sequence added by Bergman echoing back to an earlier style appears uncharacteristic in *Port of Call* suggests that there is a tendency towards the end of the 1940s, though not in any rigid logical sense, of a move away from the sole identification with the male and the more stereotypical representation of the woman as victim or 'other'. In *Prison* (1949), the first film to be both directed and wholly written by Bergman, there is a further attempt to overcome stereotypical images of the female prostitute, by contrasting the self-assured real-life prostitute with Birgitta, her celluloid substitute in the film-within-the-film, who plays the role of victim and eventually commits suicide.

Despite the increased emphasis on the social predicaments of the female in the films of the late 1940s such as *Port of Call* and *Prison*, the narrative remains centred on the male protagonist who needs to tran-scend youthful illusion by encountering a disillusioning experience, which leads to a level of maturity. Though this maturity involves compromise, *not* to escape – or try to escape – is seen as unhealthy. Paralleling this series of events is the seasonal cycle; typically in early Bergman films, couples meet in spring, have their summer and become disillusioned and 'mature' in autumn/winter.

Bergman's vision of the Swedish summer as 'full of deep undertones of sensual pleasure, particularly June'[16] may be said to reflect more gen-eral Swedish sentiments. Paul Britten Austin draws a vivid picture of Stockholm's December darkness, where the sun rises as late as half past nine in the morning and sets at around half past three in the afternoon. Once the summer has finally arrived, it is overbearingly bright, but extremely short-lived (about six weeks). As Britten Austin points out,

'This general contrast between light and darkness, and between warm, even hot, summers and icy winters, is basic to everything in Sweden and seems to affect all aspects of Swedish life.'[17]

In *It Rains on Our Love*, the couple's happiest moment is during summer, when they are gardening, but which is abruptly interrupted when the official comes to arrest them. They walk off in the end with an umbrella. The 'haven' they are eventually forced to leave – it is actually carried away – is significantly a 'summer' house. Similarly, summer represents happiness in *A Ship Bound for India* and *To Joy* (1950). In *Port of Call*, Berit's final words 'Soon it will be summer' indicate that there will be an interlude of happiness for the couple, however short-lived.

Bergman's early 1950s films explore this structure even more rigorously. *Summer Interlude* (1951) opens with various shots of summer such as sunlit rocky pools, with the song of the cuckoo calling out above orchestral music (the same sound as that during the first summer meeting between Marie and Henrik). Juxtaposed against this is the stark severity of the ominous church steeple, a deafening church bell and visions of bald trees and bleak weather. But the summer is the focus for the (short-lived) romance; Peter Cowie claims that 'No other film has caught so well the buoyant sensuality of high summer in Scandinavia',[18] like Bergman, selecting the word 'sensuality' to describe summer.

The ageing of the dancers is expressed seasonally; when Marie first met Henrik, it was during the spring performance. Now 13 years on, it is autumn, and they are still squeezing into tight costumes. Marie's companion asks what is wrong; is it 'autumn, and kids calling us aunt?' They, like Uncle Erland, are afraid of becoming old, linking age with the seasons in a cycle of inevitability. In such a way, the narrative revolves around the inevitability of death and rebirth, together with the seasonal cycle, as a metaphor both for the transience of the 'summer' experience and for youthful sensuality and romantic escapades. It is within this pattern that the necessary illusion of escape must fit, to convey the rite of passage through to maturity.[19]

Robin Wood discusses the antithesis of summer and autumn felt in the counterpointing of flashbacks and present time in *Summer Interlude*. He examines Marie's arrival on the island, where she follows the old woman in black signifying death (only much later identified as Henrik's aunt) through a bleak landscape of autumnal trees and dark skies. Wood discusses Bergman's 'unobtrusive use of dead trees, present in nearly every outdoor scene, seemingly naturalistic, but a reminder of death in life . . . especially poignant in the wild strawberry scene'.[20] This clearly signals the concept that already in the life of summer lies the death of winter, underlined by the consistent presence of the older more mature Marie, controlling the tone of the flashback.

In *Waiting Women* (1952) the seasonal cycle operates as a means to explore the learning processes that mark the boundaries between youth and womanhood. As four women await their businessmen husbands to join them from Stockholm, they begin talking about their experiences with men, and when they have had to 'face up to life'. Three of the women tell their stories about the moments that led to disillusionment, compromise or truth. The older woman, Anna, has no story to tell; there has been 'no warmth or comfort' in her long marriage.[21] The youngest woman, 17-year-old Maj, also remains silent, as she will not or has yet to experience her disillusionment: 'I refuse to believe that life has to be like this.'

Just before the first story begins to unfold, the age gap between the older women and Maj is expressed visually, in the order of places and the camera angle. Sitting roughly in a v-shape formation, the women's positions make reference to their various current occupations. The two women in the front are preoccupied in sewing and nail filing, respectively. Sitting behind them, within the v-shape, the next two are engaged in knitting – one holding the wool in a loop, the other balling it up. However, at the back, at the central point of the 'v', sits Maj, writing and observing. She has not yet been absorbed into housewifely duties, and is all too keen to create something new, to form a perfect relationship with her boyfriend, Henrik. (There are clearly many connections with the young couple in *Summer Interlude*, in name as in other respects.)

The outcome of *Waiting Women* implies – on one level – that the youthful idealism of love is a mere illusion. This is depicted seasonally, with the climax of the young couple's relationship occurring during the long summer evenings. When Henrik and Maj elope at the end of the film in the small motor boat to foreign places, rejecting the family business, Paul, the oldest family member, remarks:

> Let them go, they'll soon be back. Don't break the rule. Let them have their summer. Suffering and sense and all that all come soon enough.

This sense of cyclical inevitability is borne out by the three stories already told. As the young couple slip romantically away into the sunset to the bell-like music, their personal dreams – faraway lands (Henrik), 'no compromise, be faithful or die' (Maj) – go with them. The illusion is left hanging, ambivalently, with the possibility/hope of the dream remaining, in contrast to the outcomes of the previous relationships. To Maj at this stage, death is preferable to compromise, a telling statement which could be interpreted as a pre-echo of Monika's lack of compromise in *Summer with Monika*.

While Bergman's comedy *A Lesson in Love* (1954) focuses on the effects of an affair on a marriage rather than the theme of the youthful illusion of escape, there is a similar concern with the seasonal cycle. The fleeting illusions of an affair instigate the breakdown, and then final reestablishment of a marital relationship and loving family. David, a gynaecologist married for 15 or 16 years, is seduced in his office by the youthful Susanne. The subsequent affair, recaptured in flashback sequences, from the back of the car on the way to the train station, is envisioned romantically in contrast with the 'reality' of the journey. Half awake, half asleep, David's dreamlike voice-over begins 'I saw her first last spring' and continues 'I saw you every day, like summer itself.' A later dissolve reveals memories of his 'Summer with Susanne . . .' in a static shot of their boat out across the lake. The flashback continues ('Yes, that was a summer') presenting Susanne waking up with glistening water reflected on her skin. These magical moments are comically disrupted and undermined by moments of realism such as Susanne snatching David's pipe – symbol of his age, sex and stability – and David sulking childishly. Once again, the relationship is seasonal, and when summer is over, the bickering begins. This is represented symbolically at the start of the film when a musical box figurine couple, in eighteenth-century dress, dance mechanically until lightning forks flash across the screen and an abrupt thunderclap dissolves the twinkling music.

Blackwell proposes that 'in the pre-trilogy works, not surprisingly the imaginer is male, while in the post-1960 films it is female',[22] citing Jessica Benjamin's suggestion, in relation to Freud and the supremacy of the father that 'revolt is always followed by guilt and the restoration of authority'.[23] These are extremely helpful observations. Common to *Summer Interlude, Waiting Women* and *A Lesson in Love* is the transience of youthful summer illusion, emphasized in each case by its location within a flashback, controlled by the imagination of the protagonist. The urge for revolt is thus destabilized by the necessity of a return to patriarchal norms, albeit that these norms are starting to be represented as comical clichés in *A Lesson in Love*.

As its title suggests, *Summer with Monika* is also bound to this structure of cyclical inevitability. Opening with shots across the industrial smoggy port, there is a sense of a crying out for sun, strongly reminiscent of Carné and Rossellini. When Monika first encounters Harry at the café, she declares: 'Spring is here . . . too nice for work. Let's clear off and travel and see the world. How about it?' As they chat, Monika describes the coldness of her workplace: 'Last winter I thought my arse would freeze off', as she leans up against Harry, as if to get warm. When the couple leave the café, a drunken old man laughs, 'There's a touch of spring in the air', and his fellow drinking companion's snores seem to suggest that disillusionment is inevitable.

Weather is certainly a factor in the possibility of escape. In a plan to shelter Monika, Harry tells his aunt, who is staying while his father is in hospital, that he needs a sleeping bag for a mate who is camping. Reference is made to the fact that it is too cold to camp, and as he takes Monika to his father's boat, wind rattles against the water. A pan up from the outside of the tiny boat on this chilly night focuses on the dwarfing bridge. As the shot pans back down again, it is the following day and the water is bathed in sunlight, indicating an overnight transition from spring into summer, and anticipating the transition from city to nature that will follow. The journey out to the archipelago occurs through the blazing sunlight, and Monika wakes up at around ten past five the following morning with the sun glistening on the roof.

The effect of passing time is depicted with the occasional rainstorm followed by sun shining through a dark cloud. The onset of autumn brings with it, as far as Harry is concerned, the necessity of returning to Stockholm, when Monika casually mentions that she is pregnant. Their baby's name 'June Monika', decided by Harry, forges an obvious link between Monika and the summer interlude. However, Monika's 'No, I'm not going back, I want this summer just as it is' offers a bold new perspective that battles with the overt message of the film's ending. Alongside the suggestion that Harry has matured from his summer illusions is the possible alternative suggestion that he has not moved on at all. After all, there can be little consolation in the final shot of Harry walking off round the drab street corner passing Monika's father with his drunken colleagues. The lyrical intensity of the summer lingers on. As Jörn Donner suggests, the summer sequences recollect a very different form of Italian neo-realist film-making: 'de Santis' almost commercial sensualism'.[24] Moreover, what makes *Summer with Monika* unique among Bergman's early films is that summer is first conveyed not in flashback but with the full potential of what that summer might achieve, taking up half an hour of screen time.

It is worth noting that the extremely popular Swedish film *One Summer of Happiness* (Arne Mattsson, 1951) was made between *Summer Interlude* and *Summer with Monika*. Like *Summer with Monika*, it was censored abroad because of its explicit love scenes beside a lake and its nude bathing scene. Other aspects also make it a precursor of *Summer with Monika* such as the pastoral photography, the dance scene, the repressed authorities and the frequent use of close-ups. However, in terms of narrative, it strongly resembles *Summer Interlude*. As Brian McIlroy asserts, it is 'a quest for validity'[25] in which a student called Göran remembers at Kerstin's funeral his 'true' romance with her. The film is more retrospective than *Summer with Monika* and the themes such as the Church's interference in the lives of the young people, echo Bergman's 1940s films, in particular *It Rains on Our Love*. Again, while many similar traits are evident in Swedish film-making during this time, the focus on the potential of the woman's dreams of escape seems to be unique to *Summer with Monika*.

Monika's dreams of escape are closely connected with the cinema. She prompts Harry to ask her on their first date to see the recent movie *Song of Love*, and she is shown to be completely absorbed in the glamorous female star's face illuminated against the darkness during the big screen kiss, following her words 'You may kiss me now, honey.' On the way back, Monika dreams about the elegant things surrounding movie stars as she looks at a blouse in a shop window, inviting Harry to put his arm around her saying, 'You may kiss me now, Harry', directly echoing the film. As she says this, shot in darkness, she faces towards the camera, her close-up face lit against a dark background, mirroring the film star and an anticipation of the close-up of her stare in the jazz café towards the end of the film. It is her own reflection that she looks at, to top up her make-up in her small mirror compact, as she again consciously echoes the language of movie stars, saying that she is 'crazy' about Harry. Her identification with the female star suggests an absorption in the illusion of what she might be and that her role as a woman is constructed.

Escapism, as a substitute for actual escape, is a theme that can be seen in Bergman's earlier films. The fairground scene and the world of the music hall offer a sense of release and escapism for Blom in *A Ship Bound for India*, though it is clear that such escapism is only momentary and ultimately achieves nothing: Blom's ship is in reality stuck in the muddy docks of a Swedish port, and has made no journey to foreign shores. In the smoky music hall where Blom goes to see Sally sing and dance, he can forget his stagnant life and meaningless marriage. He also has a cherished room in town where he keeps souvenirs and photographs from lands he has always longed to visit, but never has. As in Henrik Ibsen's play *The Wild Duck* (1884),[26] the illusion of this cherished room helps him to get through another day and can inspire new dreams, but also hinders new growth or change.

It is via the 'other world' of the cinema that Monika's drive for escape gains force. She is the instigator of the escape, and the various shots of the city during the journey out allow for the transition to another world. The harmonica music that starts up as the two figures become just visible standing on the front of the boat is the same music that was playing outside Monika's flat when she stopped to daydream, implying that the dream of this escape is predominantly Monika's.[27] On their arrival, when Monika recalls the book *The Lawless Lover* they read the day before, they jump up and down banging their chests, fingers in mouths making 'Red Indian' calls, transforming the Swedish archipelago into the wilds of America – a constructed illusion, which we are invited to share. During their first day, the close-up of Monika's face, eyes shut, cheek against Harry's obscured face, as she places her cigarette in his mouth, vividly recalls the couple kissing in the movie previously, again indicating Monika's reconstruction of this other world.

Although the time spent on the archipelago is seen as the fulfilment of Monika's dream, the representation of Monika remains ambivalent, making her appear both as a figure for identification and an object.[28] The sequence with Monika awakening at dawn on their first morning away is voyeuristic, almost predatory. The camera tracks alongside Monika, as she walks barefoot in white shorts, followed by a cut to a long shot across the bay showing her in the distance, merged with the tall grasses beside the water. There are further shots of her running, rather awkwardly, washing and preparing the stove. All the while, Harry sleeps. There is a sense that we are seeing the 'real' Monika but, while Monika is significantly alone, allowing a situation which might potentially provide privileged access to her thoughts, such access is eschewed. The felt authorial presence of the camera hints at Bergman's relationship as lover with Harriet Andersson,[29] the actress who played Monika, the link with nature providing what might be seen as an awkward simplicity in the representation of women.

Monika certainly demonstrates survival instincts in the final stages of their escape. She insists on going to a private garden to steal apples and potatoes and, as Harry pulls helplessly at a tree, Monika goes around the back of the house. She is caught stealing in the cellar by the mother and is forced into the bourgeois house. Inside reeks of middle-class comfort, shot in a single long take to emphasize the claustrophobic effects it has on Monika. Conforming to traditional roles, the father rings the police, while the mother brings in the joint of meat, shot in close-up on the table. The clean, respectable daughter of about Monika's age, wearing a white blouse and dark pinafore dress, sits beside Monika, who now appears scruffy. When the father returns informing them that it will not take the police ten minutes by car, and goes to get a beer, Monika seizes the joint of meat, tearing at it like an animal – as Donner asserts – like an '*enfant sauvage* at bay'.[30] The father's dependence on modern transport is similar to Harry's growing association with the train (he drifts off on his delivery bicycle resting on the barrier at the train crossroads at the start of the film but he himself uses the train for business trips by the end).[31] Both the father and Harry are thus aligned with civilization or patriarchal law and order.

In contrast, Monika seems to represent a repressed rawness, having been dragged up from the cellar, now crawling through the trees, stopping occasionally to tear off bits of the meat with her teeth, as a dog barks. Shots of a dark sky and water dappled with sunlight accompany the sound of her breathing. There is a cut from a close-up of a spider at the centre of its web to Monika in the tall grass, suggesting – somewhat obviously perhaps – her own entrapment. When she reaches Harry with the boat her determination is clear, 'If you can't manage I will . . . I don't want to go back, I don't want anything! I don't want to!'

There are conflicting representations of Monika here. While she is rather conventionally associated with nature she also symbolizes the political potential of dreaming. Within the world that she has dreamed up, she is able to fabricate a new life with different codes, adopting different roles and resisting conventional discourses, suggesting that gender roles are constructed and not fixed. This is why it is so significant that ultimately her only motivation for returning to the mainland is a trip to the cinema, where role-playing is key.

We also see in Andersson a new kind of female star emerging. Melvyn Bragg recollects seeing *Summer with Monika* for the first time during his first homesick term at university:

> *Summer with Monika* spoke to the condition of many adolescents in the 50s: it could have been my story or that of thousands of others. The nerve of it was that somehow and for the first time, I think, a film tapped itself into the real root of what I knew I had in some measure or would in some measure or wanted in some measure to experience. The bait was Harriet Andersson.[32]

To Bragg, both the 'drab' town and Monika – or Andersson herself – were new kinds of representations, more 'real', and yet at the same time something 'to experience', rather than identify with. He describes how, in contrast, the cinema was traditionally a place for escapism: 'Another

World'.[33] In *Summer with Monika*, this other world helps fuel the dream of escape, which Monika comes to embody, but paradoxically the contrast between Monika and this glamorous other world also marks her out as being more 'real'.

This concept of Monika/Andersson as representing something new is complex, because there seems to be both the sense of her being a figure to identify with ('her mores and her attitudes struck chord on chord') and a sexual object ('Harriet Andersson's erotic charm, her playfulness and sense of life').[34] Similarly, describing Harriet Andersson as 'eroticism incarnate' in *Summer with Monika*, Cowie attributes references to the film in François Truffaut's *The 400 Blows* and other movies as representing 'Nordic ecstasy', but Cowie also describes Andersson's allure as having a 'carnal quality' that 'thumbs its nose at glamor'.[35] Paradoxically, Monika's iconic image is strong enough to connote active rebellion.

Truffaut and other contributors to *Cahiers du Cinéma* were, as Jim Hillier asserts, greatly impressed with Bergman's work as well as with other European directors at the time:

> There is in Godard's, Truffaut's, and Rivette's[36] writing of this period (in *Cahiers* and elsewhere) about Bergman, for example, a recognition of the proximity between Bergman's situation as film-maker and their own actual or potential situations, as well as a recognition of some shared attitudes to both the world and the cinema . . . Truffaut emphasizes Bergman's simplicity, his exploration of essentially personal concerns . . .[37]

Indeed, Fereydoun Hoveyda's article on Truffaut's *The 400 Blows* strikes a chord, since the words he uses to describe the child's predicament can also be applied to Monika:

> The child has no choice but to forge an acceptable world for himself with the means at his disposal. But how can he escape the tragedy of everyday life, as long as he is torn between his parents – fallen idols – and an indifferent, if not hostile world?[38]

In this sense, then, the reference in *The 400 Blows* plays tribute to what Monika stands for in relation to youthful revolt and the potential for overturning conventional, patriarchal codes.

As a way of concluding this chapter, it is worth returning to one of the most remarkable sequences of the film, in which Monika sits in the café, with an unknown man, and gazes into the camera in a long take, while

Harry is away on a business trip. The shot is followed by the night-life montage of neon lights and dance headlines that *might* be interpreted in line with Bergman's 1940s films in which the working-class girl resorts to (virtual) prostitution in order to survive. This is Wood's view, comparing Monika to Henrik in *Summer Interlude*, suggesting that while Monika is not dead, 'we are in no doubts as to the life into which Monika is being sucked'.[39] Other critics concur. Cowie argues that Monika suffers no remorse with the new lover, and that this 'last passage suggests a return to the bleak sordid life of the early Bergman films'.[40] Donner suggests that although the film does not directly condemn Monika, she 'drifts back to her former life'.[41] Philip Mosley interprets Monika's stare as 'contemptuous' and 'partly defiant', suggesting that she is to be the 'whore/victim' of the early Bergman films.[42]

But there are other ways of interpreting this sequence. Discussing the stare itself, Wood notes the darkened screen around Monika as almost the only departure from the film's strict naturalism, interpreting Monika's eyes as paradoxically 'ashamed and defiant'.[43] Defiant possibly, but also unreadable. Wood's suggestion that this is a departure from naturalism seems here to be the most telling observation, since this moment can be taken to be an anticipation of elements in Bergman's later, more reflexive films such as *Persona* (1965) and *A Passion* (1968). The gaze at the camera marks a moving out of and beyond the fiction. It also signifies a defiant female response to the heterosexual male gaze long before Mulvey's influential article on the subject.

It is certainly not confirmed that Monika becomes absorbed into a sordid lifestyle, although the links with the earlier films suggest that this *might* be the case. Alternatively though, it is important to stress the openness and the range of possibilities here, relating to performance and reflexivity, together with the sense that this is an authorial poem to the actress Harriet Andersson (similar to Jean-Luc Godard's later work such as the portrayal of Nana/Anna Karina in *Vivre sa vie*, 1962). It is interesting that both Mosley and Wood should use the term 'defiant' to describe Monika's expression. Bergman has said that it was on viewing the film *Defiance* (Gustav Molander, 1952) starring Andersson that he decided to audition her, since she was in his opinion very 'Monika-ish' in this film.[44]

The static close-up of Monika's illuminated face against the dark background could also be taken to be the moment when Monika becomes the movie star, having just taken a puff from her cigarette like the movie star seen earlier. The dizzying montage of nightclubs and dance halls is ambivalent. It may be taken to signify her future lifestyle as a dancer and the accompanying abuse and prostitution indicated in the earlier films, or it may show Monika as she dreams to be, recalling her comment earlier, 'People in films go to clubs and dances and all that.' The montage certainly contrasts with the heavy claustrophobia of the earlier shots and is, arguably, as much a celebration of Monika's fantasies as an indication of a future downfall.

Summer with Monika marks a shift towards the prominence of the female figure for identification in many of Bergman's later films. While the film is unique among Bergman's other early 1950s films in that it depicts the female's refusal to conform, it is nevertheless significant that *Summer Interlude*, *Waiting Women* (1952) and *Journey into Autumn* (literally translating as *Woman's Dream*, 1954/5) all have female protagonists. We might also see *Summer with Monika* at the dawn of a post-war trend of European films placing importance on the female point of view. There are already signs of this in Italy, for example, with the focus on the personal development and conflicts of the female characters played by Ingrid Bergman in Rossellini's films such as *Viaggio in Italia* (1953) and *Fear* (1954). We might also think of some of Michelangelo Antonioni's works such as *La Signora senza camelie* (1953) and *Le Amiche* (1955) during this period. Similarly, in France, Louis Malle's *Lift to the Scaffold* (1957) depicts Jeanne Moreau's character wandering through the streets searching for her missing lover. Such signs can be seen perhaps even more markedly in the 1960s. For example, Alexander Kluge's *Yesterday Girl* (1966) strongly identifies with the young female refugee from East Germany, wandering destitute through the 'Economic Miracle'.

There is a discourse around the necessary illusion of escape in Bergman's 1940s and early 1950s films, which seems to be breaking down in *Summer with Monika*, to some extent challenging the reinstatement of authority in the father's image. As the escape is conveyed in full, not simply in flashback, with the full potential of what that summer might achieve, so is the cyclical inevitability challenged. Monika's 'I want this summer just as it is' offers an enlightenment beyond the dreariness of Harry's compromise and a cyclical return to the film's beginnings. The escape gains importance, not simply as a *dis*illusioning experience, opening up another world where Monika can play out new roles, and more traditional nurturing roles are questioned, moving beyond the binary relationships evident in *Summer Interlude*. The final flashback reflections, reducing the summer to an illusion – necessary to attain maturity – are (at least) balanced by Monika's challenging, active and defiantly illegible gaze at the camera, in a film that remains ambivalent, perhaps unresolved.

4
Religion, Truth and Symbolism from *The Seventh Seal* to *The Silence*

Thematic developments

Religion has been a major preoccupation throughout Bergman's career, but it became the main focus for the films of the late 1950s and early 1960s, coinciding with the period when Bergman became known outside Sweden. While films of the late 1950s (*The Seventh Seal*, 1956; *The Face*, 1958) are critical of orthodox religion and outdated religious ritual, there is nevertheless a quest for a more internally spiritual or 'truer' faith. Unique moments of happiness, like the wild strawberry sequence in *The Seventh Seal*, symbolize the truth in human communion, both in contrast to and as original source of religious rituals of more conventional communion ceremonies. The quest to unveil a raw, original source of truth beneath religious convention recalls the de-masking process in *Summer Interlude* (1950). The quest for truth begins to crumble in *Through a Glass Darkly* (1960), marking the advent of the three films later to be termed the trilogy,[1] which focused to a far greater extent on human characters than Bergman's work of the late 1950s. With *The Silence* (1962), the last film of the trilogy, also comes a questioning of words and images as signs or symbols of meaning.

The quest for the secret of existence drives the narrative of *The Seventh Seal*. The title's reference to Revelations suggests that there can be no proof of God until the Last Judgement and the opening of the seals:

Even if these seals are broken, the scroll remains sealed and God's secret preserved. Not until the seventh seal is broken may we learn the secret of existence.[2]

While the seventh seal signifies the situation of mankind at the end of existence, as Egil Törnqvist asserts, it may also relate to the individual's last judgement when faced with death.[3]

The film's apocalyptic opening introduces fixed character types – Antonius Block (the knight), Jöns (his squire) and the allegorical figure of Death. The time granted by Death via the game of chess allows the knight a chance to delay death. Ultimately, though, this delay allows a brief moment of insight into the secret of existence, which the knight finds embodied in Jof, Mia and their baby Mikael, and time to perform a truly good deed, when he saves them (however temporarily) from death. The implication of this discovery of a meaning to his life is that the church that has sent him on the crusade holds no real value for him. There is a clear distinction between what is seen as internal truth or faith and more external ritual or orthodoxy, mirroring the truth/falsity dichotomy of the mask evident in *Summer Interlude*.

Jof represents the simple, good life, but is also a visionary, who exaggerates his visions. Mia visually resembles Jof's vision of the Virgin Mary, and walks Mikael like the virgin walks Jesus in the vision. This gives Mia a celestial quality that lasts through the film and connects with the holy connotations of their names. Jof's description of his vision to Mia indicates a point of view far closer to the image than the viewpoint taken by the camera in this scene. This conveys Jof's predilection for fabrication, but also allows him to make further comparisons with Mia. He talks of the virgin's small brown hands and bare feet as she walks with the child, mirroring the depiction of Mia in this sequence.

These descriptions compare with the medieval frescoes Bergman describes as the influence on his one-act play, on which the film was based, *A Painting on Wood* (directed at The Theatre School, Malmö, in March 1955) in particular the representation of Mary as a peasant woman, making Bergman's play a kind of 'Biblia pauperum'. As a Lutheran priest, Bergman's father preached in small country churches, where Bergman as a child would look towards the sunlit images of medieval paintings and carved figures above his head, especially those at Haskeborga Church. Among the images were angels, saints, dragons, prophets, devils, humans, serpents in paradise and the eagle of Revelations:

> In a wood sat Death, playing chess with the Crusader. Clutching the branch of a tree was a naked man with staring eyes, while down below stood Death, sawing away to his heart's content. Across gentle hills Death led the final dance toward the dark lands. But on the other arch the Holy Virgin was walking in a rose garden, supporting the Child's faltering steps, and her hands were those of a peasant woman . . . My

intention has been to paint in the same way as the medieval painter, with the same tenderness and joy.[4]

These images clearly influenced sequences from *The Seventh Seal* as well as *A Painting on Wood*. Charles B. Ketcham observes that William Barrett, writing at the same time as Bergman was directing *The Seventh Seal*, discussed the decline of religion in Western history: 'The loss of the Church was the loss of a whole system of symbols, images, dogmas, and rites which had the psychological validity of immediate experience.'[5] *The Seventh Seal* criticizes 'religion' as an institution and the subservience of the masses to the fear generated by the church. The depiction of this is particularly heavy-handed in the sequence with the squire and the painter. The painter points out the 'small, terrified human face' of a character facing death depicted on his church fresco, reflexively referring to the fresco that was the original stimulus for the film. The squire asserts that if the picture scares people they will go running 'right into the arms of the priests'. The painter justifies it, 'I have to make a living – at least until the plague takes me', implying that he follows the church's orders out of financial necessity. In addition to condemning the church, this sequence also highlights the artist's easy rejection of his own free will, contrasting him with the knight, who recognizes his freedom.

Occasionally *The Seventh Seal* alludes to an inconclusive form of existentialism[6] via the changes that occur during the knight's reprieve. A transition occurs during the confession, when the knight reveals his recent anxieties about the existence of God and the 'phantoms', 'dreams' and 'fantasies' of his life's expectations. He wants 'knowledge' or proof that God exists, again conveying a variation on the morality play counterpart:

Is it so cruelly inconceivable to grasp God with the senses? Why should he hide himself in a mist of half-spoken promises and unseen miracles?

The possible consequence of the knight's unanswered questions is that 'all is nothingness'; as Death suggests, 'Perhaps no one is there.' The knight speculates that God is an illusion forged out of fear, a viewpoint developed further in *Through a Glass Darkly*. It is this internal development that leads the knight, at least temporarily, to the philosophical standpoint where he must 'carry out one meaningful deed'. This intent is not linked with any idea of personal redemption, salvation or approval from God. To some extent, Block's questions represent the first steps in philosophical discovery towards aspects of Being, relating *The Seventh Seal* to 1940s existentialism such as Jean-Paul Sartre's *Being and Nothingness* (1943), which set out a radical doctrine of human freedom. The knight's decision to carry out one meaningful deed signifies a quest for authentic personal being, and fits in with the existentialists' 'il faut s'entraider' ('you [one] must help one another'). The suggestion here is that, as Sartre argues, 'existence' comes before 'essence' and that:

> Man is nothing else but that which he makes of himself . . . man will only attain existence when he is what he purposes to be.[7]

While such existentialist impulses are evident in the film, its resolution and the wild strawberry sequence in particular offer the possibility of a spiritual significance, an essence before existence that pushes against existentialist belief.

Moreover, despite aiding the 'holy family' and realizing momentarily the value of their company, claiming that it will be enough for him, the knight continues to seek the existence of God (suggesting that ultimately it is not enough). He is also, therefore, Everyman facing death, and the film structurally resembles *Everyman* in many respects. It is not surprising that Bergman directed *Play of Everyman* by Hugo von Hofmannstahl, in which Max von Sydow was highly praised for his 'pious emotional power',[8] just before beginning *The Seventh Seal*. However, there are crucial variations. As Ketcham points out, 'A mediaeval knight might have raised the question of salvation because of his sinfulness or his unworthiness, but he would not have raised the anguished question: Is there a God?'[9] Here the allegorical structure of a morality play is adapted to fit the contemporary questions of doubt rather than guilt. Unlike *Everyman*, the God who/that the (cerebral, high-born) knight seeks does not appear in the film, leaving questions hanging ambivalently; the knight dances off with Death at the end. Prior to this, while the other characters face Death, Block is kneeling, head turned upward and away from Death to the one glimmer of light from the distant window. This denial of death conveys an isolated figure, either about to achieve enlightenment or arrogantly deluded.

Conversely, Block's squire Jöns ('everyman' John), played by Gunnar Björnstrand, signifies the self-parodying carnal body of lust and action, sweating and wiping his mouth with his hand:

> This is squire Jöns. He grins at Death, mocks the Lord, laughs at himself and leers at the girls. His world is a Jöns-world, believable only to

himself, ridiculous to all including himself, meaningless to Heaven and of no interest to Hell.

While Block saw the metaphysical vision of Death, Jöns sees an actual corpse. Both are blind to each other's visions. Jöns is more individualized than this, though; while he scoffs at pictures of corpses, he then asks for a brandy, out of fear rather than gluttony. He is of a lower social standing than the knight, but his cynicism reflects a heightened sense of learning. Jöns's importance as a character in *The Seventh Seal* is suggested by his prominence in *A Painting on Wood*. While Bergman's play contained more or less the same characters and even some of the same actors as the later film, 'only one character may be found full-blown, and that is Jöns the Squire, whose dialogue in play and film is almost identical line for line'.[10] Significantly, Björnstrand had also played the stage character.

Despite being opposites, Jöns and Block work together and mirror each other. For instance, both go some way in helping Tyan the 'witch'; Jöns hands Tyan the water, while the knight gives her the sedative potion.[11] Similarly, Jöns's protection of Jof in the inn anticipates the knight's safeguarding of the 'holy family' later. At the end, though, their extreme opposition to each other is again emphasized. While the knight kneels in the background, the squire – adamant to the end that there is nothing there – is in the foreground with the other four. There is a medieval style 'conflictus quarrel' between the two halves of the double protagonist.

When Jöns saves the girl from Raval, recognizing him from theological college, Jöns mocks Raval's previous pretensions to academic religiosity. It was also Raval who, ten years before, convinced the squire's 'master' (Block) to 'join a better-class crusade to the Holy Land'. The squire's comment to Raval ('now you know better . . . now you are a thief') links Raval's thieving nature with the High Church and orthodox religion institutionalized at the time. Both steal money from the dead. It is also a further commentary on the futility of the crusade and the fragmentation of the church during crisis.

While the squire's heroism and hedonism, reminiscent of a Camus anti-hero, are appealingly humorous, his subsequent ill treatment of the mute girl and his ill opinion of women, compromise or complicate his position as a character of sustained identification. He is a valuable comical counterpart to his master, denouncing religious faith as an illusion – 'Everything is worth precisely as much as a belch, the only difference being that a belch is more satisfying' – but not an answer to the film's central questioning.

Death represents both the knight's fear and the possibility of knowledge, since Death's actions will lead to the revelation of God or nothingness. In the opening, he is given a celestial quality; as Törnqvist points out, his reading of Revelations relates to the Prologue of a medieval morality play such as *Everyman*, and also suggests that he may have divine status.[12] However, as Törnqvist goes on to argue, he approaches the knight from behind like a traitor, suggesting that he might be an angel of the devil.[13] It is thus significant that Death is represented as a white clown, as discussed in Chapter 2, signifying the 'falsity' or sham of his role,[14] and linking him with the illusory nature of 'God'.

The final 'Dance of Death' and the salvation of the 'holy family' Jof, Mia and Mikael serve as a resolution to the film and a reworking of Revelations,[15] adapting it to the more humanist viewpoint that heaven exists on Earth, as opposed to the arrival of *God* on Earth, with the wiping away of tears by rain rather than God. The 'holy family' are saved from Death, as Joseph, Mary and Jesus were saved from Herod. But it is also due to Jof's visionary capacities (he sees Death playing chess with the knight) that they are 'saved', as well as the knight's actions, suggesting that there is a celestial truth to his existence. Significantly, the film ends with angels singing 'Soli Gloria Deo', echoing the angel's singing to the Glory of God in Revelations, and contrasting with the 'Dies Irae' of the opening.

Similar visionary endings are evident in *Wild Strawberries* (1957)[16] and *The Virgin Spring* (1959). While Bergman was reliant on the original folk song and legend[17] when directing *The Virgin Spring*, and it thus lacks the doubt and complex questioning of *The Seventh Seal*, it is useful to note that Bergman was still attempting to resolve his films of the late 1950s with an element of hope:

> . . . the welling up of the spring was not meant as simply the tidy expression of a religious miracle. The spring was the medieval symbol for the water of the feelings. I didn't see how it was possible to allow the picture to end without the spring without there being a 'great silence' and 'no release' for the characters or the audience.[18]

The paradigm of this truthful way of being in *The Seventh Seal* is the wild strawberry sequence, where the knight comes nearest to peace.

As Birgitta Steene suggests, Mia officiates at the communion of humans; wild strawberries are sometimes linked with the Virgin Mary in late Northern iconography.[19] The bowl of milk is raised and held between the hands like the communion cup. Block recognizes the value of this tranquil occasion, 'And it will be an adequate sign – it will be enough for me.' The film places emphasis on *the moment*, when a celestial God is evident in infinite love. This kind of iconography, embodied in the bowl of milk, the wild strawberries and the celestial sunlight, begins to evaporate in the trilogy.

The trilogy

Through a Glass Darkly (1960): 'certainty achieved'
Winter Light (1961/2): 'certainty unmasked'
The Silence (1962): 'God's silence – the negative impression'

In terms of Bergman's additional subtitles to the newly formed 'trilogy', *Through a Glass Darkly*'s 'certainty achieved' is transformed into an illusion. The film ends with the coming together of father (David) and son (Minus), when David tells Minus that God is love in all its forms, 'We can't know whether love proves God's existence or whether love is itself God.' When David has left the room, Minus says wistfully, 'Papa *talked* to me' and the statement verges on cliché, since 'papa' can also connote 'the Father' or 'God'. David's suggestion that love overpowers all the angst that has gone before may be seen to offer a hopeful resolution to the film, in line with *The Seventh Seal*, *The Face* and *The Virgin Spring*.

However, it is difficult to accept the film's ending as a resolution. When Karin sees God coming out from the wall, it is a cruel vision of a spider God. It is not a vision we share with her, but a link is made with the helicopter that arrives at this moment to take her away.[20] In *Winter Light*, Tomas describes to Jonas precisely what the spider god means. It is the monster creator contrasting with the security God, the 'fatherly God . . . Who loved all men' but oneself most of all, allowing one to refuse to 'accept reality' and deny evil. The helicopter represents a horrific world that a monster creator might be responsible for, symbolizing institutional control.

David's words *as* ending imply the denial of both the spider god and nothingness (no God) in favour of the security God. Robin Wood sees the ending of *Through a Glass Darkly* as the weakest ending in mature Bergman, because, he claims, it undermines Karin, who he perceives to be the key character.[21] Wood sees it an error to make Karin insane, arguing that Bergman is obviously 'half-afraid' of her. Wood asserts that Bergman pretends, along with David, that 'God is love, in all its forms'.[22] However, Karin's madness does not necessarily function on the level of making all Karin's visions delusions. Karin possesses acute perception of inter-family relationships, perhaps suggesting that those who see the world's horrors cannot remain deluded by the security God.

Bergman has claimed that doubts about the ending caused him to write a 'sequel' refuting David's self-protecting 'security God':

> It (*Winter Light*) is a pendant to *Through a Glass Darkly*. An answer to it. When I wrote *Through a Glass Darkly* I thought I had found a real proof of God's existence: God is love . . . and I let the whole thing emanate in that proof, it came to form the coda in the last moment. But it only seemed right until I started shooting the film . . . For that reason I smash that proof of God in the new film.[23]

As a *resolution*, as John Coleman asserts, it 'hardly winds up a wet afternoon of incest and horror on the helpful note it appears to by itself', and the closing line by Minus does seem uncomfortably 'starry-eyed'.[24] Jonas Sima suggests that Jörn Donner's only objection to the film is Minus's final line, losing credibility on the basis of the preceding narrative. Bergman's response in this instance is useful:

> He's right. But wrong too. What makes him feel its inadequacy is that the film, as such, could never have been naturally one with its final sequence. They stand there side by side, quite dead. The simple reason is that there was no natural emotional bridge in me between the somewhat hopeful message of the end and the pessimism of the rest of the film.[25]

Minus recognizes the self-delusion of his father's words, and distinguishes them from his father's genuineness: 'Your words are terribly unreal, Dad. But I see that you mean what you say.' While out fishing Martin criticizes David's 'monstrous inventiveness'; 'Have you ever written so much as a true word in any of your books?' David's problems with communication and paternal care are presented early on, during his tearful breakdown in the opening sequence. As Tony French suggests, the evidence of David's own realization of his flaws serves to question 'whether we are being encouraged to believe that David's words are true even for him'.[26] As Ketcham asserts, the suggestion is that 'Truth' exists 'somewhere and that language functions merely as its conveyor'.[27] In this respect, David's words are a *lie* (not consciously told), suggesting discordance between word and truth that will increasingly become apparent in *Winter Light*, *The Silence* and *Persona* (1965).

Steene, Wood and (sometimes) Bergman[28] see *Through a Glass Darkly* as 'faulty' for attempting to cling onto the 'security God' that they suggest is replaced in *Winter Light* by humanism. In striking contrast,

Arthur Gibson sees *Through a Glass Darkly* as a film in the process of discovering 'humanistic insufficiency':

> ... man must learn that his loving (of fellow man and, above all, of God) must be a steady self-transcendence, never a retrograde involution upon himself or upon his species.[29]

These diverse readings warn against claiming any singular 'meaning', but the ending does not necessarily attempt to uphold an ill-fitting desire for the security God. Minus does not agree with David's words *per se* but rejoices in human contact, suggesting a move towards humanism, but not necessarily a resolution. Once the security God has been abandoned, there is a choice between the spider God, a transcendental God (Gibson), humanism (Wood/Steene) or nothingness. In short, *Through a Glass Darkly* begins to challenge the overriding belief in a true vision apparent in *The Seventh Seal, The Face* and *The Virgin Spring*.

Although interpretations of *Winter Light* vary tremendously, it is generally agreed that the film attempts to 'smash that proof of God'. As Steene asserts, the 'smashing of the coda' involves abandoning the 'security God',[30] a God that is represented as an illusion, created for personal security, in denial of the horrors of the world. However, critics differ on what is being suggested as a replacement, if anything at all.

At the end of *Winter Light*,[31] in a remote church at Frostnäs in Southern Sweden, Tomas Ericsson, Lutheran pastor, officiates at an evening communion, thus celebrating the Eucharist, sacrament of the Lord's Supper. Four hours have passed[32] since the communion service at Mittsunda, another church not far away, where Tomas lives. At Frostnäs, the only communicant present is Märta (also present at the previous service) who has travelled there with him. Her presence is all the more poignant for her adamant disbelief in the existence of God:

> God doesn't speak. God hasn't ever spoken, because he doesn't exist. It's all unreservedly, horribly simple.

Even though there is no congregation, apart from Märta, the sexton and the organist, and the latter two seem keen to go home (it is a bitter, frosty evening), Tomas decides to go ahead. Before a bare church, he proceeds with the ritual, ending, 'Holy, Holy, Holy, Lord God, Almighty. All the world is full of your glory.' These words, echoing out in the silence, within a similar space to the opening service, might emphasize the meaningless ritual religion has become.[33] Since the earlier service, one of the communicants, Jonas, has killed himself through despair of the world and fear of Chinese bombing and after a conversation with Tomas. Tomas's initial hopeful advice that God is full of love is refuted soon after by Tomas himself in a sudden revelation of his brewing fears. Tomas tells Jonas that his security God was established during his protected upbringing. The horrors of 'bloody real life' such as the Spanish civil war, 'turned God into a spider God', leading him into hiding and denial. He suggests that there may be no God at all:

> Well, and what if God doesn't exist? . . . What a relief! And death – extinction, dissolution of body and soul. People's cruelty, their loneliness, their fear – everything becomes self-evident – transparent. Suffering is incomprehensible, so it needn't be explained . . . There isn't any creator, no-one holds it together, no immeasurable thought to make one's head spin . . . We're alone, you and I.

However, the tone is, as Ketcham suggests, one of 'defiance' rather than of 'doctrine'.[34] The security God is replaced by earthly beauty:

> You must live, Jonas – summer's on the way. After all, the darkness won't last forever. You've got your strawberry beds, haven't you, and your flowering jasmine? It's the earthly paradise, Jonas.

Tomas tells him that they can be good friends, 'You've given me your fear and I've given you a God I've killed.' The 'killing' of God has been read diversely: as a movement towards a transcendental God (Gibson) and as an affirmation of humanism (Steene and Wood). Alternatively, it might be interpreted as a complete refutation of God.

The representation of the opening communion (also based on the Last Supper) as a now meaningless ritual is suggested by the single long take used to distribute the 'bread' to the five communicants around the circular bench. The shot remains static on the medium close-up of Tomas throughout this opening recital, emphasizing his monotonous tone. A cut across 180 degrees reveals in a long shot that Tomas is standing centrally with his back to the congregation further emphasizing his alienation from his congregation. The crucifix over the arch above his head suggests his clinging to iconographical faith. As they pray, there is a dissolve to shots across a landscape that in its bleakness confounds transcendence; the church a dark sombre block in a frosty landscape. The dissolves to a higher line of horizon across water also suggest a ghostly anticipation of Jonas's suicide at the rapids, against Tomas's voice over, 'Lead us not into temptation, and deliver us from evil.'

After a slow dissolve back to Tomas, followed by a cut to depict him turning round to face the congregation, cutting is used much more frequently to highlight each character's response to the service. For instance, there is a cut from Märta, who is not singing, to a close-up of the 'bread' on a plate, with Tomas's thumb just in view. This is followed by a long shot of Tomas standing. The symbolism of this becomes clearer as the film develops. After the ceremony, Märta says that she sees the taking of the communion as a love feast. While Tomas is fixated on transcendental 'love', Märta attempts to share a physical love. The camera tracks forward towards Tomas's face, as he says, 'Our Lord and Heavenly Father, we offer and present unto thee ourselves, our souls and bodies to be a reasonable, holy and lively sacrifice unto thee.' This is followed by a cut to Märta's saddened face, as the camera tracks forward to close-up, mirroring the previous pattern. When Tomas later reads Märta's letter, it echoes these words but in human terms, 'I love you . . . I love you for you. Take me and use me.' Märta offers a 'real' physical love, or sacrifice, in contrast to the transcendental offering. Following his discussion with Jonas, Tomas stares hopelessly out of the window, uttering, as the camera tracks in to close-up, 'God, why hast thou forsaken me?' As the camera tracks back, Märta is revealed falling back into the shadows, unbeknown to Tomas: *she* has not forsaken him. They proceed to embrace passionately.

Tomas's and Märta's physical reunion leads into the sequence where Tomas visits the scene of Johan's suicide, singled out by Wood as the 'core',[35] and Steene as the 'Nadir',[36] occurring halfway through the film. There is a cut from Tomas's departure alone in the car to his arrival at the rapids, spanning the longest period so far in the film. The long shot of Tomas's arrival and the long take as the camera tracks Tomas's journey from the body to the car and back to the body, against the roaring of the rapids, detach us from the events and emphasize Tomas's isolation. Märta comes over from the car, but is gestured away by Tomas's harsh arm movements. It is a surprise to see her, since it seemed that Tomas left alone in the previous sequence, suggesting that Tomas has stopped for her, which will add to the narrative developments in the schoolroom later.

Wood and, independently, Steene see the moment when Tomas pauses at the door after criticizing Märta in the schoolroom and asks her to come to Frostnäs, as a turning point in the narrative. Although we know that he has stopped for her already once today, this is the first moment actually shown in the film. However, the motivation is ambiguous; it is possible to question, as Märta does, 'Do you really want me to? Or are you just afraid again?' It can thus be taken as a crucial moment, or just another repetition of a habit drawn out of fear. However, when they leave the schoolhouse, Tomas gives Märta the car keys, and she now drives the rest of the journey to Fröstnas, suggesting her new-found importance to Tomas.

According to Wood's and Steene's accounts, the scene with Märta in profile, head bent down praying, saying 'If we could believe in a truth', juxtaposed with Tomas in profile, head in the same position, marks the coming together of the two in a faith bearing humanistic traits. Tomas's new approach to God must begin on Märta's deeply personal level. Before this, the organist has deflated the idea of Tomas's ideal dead wife. Wood sees the ending as an explicit communion between Tomas and Märta, 'an ending of uncompromising honesty'.[37]

However, writing at the same time as Wood, Gibson takes a wholly different view, with *Winter Light* playing its part in the movement away from humanist beliefs, a progress through to a 'radiant, austere, celestial God' in *Persona* after the 'awful interposition of the supreme alienation of *The Silence*'.[38] For Gibson, *Winter Light's* ending marks the unmasking of the 'humanistically restrictive pseudo-identification of love with God'.[39] While I do not share Gibson's view, it helps to show that the trilogy is open to a number of very different interpretations.

Bergman later claimed that *Winter Light* represents the final break with 'God', moving towards a focus on human relationships; he wanted to say 'Paul became Saul', simply, 'without symbols'.[40] Robert E. Lauder also argues that the ending points towards human love as the only salvation available.[41] This viewpoint, along with Bergman's retrospective opinion also in the 1980s, seems to suggest that in *Winter Light* God ceases to be an issue, that it is human love *alone* that exists, in other words giving a slightly different emphasis from Wood and Steene.

The final sequence at Frostnäs Church does seem to highlight in a graphic way the growing connection between Tomas and Märta. In the vestry, the sexton suggests that people dwell too much on Christ's physical suffering, observing that what must have been most painful was the desertion of Christ by his disciples and the (seeming?) desertion by God. He quotes Christ's last words, 'God, Why hast thou forsaken me?' echoing Tomas's words earlier. Such horrible doubts plague Tomas, who is also 'not long for this world'. The subsequent slow dissolve from Tomas's face to Märta's face can suggest various 'meanings': that Tomas, finding there is no God, realizes that Märta is the only one who has not forsaken him; or that Tomas realizes that he must continue to believe since all Christians, even Christ, are tested by God's silence; or that, as Steene and Wood suggest, Tomas's relationship with God from now on can only exist on Märta's human level.

Even Bergman's 'Paul became Saul' is complicated in his later writing:

> If one has religious faith, one would say that God has spoken to him (Tomas). If one does not believe in God, one might prefer to say that Märta Lundberg and Algot Frovik are two people who help raise a fellow human being who has fallen and is digging his own grave.[42]

Or, it is possible to interpret that there is no such happy ending either way. The denial of any dominant system of signifiers makes it difficult to offer an absolute reading of the film. All that can be said with any certainty is that Tomas's belief in the security God crumbles in the light of modern horrors. The profile close-up of Märta sitting in the pew, cut with the final medium close-up of Tomas, muttering 'Holy, holy, holy is Lord God Almighty' does heavily insinuate an intimacy between the two of them absent at the start, making it hard to agree with Gibson's interpretations of the film. Although the words of the final communion themselves are more optimistic, their monotonous delivery echoes the opening, suggesting that words are meaningless as *The Silence* suggests.

The Silence, implying absence of sound, assumes 'The Silence' not only of God, but also the collapse of communication between human beings. Communication is central to *Winter Light* which, analysed in its most positive light, affirms a renewed importance in the communal link between Tomas and Märta as humans. But in *The Silence*, which will be discussed in more detail later, ritual and communication are empty of all value. Significance and meaning dissolve away in this 'negative impression' where God is not, and where actions and thoughts are only as important as the individual sees them to be. *The Silence* observes the breakdown of language[43] focusing on the smallest hints of other more valued forms of communication.

Stylistic developments

Discourses emerged in Britain and North America during the 1950s and 1960s, formulating distinctions between mainstream and art cinema. Discovered as the 'new', 'foreign' or 'art film' director by British and North American newspaper critics, it was via this medium that Bergman was loved and loathed with a great intensity and rapidity. Here, the Bergman phenomenon was exposed, debated and disputed, which entailed some detailed analysis of film style as part of critics' attempts to define broader concepts such as what 'art cinema' was or should be.

Bergman was first discovered outside Sweden when his sixteenth film *Smiles of a Summer Night*[44] triumphed at the Cannes Festival. But Bergman's reputation reached its peak in the UK around 1958, coinciding with the screening of *The Seventh Seal*, which had won the Special Jury Prize at Cannes in May 1957. According to Leslie Mallory's account in the *Evening Standard*:

> No director, British or foreign, has ever been honoured in this country as Bergman has. No director in history has ever had three of his pictures included in the best ten of the year, as he has! You can get tickets for 'My Fair Lady' more easily than for the summer-long season of Bergman's pictures now running at the National Film Theatre. Cinemas in Hampstead and elsewhere are trying to mop up this frustrated overflow by arranging Bergman seasons of their own.[45]

By 1960, Bergman's films were acclaimed widely in the US.[46]

The Seventh Seal's 'modern' questions about religion and the meaning of life, conveyed in an allegorical style more generally associated with literature than with film,[47] made it stand out. Melvyn Bragg even singles the film out as a turning point in cinematic history:

> . . . generally the screen was for entertainment: for the real stuff of thought you opened a book. Bergman upended all that in the one film.[48]

Bragg's further suggestion that via Bergman 'a generation sought out De Sica, Fellini, Visconti, Rossellini, Carné, Renoir, Truffaut, Buñuel, Kurosawa, Ray' is extremely misleading as a general view. However, it does indicate the way that Bergman became labelled, along with other European directors, as a 'foreign' or 'art' film director.

There is a connection between the knight's moral free will and Bergman's persona as 'art film' director, choosing to follow his own ideas, resisting the alleged ideological dominance of Hollywood. The fact that Bergman had never visited the US, or taken up the offer to make a film there, became part and parcel of the Bergman myth at this time. It was mentioned in all the lengthier contemporary newspaper articles, particularly in the US. For example, Hollis Alpert describes Bergman's rejection of Hollywood, despite an American executive's offer of fruitful returns: 'The executive mentioned money, upon which Bergman proceeded to outShaw GBS by implying he was more interested in art.'[49] Svensk Filmindustri, at which the 'bright directional star Bergman' preferred to work, free to edit from beginning to end, came to represent independence from US censorship and economic power and the triumph of art over commercialism.

Newspaper critics frequently interpreted the backdrop of the plague in *The Seventh Seal* as an allegory of the atom bomb. Dilys Powell implies that it amounts to little else, 'What he [Bergman] has done is, drawing on the figures of medieval religious painting – Death, the Holy Family, the Crusader – and using a mixture of historical imagination and, as I say, allegory, to make a film about fear of the H-bomb.'[50] Few articles failed to use the term 'allegorical'. Thus, in addition to the apocalyptic mania specifically invoked by the plague, there is also the suggestion of a whole civilization in crisis, which – if godless – is a threat to all institutions, conventions and illusions of stability.

The question of whether the characters, 'evidently meant to portray various types of simplified humanity',[51] are simply symbolic provoked much debate:

> Nor should the film simply be labelled 'symbolical'. Its characters do not 'represent' something other than themselves; they are what they appear to be.[52]

> All these people, as in Langland's 'field of folk' are live individuals – not only the world in microcosm.[53]

At the same time, Isabel Quigly denounced these 'fantasies involving puppets, not people'[54] criticizing the 'shiny' film's moral poverty compared with its visual richness:

> . . . the formal beauty of his groups and landscapes is breathtaking: but when he tries to get to grips with the real world, however allegorically, and to ask questions about the human condition, he seems bankrupt.[55]

As Lloyd Michaels suggests, engagement with character generally relies on 'a represented person that corresponds by analogy to our understanding of personhood in real life without being confused with reality'.[56] That Nina Hibbin attributes the knight's and squire's failure to rescue the 'witch' as 'excruciating sadism'[57] suggests an apparent scarcity of character-motivated cause. Powerless to save her, as discussed earlier, they give her water and a sedative to ease her suffering. However, Hibbin's response suggests that the *cause* for their lack of action is not foregrounded (enough).

By the end of the 1950s, with films like *The Face* (1958), *The Virgin Spring* (1959) and *Devil's Eye* (1960), critics began to tire of the all too familiar allegorical style, so established for well-informed filmgoers that it began to be seen as pretentious and easily parodied.[58] Bergman's popularity plummeted across Europe and then America. *The Virgin Spring* was loathed as *The Seventh Seal* had been loved.[59] The extent of this sudden fervour against Bergman at this time suggests that he was suffering at the hands of fashion. By 1960, as quickly as he had risen to fame, Bergman became 'unfashionable' in Britain and then North America, or stopped attracting fashionable audiences and exciting the young, even when his work was acclaimed in other directions.[60] The symbolism, the visual imagery, the emblematic characters, the fairytale setting[61] and the nostalgic screen of a bygone age were becoming a cliché.[62] Critics were demanding a change in style.

Through a Glass Darkly (1960) seemed to offer a direct response to this demand for change. It was critically acclaimed as a 'powerful, personal experience',[63] forging a new stage in Bergman's career.[64] An article in *Time* magazine helps to clarify the term 'personal' in this context, describing the film as Bergman's 'ripest' because it consists of 'characters for whom the audience cannot help but care', taking the tinge off the cold irony and giving everything a 'kindly glow'.[65] The characters no longer emerge as symbols.

W.J. Weatherby (in the *Guardian*) maintains that *Through a Glass Darkly*'s reduction of characters to just four and its remote setting make it 'more real' than most of Bergman's earlier creations, enabling a 'close study of the interplay between personalities' as opposed to penetrating ideas or themes.[66] The move away from celestial preoccupations towards a focus on human relationships seems to call for a style that is less 'shiny'. As John Coleman remarks:

> . . . this is the sparsest film he has yet made. Everything which he has thought to be irrelevant has been squeezed out.[67]

Like *The Seventh Seal*, *Through a Glass Darkly* opens with a quotation from the Bible. However, rather than the dramatic voice-over, white words appear silently on a black background. As Ketcham asserts, the quotation marks a shift 'from the apocalypticism of "The Revelation of St. John" to the personal confrontation supplied by a reference to what is the most widely known passage in all of St. Paul's letters, the thirteenth chapter of his "First Letter to the Corinthians"'.[68] The thirteenth chapter ends:

> When I was a child, I spoke like a child, I thought like a child; when I became a man, I gave up childish ways. For now we see through a glass darkly, but then face to face. Now I know in part; then I shall understand fully, even as I have been fully understood. So faith, hope, love abide, these three; but the greatest of these is love.

Following the words, sombre and restrained cello music by Bach plays as the credits appear. In contrast to the mood music of *The Seventh Seal* which punctuates the atmosphere and themes, cueing the spectator in a more classical way, the music here is used to create a tone, and it is chamber music, using a single cello rather than an orchestra. No music is used in the remaining sequence, creating a sense of sparseness or lack of (a need for) dramatic punctuation. The personal dedication, 'To Kabi, my wife', makes this film unlike any Bergman film previously, or since, until the final dedication 'To Ingrid' (Bergman's deceased wife) in *Saraband* (2003).

The coastal location of *Through a Glass Darkly*'s opening also recalls *The Seventh Seal*, but here the characters wade through the sea to the shore, suggesting a more naturalistic edge, beginning with the everyday activity of bringing in the net, carried out by contemporary characters, indicated by costume and use of 'modern' terms and categories such as Karin's 'schizophrenia'. After the credits, nothing but naturalistic sound is used, and there are long periods of no dialogue. The four characters are portrayed equally emerging from the sea, their voices echoing out in a loud cacophony of laughter and shouting. An extreme long shot is used, and held, emphasizing the length of time that it takes them to walk up to the beach. As they approach the pier, they argue jokingly over the various combinations of who will share which task, denoting complex human relationships and the randomness of events.

There follows a series of parallel edits between Karin's father and husband (David and Martin, respectively) taking out the net together, and Karin and her brother Minus collecting the milk. Visually, the men are more ordered in their activities, winding up the net, rowing in the boat, talking constantly and joking. The entire sequence with Karin and Minus is less rigid, filmed as a long take, as Karin spirals around her brother twice, and for some time they do not speak.

The Seventh Seal seems to be filmed with a confidence in how to show and how to tell. *Through a Glass Darkly* does not seem to have that confidence. *The Seventh Seal* uses a more expressive style along with conventional or classical modes of editing; it was the philosophical content that made it stand out as a new type of film for its era. With *Through a Glass Darkly*, however, there is a sense that some of the security props that have previously been relied upon are discarded in favour of a new approach. The characters contain various layers and discuss trivia such as the details of Minus's Latin lessons, making the film different not only from *The Seventh Seal*, but also from more classical film-making.

The horrors of Karin's madness begin to confound the idea of a God. While Mia teases Jof about his visions, the subject of madness is not touched on in *The Seventh Seal*. Karin's delusory state draws attention to subjective perception, making cues for what we are to take as true and untrue much hazier than in the earlier film. The arbitrary nature of existence is brought to light as David and Martin discuss Karin's chances of survival, which confounds the more comforting concept of a personal last judgement. The concept of God's reflection in the goodness and beauty on earth would seem trite in this context.

Arthur Knight's contemporaneous review of *Through a Glass Darkly* observes a general reduction of everything that is not of vital necessity:

> He seems deliberately to have eschewed the symbolism, the convoluted flashbacks and the lush imagery of his most popular films to create a new style with its own rewards – all sinew and bone, stripped down to the essentials. Its story takes no sudden tangents; its conclusion is stated with unabashed baldness.[69]

However, symbolism is present in *Through a Glass Darkly* even though the film lacks the *kind* of symbolism evident in *The Seventh Seal*. Lennart Nilsson (in *Time*) defines symbols like Karin's spider god as 'metaphysical insights'.[70] The door is opened for Karin by the breeze of the helicopter that will take her away to the mental hospital. The helicopter is also metaphysical incarnation of the spider god, an expression of Karin's schizophrenic state of mind, as opposed to a symbol of the type used in Bergman's earlier films. 'Darkly', a contemporaneous review in *The Times*, describes Karin as a

> schizophrenic who is disintegrating under the strain of living in two worlds, the visible, tangible world where all seems orderly and secure, and her inner world of madness and delusion. Even the world Karin thinks to be rational is not, however, quite as she thinks it, and so Bergman is concerned with a double aspect of illusion, with metaphysical subtleties which he presents with an air of straightforward

realism. This again, however, is not what it seems to be, and it is by means of symbol and suggestion – Karin's incestuous love for her young brother finds expression in the hold of the stranded ship – that he feels his way towards an understanding of Karin and those who stand in such close and tragic relationship.[71]

The film works on several levels, conveying events which happen as part of the narrative with a linear orderliness, events which do not seem to fit into the narrative and events which may not happen at all, or happen in a metaphysical sense. Within these psychological dimensions the incest may or may not occur, anticipating some of the ambivalences of *Persona*.

Winter Light works with a similar concentration of characters, predominantly just two: Märta and Tomas. Like *Through a Glass Darkly*, there is no single protagonist. Characters are once again located within a small, cut off community, and time is limited still further, to four hours. Developments through the film are on a personal level. Symbols in *Winter Light* are uncomfortably obvious, rather than part of an overall allegory. Tomas's doubts are conveyed in relation to Christ on the cross. The dying Christ hovers tragically behind him during his most dark moments, but also exists as part of the diegesis. It is a comment on the silence of God in the same way that the prominent flask of coffee reflects his tiredness. These are not symbols on the allegorical level of, for example, the chessboard in *The Seventh Seal*.

In *The Silence*, characters continue to rise in prominence above plot. The anonymity of Timoka, where even the language is made up,[72] helps to establish it universally as a place on the verge of war or during the aftermath of a war, as Bergman asserts:

It's a country preparing for war, where war can break out any day. Whether it's a civil war or what, I couldn't say; but all the time one feels it is something perverse and terrifying, these tanks in the streets. I happened to be in Hamburg just after the war, and one saw a lot of that sort of thing. The city had already been massacred; but at night tanks drove about the streets, or simply stood silently sleeping at street corners.[73]

Any film that contains the inexplicable emergence of tanks around street corners inevitably lends itself to interpretation in the symbolic sense. However, Bergman claims that *The Silence* 'tells its story by simple means, not with symbols and such antics'.[74] It may seem that Bergman is being provocative with this statement, since *The Silence* has rarely been received as a 'simple' film. However, it can be said that the film constructs a mood or atmosphere, 'closer' to each character, in a similar style to *Through a Glass Darkly*.

Links with music are evident throughout the trilogy, which have not been so apparent before. *Time*'s description of *Through a Glass Darkly* as a 'quartet' with its 'thematic analysis of four lives' implies that the film presents a theme, with variations on this theme, focusing on the unravelling of the four characters.[75] Bach music plays at key moments through the film, and is the only form of extra-diegetic music. For instance, Bach starts up during the scene when Karin and Minus are together on the rotting boat, conveyed at the far end of the hold. The first time we hear it (apart from the credits) is when Karin reads her father's diary. French asserts that 'this marks her exit from anything but sporadic sanity'.[76] In this case, the music draws attention to the melancholic stages of Karin's illness. The music is slow and contemplative, in sharp contrast to the dramatic cues of the earlier films such as the music accompanying Jöns's point of view as he looks at the skull (*The Seventh Seal*).

While *Through a Glass Darkly* began with Bach, Bergman has claimed that *Winter Light* began with Stravinsky's *A Psalm Symphony* and *The Silence* with Bartok's *Concerto for Orchestra*. It was his original idea with *The Silence* to attempt to obey musical laws instead of dramaturgical ones[77] presumably meaning that the scenes work by association rhythmically – with themes and counter themes. He suggests that all that is left of Bartok is the beginning with its 'dull, continuous note followed by a sudden explosion'. The 'dull, continuous note' presumably refers to the long take and whirring train sounds of the opening, as the camera pans from left to right and pauses on the three characters individually. Real time is conveyed as the boy, Johan, stands, fills the screen space and looks directly into the camera, wiping his eyes. The effect of a dull note continues with the silent visual blur when the boy, shut out of the women's compartment, looks through the window at tanks passing. These are envisioned from Johan's low angle, as menacingly huge, ever more dizzying as the camera pans from left to right, the tanks themselves facing left. Disparity between the outside world and Johan's world is created by the use of the window as screen, emphasized when he places his hand flat on the glass, attempting to make sense of the images he sees (a precursor of *Persona*). The tanks become a series of abstract patterns, black blobs on a white background. The silence heightens the abstraction and draws out the rhythm. The 'sudden explosion' comes with the cut to an extreme high angle, overlooking the town, with its heavy traffic, deafeningly loud; Johan looks out of the window at the people rushing by.

Music provides one of the few reliable sources of communication. Diegetic music is used to suggest levels of Ester's character. As she puts on some jazz, a close-up shows her hand come alive. She kisses her hand in a moment of happiness and the music becomes romantic. Only in this environment is she free to work, and confident enough to touch the sleeping Anna and Johan. The music reaches a climax. In contrast, when Ester goes out onto the balcony, the music stops abruptly, highlighting the alienating traffic sounds and the metaphysical horror of the emaciated donkey. The emaciation is caused by the effects of war, but also refers to Ester's own illness. There is a cut to a close-up of the radio, and a return to the romantic music, which Ester clicks off abruptly, reflecting her sudden change of mood highlighted by the immediate close-ups of the bottle, glass and cigarette.

Similarly, music conveys Ester's emotions, following the sequence in which Anna and Johan discuss when they may be leaving and whether Ester will be going with them. Ester, alone in the dark foreground, recalling Isak in *Wild Strawberries*, is visually alienated from the brightly lit mother and son in the back room, as they talk to each other and hug. The cut to Ester is marked by the slight rise in volume of the Bach piece. It is a moment of striking intimacy when the concierge knocks and, entering, occupies the same foreground space as Ester. Despite the language barrier, they are linked together by their knowledge of the composer's name, 'Johann Sebastian Bach', which is unchanging in each of their languages. The tension between the sisters is also conveyed by their disparate feelings towards music. Although Anna says that she cannot leave Ester like this, her failure to recognize Bach, and the subsequent close-up of her hand as she switches the music off, suggest that the sisters are already wrenched apart. Significantly, at the moment when Ester and the concierge discover a mutual appreciation in music, Johan is sitting on the threshold of the doorway between the two rooms, halfway between the sisters.

The trilogy works stylistically under new guidelines, and the musical connections tie in with the concept that these films are – to a greater extent than Bergman's previous work – chamber films:

> *Through a Glass Darkly* and *Winter Light* and *The Silence* and *Persona*
> I've called chamber works. They are chamber music – music in which, with an extremely limited number of voices and figures, one explores the essence of a number of motifs. The backgrounds are extrapolated, put into a sort of fog. The rest is distillation.[78]

The term refers to August Strindberg's invention of the term 'chamber play', used to imply, 'the intimate course of events'.[79]

In order to achieve intimacy, and to reduce the 'false' sense of a staged play, Strindberg constructed a set of dramatic principles and ideas. This consisted of the use of a small set of characters, together with the 'closeness' or sparseness of setting. A reduction in set decor should, according to Strindberg in his Preface to *Miss Julie* (1888), mean that the 'audience's imagination is set in motion'. Moreover, the use of a single set should 'enable characters to accustom themselves to their *milieu*, and to get away from the tradition of scenic luxury'.[80] Strindberg's other ideas included: the removal of footlights, the rejection of anything 'false' such as obvious make-up and a visible orchestra, naturalistic acting (with actors not being afraid to turn their backs to the audience) and the adoption of a small stage and small auditorium.

The trilogy, with its use of a small set of characters, naturalistic acting, the sparseness of setting and events and the concentration of time are thus integral to Strindberg's ideas about intimacy. This links in also with the contemporary critics' sense that these films are in some ways more 'real'. The use of music also indicates a paring down with, for example, the cello chamber music of *Through a Glass Darkly*.

The quest for religious truth ends with the last film of the trilogy. A preoccupation with God becomes a preoccupation with the interrelation of humans. The film marks an end of the appliance of religious symbolism, as Wood suggests, 'There is nothing that cannot be explained "naturalistically".'[81] Christian symbols that are evident have lost their meaning, and the film highlights their new-found insignificance. As Ketcham argues, the church bells ring but mean nothing. The first sexual encounter is inside a church, not out of anger or defiance (fornication in the presence of the Host) but out of indifference and comfort – it is 'dark' and 'cool'. The emaciated donkey pulls a cart with a potted palm tree, drops it and returns, but burdened with useless, broken furniture, the palm is the 'herald of nothing'.[82] It is not so much that there are no symbols, but that these symbols are deprived of meaning.

As Anna remarks to Ester, 'When father was alive he decided things. And we obeyed him . . . When father died you thought you could go on the same way . . . You can't bear it if everything isn't a "matter of life and death" and "significant" and "meaningful".' Ester is silent to the end, as Anna asks her why she continues to live. While 'father' might signify 'God', these words connote a challenge to the patriarchal symbolic order that will continue on into *Persona*, when Elisabet ceases to speak.[83]

The early 1960s was a crucial period for Bergman's film-making in terms of developing a less ornate or elaborate style, with reduced reliance on symbolism, almost parodying it in places and a greater emphasis on human relationships, contrasting with the pre-ordained tapestry effect of *The Seventh Seal* or *The Face*. This stylistic shift coincided with thematic shifts, the paring down reflecting a moving away from religious preoccupations to consider language and truth, the semiotics of communication and signification within fictional narrative. The next chapter will further consider the problem of legibility in relation to Bergman's next 'chamber film', *Persona*.

5
Persona: Cinema as Mask

Like the trilogy, *Persona* (1965) fits Bergman's conception of a 'chamber film', referring back to August Strindberg's term 'chamber play' used to denote a compact structure, a small cast, limited action, intimacy and a concentration on the emotions. *Persona* resembles Strindberg's *A Dream Play* (1901) with its fluid boundaries between reality, dream and the imagination, its ghostly edge, its formal repetitions and rhythms and its representation of people as phantoms, illusions and dream visions, as Birgitta Steene suggests 'taking the spectator into both a realistic mise-en-scène *and* a reality beyond the tangible world, that is, into transcendent states of mind' with 'an all-encompassing dreamer consciousness that hovers over the dramatic action'.[1]

Persona concerns the actress Elisabet Vogler (Liv Ullmann) who falls silent mid-performance (the link with the theatre suggesting that she drops the *mask* of speech). This silence continues into her everyday life. The narrative begins with her stay in hospital, where the female psychiatrist or doctor suggests that Elisabet and her nurse Alma (Bibi Andersson) leave to convalesce on an island. There the nurse and actress experience emotional and fraught moments together.

One of the main talking points about *Persona* has been the scenes and events that border on the 'unreal' such as Elisabet's visit to Alma's room at night and the visit of Elisabet's husband. These episodes may be bracketed as Alma's or Elisabet's dreams, for example, but the more thorough attempts at discovering (through use of lighting, sound, context, language) which parts might fit into the category of 'real' sequences and which fall into some other category (dream, hallucination, wish fulfilment, personal subjectivity, abstraction), though extremely interesting, have usefully concluded that such boundaries are often unclear and frequently misleading.[2] This lack of clarity points towards some of the obstacles that *Persona*, as mask, puts in the way of confident reading. In *Images*, Bergman claims that when Elisabet refuses to speak, 'in fact, she doesn't want to lie'.[3] The fraudulent nature of words is expressed in the extract that Bergman cites from his notes in preparation for *Persona*, where he created an imaginary diary for Elisabet:

> Then I felt that every inflection of my voice, every word in my mouth, was a lie, a play whose sole purpose was to cover emptiness and boredom. There was only one way I could avoid a state of despair and a breakdown. To be silent . . . reach behind the silence for clarity.[4]

As discussed in Chapter 2, traditionally the mask is a symbol of superficial and fundamental characteristics, suggesting a true, private person hidden from view. The term 'mask' might apply to the mask itself, the dramatic role, the person and the face. It also signifies voice amplification ('per sonare': 'to sound through') as well as providing, paradoxically, a bar to the face. The programme for the Academy Cinema Two, where the film was first screened in London (1967), begins to unpack the mask motif: 'Persona: the Latin word for an actor's mask, mask and face, as it were, becoming one.' The mask motif culminates in the composite close-up of Alma and Elisabet (Bibi Andersson and Liv Ullmann), alluding to the mask of cinematography.

A number of Bergman's early films such as *A Ship Bound for India* (1947) and *Summer Interlude* (1950) reflexively foreground cinema's illusions via metaphorical allusions to theatre. Direct reference to cinema is evident as early as *Prison* (1949), which uses a film within a film structure. Two characters, themselves protagonists in a film already set up with title credits half way through, view a flickering projection of a man in white bed clothes chased by a skeleton. Bergman created this farcical scene as a child, and parts of it are flashed onto the screen in *Persona*, at the opening and then, later, after the midway breakdown. With *The Face* (1958) released in America as *The Magician*, as 'tricks' of a nineteenth-century magician are put to the test by a group of officials, a face projected upon a screen anticipates the artifices of cinematography.

Narrative ambiguity: Reality, fantasy and reflexivity

Persona questions the capacity of traditional forms of narrative to communicate truth, recalling Thomas Elsaesser's search in 1971 for a way of describing the kind of truth offered in Jean-Luc Godard's films: 'Neither realistic fiction, nor documentary, nor subjective projection, their reference-point was, and remained, that aesthetic *persona*, the poetic self, bodying itself forth as "the raw realism of subjectivity".[5] While it is clear that Godard and Bergman are not always motivated by similar forces, Elsaesser's terminology here does seem to be relevant to *Persona*'s exploration of the film as body, projected as a stylistically conscious mask ('persona'). These kinds of terms can be used in an attempt to define modernism. As Marilyn Johns Blackwell argues: 'Modern art, in its anxious reflection on its own substance, has become, in Roland Barthes' phrase, "a mask pointing to itself".'[6]

After May 1968, challenges to traditional fiction, allegedly signifying bourgeois ideology, were given a more political justification. However, in his earlier work Godard was much more interested in the artificiality of appearances. As Peter Wollen suggests, Godard explored 'the impossibility of reading an essence from a phenomenal surface, of seeing a soul through and within a body or telling a lie from a truth'.[7] In addition, Wollen asserts that Godard sees silence as the only true communication and highlights Godard's horror of acting based on the 'logocentric' aversion to a person who speaks someone else's words. It is in this sense that we might begin to make links between *Persona* and Godard's early work.

This sense of distinguishing truth from lie seems to be one of the central concerns in the sequences which refer to specific historical events: the photograph of the boy in the Warsaw ghetto and the television clip of the Vietnamese Buddhist's suicide. A useful stance to take here is Penelope Houston's example of comparing the scene of the Buddhist's suicide on television with the (opening) stigmatic hammering of the nail into the hand, suggesting that though both are painful to watch, reason argues that the nail shot is faked.[8] Houston's distinction is also interesting when remembering that the suicide is shown through the medium of television, which rather than distancing us here provides a disturbing moment of reality. The link between these images and Elisabet may refer to the artist's relationship with truth, a modernist motivation for silence and the possible functions of cinema as a means of expressing real emotion or tangible pain.

Egil Törnqvist asserts that the authentic suicide of the monk serves to contrast with the 'meaningless role-playing, inauthentic Elisabet'.[9] This seems to connect on a personal level with Bergman's concern during his stay in hospital over the position of the artist in modern society and the artist's relationship with 'real' television broadcasts, the new informer to the public: 'Art used to be able to be an act of political incitement, it could suggest political action. Today . . . [it has] played itself out.'[10]

Political activity is now precipitated by the news and television. In this sense, the images used in *Persona* turn fictional art 'into a bag of tricks, into something indifferent, meaningless'. In the preparations for *Persona* these preoccupations haunted Bergman, along with the question of whether art in general can survive at all except as pure 'leisure' in the form of 'puffed up self-satisfaction'.[11]

Bergman has discussed a lack of faith in traditional forms of narrative while discussing *Persona*:

> I've become more and more aware of the theatre's, film's, and TV's limited capacity for communicating fiction. Today, when I see how badly the novel has gone off the rails and how less and less able we are to explain and accept a fictitious course of events in an elemental way, the more reluctant I have become to tell stories with a beginning and an end.[12]

Robin Wood, in 1969, discusses the way that in *Persona* the traditional work of art (ordering of experience towards a positive end) is breaking down. Susan Sontag discusses traditional narrative, in terms of causal connections and time, and describes some of the ways that *Persona* differs, concluding that its construction is best described as variations on the particular theme of doubling:

> The action cannot be unequivocally paraphrased. It's correct to speak of *Persona* in terms of the fortunes of two characters named Elizabeth and Alma who are engaged in a desperate duel of identities. But it is equally pertinent to treat *Persona* as relating the duel between two mythical parts of a single self: the corrupted person who acts (Elizabeth) and the ingenuous soul (Alma) who founders in contact with corruption.[13]

It can also be said that, in terms of questioning narrative form, there is a similarity between *Persona* and the films and theory of Godard at this time. Indeed, *Persona* can be seen in the context of a trend, especially during the 1960s, towards the birth of reflexive cinema. As Elsaesser claims:

> What has marked off the modern narrative cinema in recent years is its degree of self-consciousness – about ways of constructing a cinematic fiction, about the manipulative effects produced in an audience, about the conditions under which images can give a true picture of reality.[14]

He discusses the historical development evident in particular individuals from engaging in cinema theory to practical film-making, citing directors such as Godard, Pier Paolo Pasolini, Bernardo Bertolucci and Jacques Rivette, and places these in the context of a general reaction against (and within) traditional narrative forms. *Persona* thus appeared at a time when the processes of narrative film were being put into question.

Wollen describes how traditional narrative was seen as constituting 'narrative transitivity', by which he means 'a sequence of events in which each unit . . . follows the one preceding it according to a chain of causation'.[15] This chain is usually psychological and is made up of a series of coherent motivation, generally forming the pattern of an equilibrium that is disturbed, setting off a chain reaction, ending with a new equilibrium. Godard began to move away from this tradition early on, for example, with the use of separate chapters (*Vivre sa vie*, 1962), providing interruptions to the narrative in a formally Brechtian way. By *Vent d'Est* (1970), Godard had shattered practically all narrative transitivity, so that the story had no comprehensible sequence. These aims became politically motivated, attempting to re-focus the attention of the spectator in a politically Brechtian manner: 'He can disrupt the emotional spell of the narrative and thus force the spectator, by interrupting the narrative flow, to re-concentrate and re-focus his attention.'[16]

However, it is misleading to imply that *Persona* fits entirely within the trend. Much of the theory questioning traditional narrative evolved towards the end of the 1960s, nourished by May 1968, and was politically motivated towards liberating the spectator from the ideology associated with mainstream cinema. Allen summarizes the critical climate:

> Mass culture – classical Hollywood cinema – was deemed illusionistic and manipulative, and an alternative film-making practice was celebrated in which cinematic illusionism and the pleasures of narrative involvement it afforded were eschewed in favour of the cerebral pleasures of films that sought to foreground the manner of their construction and undermine the effect of cinematic illusion.[17]

There was an attack on 'entertainment' cinema, as part of a broader attack on 'consumer society', as Wollen's observations demonstrate:

> Cinema is conceived of as a drug that lulls and mollifies the militancy of the masses, by bribing them with pleasurable dreams, thus distracting them from the stern tasks which are their true destiny.[18]

Bergman's work in general seems to be slightly different, intending, like much Hollywood cinema, to bring the spectator closer in some intensely emotional way rather than to distance them and obtain an objective form of cerebral pleasure, or what Wollen terms 'unpleasure'.[19] Elsaesser clarifies this distinction:

> Only Bergman among other European directors manages a similar physical immediacy in his films, for he uses aesthetic processes specific to the cinema (the manipulation of space for example) not to create intellectual effects, but to convey psycho-physiological states . . . that are an integral part of his moral themes.[20]

This seems to be the case with the non-naturalistic edge that is cast onto the hospital scenes,[21] especially when Elisabet views the television newsreel of the Buddhist monk setting fire to himself. The sequence opens with Elisabet pacing the room, conveyed via a straight-on long shot, with the television to the right and Elisabet's bed to the left. A huge shadow of Elisabet is cast on the wall behind her, as her eyes remain fixed on the television. Low voices gradually grow louder. There is a cut to images on the screen. Initially framed within the television, there are images of a street, a woman walking her dog, as the camera tracks left to right and people run towards a fire. Cuts to closer shots depict various angles viewing the Buddhist monk. The male newsreader voice-over is detached from the horror, discussing aspects of military warfare such as 'artillery', 'forces marching in' and 'machine guns'. A cut to a medium close-up shows Elisabet watching, and intermittent cutting gradually focuses in on Elisabet's eyes and her hand across her mouth in horror. As the monk falls there is an abrupt cut to an extreme long shot, in a now silent room, with Elisabet into the left-hand corner as far away from the television screen as possible. The final cut from Elisabet in the flickering glare of the television to her still standing at the back of the room, the television off, suggests that the scene was too alarming, and that a response is literally to switch off from it – thus representing an almost abstract fear or horror. Despite the disruption in continuity here, which seems to be 'felt'[22] rather than noted intellectually, identification with Elisabet is heightened.

There is also the sequence before this, in which Alma leaves Elisabet alone after switching over the radio to Bach. Here, there is a long take of a static close-up of Elisabet looking almost straight at the camera (it is difficult to ascertain the precise direction of her gaze). As the sombre music continues, her head rolls back on the pillow so that we see a dark silhouette of her facial profile and her hands which have come up to cover her face. The music is continuous, but time seems foreshortened, stretched out unendurably here, as Elisabet's pain is transmitted. This is one of the few moments where we feel confident in experiencing some kind of truth in relation to Elisabet, in the gesture of despair. While this seems to be unendurably long (a couple of minutes), there is also the sense that this Bach sequence is only a brief representation of the whole night for Elisabet, since the room gradually grows dark. Another paradox is the swift cut to Alma getting into bed, seemingly seconds after she has left Elisabet's room and entered hers. This would suggest that either there has been an ellipsis and we are seeing parallel time or that it was merely seconds ago that Elisabet was left alone, and the long take was representative of Elisabet's state of mind. This suggests that temporal–spatial distortions here bring the spectator closer to character.

Similarly, critics[23] have felt that the mechanical breakdown halfway through does not have a distancing effect in a Godardian or Brechtian sense, but in some way adds to the psychological breakdown of the characters. As Blackwell suggests, the destruction of the illusion cannot be isolated from the narrative.[24] *Persona* provides a distinct form of reflexivity, as Christopher Orr observes:

> Bergman does not possess the French director's didactic political consciousness . . . Nevertheless, the editors of *Cahiers* are correct to suggest that even though Bergman is not following a precise political agenda, his film is 'progressive' and arguably Brechtian because its forms break down traditional or ideological ways of depicting reality so that its content takes on a political dimension.[25]

Certainly, connections can be made between *Persona* and Elsaesser's remark that 'the cinema has lost its primary social function of providing mass-entertainment and is looking for a new definition of its role and purpose'.[26] Similarly, the target was the narrative fiction film, and the requirement of the 'director to play along with the way the industry is organised'.[27]

Ambiguity of meaning: A question of cause and effect

Attempts to extract a coherent meaning from *Persona* are common and, as predicted by Sontag,[28] sometimes problematic. Wood revisited his previous article on *Persona* that appeared in *Movie* (1969), in a new article in *CineAction* (1994),[29] reading *Persona* in terms of Elisabet's rejection of her patriarchically prescribed role, escaping words (signifiers of male domination) and conveying the female doctor as a paradigm of a female following the male system. What forms on the island, Wood suggests, is a type of female bonding that goes wrong. Wood argues that although Bergman has gone a long way in attempting to show what female companionship might achieve, this is eventually broken down in a Bergmanesque diatribe against women.

In his responding article in *CineAction*, Göran Persson[30] claims that he read Wood's article with 'great interest and a growing sense of missing what the film was about'. His thesis centres on the idea of the development of a person (Alma) from the desire 'to merge with someone all powerful to being able to enjoy standing alone, from symbiosis to individuation'.[31] These articles reveal the potential for extracting opposite meanings from *Persona*. While it is possible to prefer one reading over the other, it is not possible to state conclusively that one is more accurate. Disparities seem to lie in interpretations of cause or projections of causal connections onto the film.

Wood and Persson locate the key to the cause of Elisabet's silence within the brief shot of Elisabet's performance as Electra at the start of the film, when she stops speaking and then begins to giggle. Persson sees this as the moment when the wishes of the role figure – the death of the mother – suddenly become real to Elisabet, resonating from such wishes against her own mother, awakened by the death of the woman in the morgue (depicted in the opening montage) who acted as a mother to her own boy.[32] Wood makes links with the female Oedipus complex (originally termed the Electra complex). He claims that this is the process by which the female learns to accept her patriarchically prescribed role, 'relinquishing the father and her own innate masculinity, identifying with the symbolically castrated mother'.[33] By desisting from this, Wood asserts, Elisabet rejects her 'correct' position in the Symbolic Order.[34] Alternatively, this shot might be interpreted more generally to suggest Elisabet's rejection of (false) performance, and specifically the limitations of the female role, since it was Sophocles's Electra who was unable to speak a lie, while her sister, Chrysothemis, insisted on pretending to go along with their mother: 'Do you not reflect/You are a woman, not a man?'[35] However, these readings are based on interpretations of definitive meanings that are not openly offered. After all, the psychiatrist's account that Elisabet was playing Electra may itself be misleading.

Furthermore, Wood's theory that the film takes an appalled stance at each female's rejection of their natural nurturing female role is rooted in the 'disturbing' episode, where, as he sees it, Alma repeats a monologue implicating them both as bad mothers. Persson, on the other hand, suggests that Alma has somehow found out about Elisabet's past. In this register, Elisabet has also been betrayed: 'How does Alma know all this, which apparently is true, given the reactions of Elisabet? Has she been informed by the psychiatrist?'[36] He is trying to project onto the film a cause that may not be given.[37]

It is interesting to compare these interpretations with David Boyd's alternative reading 'that Alma is not revealing Elizabeth's history, but rather inventing it, extrapolating a past out of her interpretation of Elizabeth's present'.[38] Boyd's 'alternative possibility' suggests that the sequence has multiple functions. While Boyd reads this as a performance actively invented by Alma, it might also be seen as simply a performance that does not necessarily stem from a causal motive such as Alma getting back at Elisabet. It is possible to see Alma as mask voicing Elisabet's story, in a performative sense, speaking or projecting possible causes.

Performance: Manipulating the grip of narrative

This kind of play with performance becomes more noticeable if we look at the words of the radio play near the start of the film. The radio play is set up very much as a performance: Alma opens the curtains to let in the twilight for Elisabet; Alma switches on the radio; light shines from it, illuminating Alma's face as she leans over Elisabet. The words of the play resonate:

Forgive me, my darling
Oh, you must forgive me!

Elisabet, obscured by Alma's face, begins to giggle. Alma turns to face her:

Your forgiveness is all I crave . . .

Alma asks Elisabet why she is laughing. As Elisabet turns to face Alma (or the camera, her eyes shaded in darkness), Alma asks, 'Is the actress so funny?' Elisabet turns away, hand over mouth, as the actress demands:

What do you know about mercy
What do you know

Elisabet continues to giggle, then flashes a look up, switches the radio off angrily, looking up to Alma grimly in the darkness. Alma interprets

Elisabet's reaction in terms of the bad acting, and says that she has a tremendous admiration for artists. The extract ends with Alma putting on some music by Bach.

Around the radio play, we can conjecture a number of meanings. It represents the stereotypes of an amateur melodrama, with a woman who has sinned begging forgiveness from a stalwart husband. In this context, Elisabet's reaction is not (only) against the standard of acting but (also) against the supplicant female role. It is also possible to make links here between the radio play performance and the glimpse of Elisabet's performance at the start of the film. In this brief shot we see Elisabet, as Electra, fall silent and after a short interlude giggle. In both cases Elisabet seems to find the role intolerable and humorous. Both are conveyed as performances. In neither case do we become absorbed in the narrative. In the case of the radio play, attention is drawn to the role (Elisabet's reaction) and to the melodramatic style (Alma's comment).

What is perhaps most intriguing, however, is the direct parallel between these words and Alma's words later in the film as she runs after Elisabet begging forgiveness. Alma has been hurt by Elisabet's letter to the doctor that trivializes Alma's personal confidences. Elisabet's compassionate mask (her facial expressions and warm touch) is now seen as a lie. It is worth noting here that the unreadable nature of a face is also one of the major themes of *A Passion* (1968), for instance, when Andreas looks at a catalogue of photographs and sees one of Eva just starting a migraine: 'You can't read another person with any claim to certainty . . . Not even physical pain always gives a reaction.'

When Alma pleads with Elisabet, the grip of the narrative is at its strongest. The effect of the long shot, viewing the figures making their way along the beach, disappearing at times behind trees, bushes and walls, makes the scene more naturalistic, heightened by the long take. Alma's words as she runs after Elisabet are expressed with an emotional force:

Elisabet forgive me
I don't know what came over me

She then proceeds to explain herself, her reasons for her actions, the letter, the terrible blow of having her confidences shattered, the *causes*, and we identify with Alma because of this causal connection. It offers a truth to grasp onto; her explanations are real. Running while Elisabet strides, she humbles herself to the idol:

And I was flattered that a great actress bothered to listen

She states that she now realizes that it was sheer exhibitionism, begging:

> I want you, please, to forgive me
> You mean so much to me
> Don't let us part as enemies

They come to a clear section in the trees. There is a dramatic cut from the distant shot to a close-up of Elisabet's face. She moves her lips as if about to speak. There is a cut to a close-up of Alma's face, they are face to face, Elisabet facing away from the camera. She turns and walks off screen with Alma watching her. A cut back to the long shot emphasizes Alma's isolation as she walks, then starts up a run through trees, around rocks and turns round, yelling:

> You won't forgive me because you're proud
> You won't condescend
> (*Stepping back.*)
> I won't. I won't

Alma's words and those of the actress in the radio play are strikingly similar, and in this light Alma is playing the role of the supplicant female. However, while the radio play was defined as a performance, the emotional forces causing Alma's outburst as she runs after Elisabet are much more clearly signalled. Although in general film viewing we may always remain medium-aware, it is possible to fluctuate from seeing the actors to seeing the characters they play.[39] As Alma runs after Elisabet, we are gripped by narrative, drawn much more into the causal chain of the fictional world and less inclined to register it as a performance in this sense, in a similar way to watching a piece of conventional illusionist narrative where, as Richard Allen describes it, the spectator 'actively participates in the experience of illusion that the camera affords'.[40]

Christopher Orr sees this sequence as 'probably the most melodramatic in the entire film'.[41] It is interesting to see that he discusses such melodramatic 'moments of intense emotion' *in contrast* to other more Brechtian or self-reflexive moments of the film to formulate the theory that *Persona* is a 'Brechtian melodrama'. However, the parallels between this sequence and the radio play suggest that this sequence might also be seen as Brechtian adding a political dimension to this melodramatic moment. Erik Hedling also detects a political dimension in this sequence. For him, the depiction of the bleak shoreline breaks down or deconstructs long-established, chauvinistic representations of Swedish-ness: 'And in his creation of a cinematic landscape Bergman was certainly a social heretic, challenging – whether he was aware of it or not – a traditional cinematic discourse which had so far been clearly connected to strong nationalist sentiments.'[42]

The conventions of melodrama evoked by the radio play suggested that the woman was pleading with a dominant male. But the female voice was all that was heard. In this later sequence, there is a play on masculine and feminine roles, with Alma, the smaller figure, running in a black dress, while Elisabet takes the long strides, here wearing trousers. Alma also seems to be answering her own questions as though performing Elisabet's role. It is clear that gender roles and sexual identity are important to the film. As Gwendolyn Audrey Foster asserts, '*Persona* challenges the regime of heterosexuality.'[43] The repeated 'mirror' shot of Alma and Elisabet staring into the camera as Elisabet strokes Alma's hair, for example, challenges conventional representations of heterosexuality,[44] most notably when this image cuts to the shot of Elisabet taking a photograph of the camera/spectator, further challenging the heterosexual male gaze.[45]

The visit of Elisabet's husband can also be interpreted as a performance, specifically the part where Elisabet arrives, clad in black, through trees behind Alma. We do not see the husband until Elisabet's hand takes Alma's up to the face of the man in dark glasses. Alma then uses the words of a loving wife to comfort the man. Elisabet's face appears from behind, in-between the two faces. There is then a close-up of Elisabet's expressionless face only, as Alma and the man talk about a young son and Alma reassures:

Tell your[46] little boy that Mummy will soon be home that Mummy is ill

Then, like rear projection behind Elisabet's sharp contours, the hazy profiles of the two figures talk about tenderness. The cut to the bedroom scene is preceded by a close-up of Elisabet's face, which turns at the husband's clichéd words, 'Is it good for you?' As the camera pans, we see the couple lying down, the man's hand around the woman's face. Alma responds, expressionless:

You're a wonderful lover,
You know that

Alma thrashes, kicks and shakes her head:

> Leave me alone, it's shameful
> Leave me alone. I'm cold and rotten and bored.
> It's nothing but lies and cheating

Alma bashes her head. The camera pans round again to face Elisabet against a deafening non-diegetic sound.

It is important that the many levels on which this sequence may be read are kept in view. However, it is interesting to see this as a part where Alma adopts the role of Elisabet's husband's wife.[47] Alma's words at the end in this light, rather than expressing guilt at having slept with Elisabet's husband, invite an insight into Elisabet's possible history. Read this way, it is through the mask of Elisabet that these words are performed. As Lucy Fischer argues, their female gender is an essential aspect of this performance: 'Elizabeth not only has to fake her maternal role but must feign the conjugal duties of a wife – further evidence of her need to perform off-stage . . . Alma enacts the role of Elizabeth, as the actress voyeuristically looks on . . . Alma's dramatization casts the actress's sex life as a scam . . .'[48]

Bergman suggests that the two women's roles are interchangeable throughout the film:

> Could one make this into an inner happening? I mean, suggest that it is a composition for different voices in the same soul's concerto grosso?[49]

This resembles the breakdown of identification in Godard's earlier films, with the non-matching of voice to character. Later, Godard uses the same voice for different characters or different voices for the same characters (for example, in *Vent d'Est*).[50] However, whereas Godard's motivation for this was unambiguously Brechtian, closely linked with the break-up of narrative transitivity, Bergman's projection of words via another person's mouth also highlights the affinity between the characters as women as well as suggests that outward appearances and words may lie.

With Alma's breakdown in language later in the film, it is possible to argue that she now experiences the inadequacies of language to express inner thoughts: 'us . . . we . . . no . . . I . . . Many words and then nausea'. It is hard to claim that Alma has conscious control over these words or that, as Sontag suggests, she is trying to get Elisabet to say something: 'Alma at one point begs Elizabeth just to repeat nonsense words and phrases that she hurls at her.'[51] It is also difficult to accept that Alma is begging at all at this point. Elisabet stands in front of Alma to start with, increasingly mouthing the words Alma comes out with, rather like a ventriloquist's dummy. This is another instance of a performance, where the process of speech is breaking down.

Performance permeates the play with narrative techniques such as the male voice-over that accompanies Elisabet and Alma as they set off on holiday. The two women walk (in long shot) in their large sun hats among trees, bobbing down (behind the wall that separates them from the foreground) to pick mushrooms. It is possibly Bergman's voice offering present tense sweeteners such as 'being near the sea does the actress good'. Alma turns in the sunshine, placing mushrooms in Elisabet's basket, as the voice-over remarks that she 'takes good care of her patient'. There is then a cut to the harmony at the table, where the two of them hum as they prepare the mushrooms. The voice-over narration in some ways provides something comfortable, drawing on conventional film-making practices. However, it also poses problems; this voice-over is not used at any other point in the film, and thus jars with the coherency, making us question whose voice it is and why it is here. There is also a sense of an over-sanitization of the sequence, by reinforcing the distinct roles of 'actress' and 'nurse', patient and carer that are about to be shattered.

Later in the film, Alma tells Elisabet the story of her experiences with Katarina and their beach affair with two young boys. Significantly, the story is not supported with flashback images, but foregrounds Elisabet's response as silent listener. Bergman suggests that Elisabet's face becomes a 'cold, voluptuous mask' and that her lips 'grow' through the scene[52] (they do not, but the camera cuts to closer shots of her face and Ullmann moves her lips slowly). In addition, Bergman states, the audience as listeners must visualize the story internally and experience their 'own cinematography'.[53]

A beginning and an end

Initially Bergman wanted to call the film *Cinematography*, to make film projection itself the central focus. Perhaps the most brutal and distancing moments are the opening and ending frames. The opening is reflexive, looking both backward at previous films and forward to the film itself. It presents a series of images relating to film projection: a white square, a blank screen, the leader, flashes of the upside-down numerical countdown, the inverted cartoon of the fat woman washing, following on with the farcical scene (from *Prison*) already mentioned. This relates to avant-garde film-makers such as Paul Sharits and Peter Gidal, who expose the material properties of the cinema with the projection of a still photograph and the film strip in projected light.

Persona can be seen as quite revolutionary for the time. Godard's early films introduced cinema as a topic in narrative, with the 'Lumière' sequence in *Les Carabiniers* (1963) and the film within the film in *Le Mépris* (1963). But it was not until his contribution to *Loin du Vietnam* (1967) that the camera was shown on screen. Post-1968, the process of production was systematically highlighted. In Godard's *Vent d'Est* we see the camera, but there is also an actual altering/scratching of the celluloid surface. This might seem to fit in with other avant-garde film-makers, the American underground particularly. However, while, as Wollen suggests, the American avant-garde film-makers worked alongside the developments in painting, and worked to foreground the film in a similar way to foregrounding the canvas, Godard seems to be looking for a way of expressing 'negation'. He was considering the film as a process of writing in images rather than a representation of the world, scratching as an erasure or a crossing out of the image.[54]

Persona attempts to show ideas with images and it depicts burning/splitting celluloid. The presentation of projection is both there to remind the spectator that this is a film, and to express, as a 'poem', the initial ideas around the film's conception. The images used after this are reflexive, since they relate to images used by Bergman in previous films: the farce derives from *Prison*; the spider relates to the spider God described in *Through a Glass Darkly* and *Winter Light* (1961); other images relate to discussions about faith such as the slaughtered lamb (Märta in *Winter Light* wears the sheepskin coat during the Eucharist hymn 'God's pure, innocent lamb' at the opening) and Christian sacrifice (hand-piercing occurs in *The Seventh Seal*, *Wild Strawberries* [1957] and *Winter Light*). As Törnqvist asserts, the image-filled frames contrast with the imageless white frames,[55] linking with the psychological dichotomy between the mask and the face in the film proper.[56] Bergman associates the images with the processes of creativity:

> But when the projector was running, nothing came out of it but old ideas, the spider, God's lamb, all that dull old stuff. My life just then consisted of dead people, brick walls, and a few dismal trees out in the park.[57]

By 'dull old stuff', Bergman seems to refer to the earlier explicit symbolism used, for example, in *The Seventh Seal* and even to the religious preoccupations in the trilogy (spider, God's lamb), which can be said to be lacking in *Persona*.

Once again, problems arise when attempting to interpret absolute meanings that are not offered. For instance, Persson suggests that the boy is Elisabet's son and the old woman in the morgue is the relative who looked after him.[58] It is just as feasible to suggest that he is, or represents, Bergman himself:

> So I made believe I was a little boy who'd died, yet who wasn't allowed to be really dead, because he kept on being woken up by telephone calls from the Royal Dramatic Theatre. Finally he became so impatient he lay down and read a book. All that stuff about The Hero of our Time[59] struck me as rather typical – the overstrained official lying on his sickbed.[60]

It is also possible to see the boy as relating to the viewer, that we are seeing through his eyes and that he may represent the notion that we see and are seen through screens. A reflexive moment occurs when the projected image of the woman (Alma/Elisabet) that the boy looks at and strokes is placed, via a sudden cut, in the auditorium. The boy stares directly into the camera running his hand across the camera lens. It is also possible to trace links between these opening images and the contents of the main film narrative, as Houston has done, for example, in linking the more clichéd shots of the opening with the images of real-life horrors later on. There is also the extensive work of Törnqvist who makes links between all the images and the film as a whole. Inherent in all of this is the idea that representation is a fluid process, symbolized by the representation of the two merged faces, as Bergman puts it, 'floating in to one another',[61] subject to multiple interpretations ('as with any poem, images mean different things to different people'[62]).

The difficulties with interpreting concrete meaning, the problems with interpreting which scenes are 'real' or 'unreal' and the temporal–spatial challenges to traditional narrative suggest that *Persona*'s interest is in the spectator's relationship with the cinematic fictional world. The film experiments with the nature of cinematography itself. *Persona* plays with dramatic form, occasionally amplifying the stylistic conventions of storytelling.

While the ending would seem to be a crucial part of the film, especially for those extracting a coherent meaning from the film as a whole, most critics have not paid close attention to it. Moreover, most interpret the second brief shot of Electra as Elisabet's return to the stage. Persson's argument is a classic example:

> Elisabet returns to acting, from a better base. It is not possible to inter-pret the last picture of Elisabet, acting again, in any other way. That must also be the idea of the director. In the published screenplay the psychiatrist sums up what happened: Elisabet returned to her work – Bergman probably found that it was unnecessary to include this in the film, evident as it must be to the audience who had understood it.[63]

It is possible to question many aspects of the above argument (a) that Elisabet returns to acting; (b) that it is from a better base; (c) that the shot of Elisabet acting again signifies (a) and (b); (d) that it even is a shot of Elisabet acting again; (e) that any of this is the 'idea of the director'; and (f) that the screenplay should provide the key to either the direc-tor's ideas or to the film itself. However, putting these reservations aside momentarily, it is interesting to analyse what such a reading might imply. A return to the stage 'from a better base' might imply that the ending of *Persona* is similar to the final resolution in *Summer Interlude*. As discussed in Chapter 2 the earlier film depicts Marie dancing again at the end, having restored a healthy relationship with her art. It is possible to impose a similar meaning onto *Persona*: Elisabet reached an unhealthy relationship with the mask; she had begun to believe that she was what she pretended to be to the point where her inner self stagnated; the break from acting, both in the theatre and in real life, via the dropping of the mask of speech, enabled a recovery and an insight into her true self. The ending, with the brief shot of her once again on the stage, would then show that she has established a healthy relationship with the mask. This would also conform to the conventional structure of narrative tran-sitivity, where there is an initial equilibrium, followed by a break with this equilibrium, resolved by a new equilibrium (restoration of health). However, even with Persson's psychological 'better base', there are still elements of circularity in this reading which seem to press against the more traditional concept of moving forward at the end of a film.

Moreover, even if it were necessary to rely on the screenplay as a means of explaining the film, there are discrepancies between the screen-play and the meaning that Persson attaches to the film. In the published screenplay, the psychiatrist tells the spectator that Elisabet returns to her home and to her acting, stating that she is welcomed with open arms. Elisabet's silence 'was a role like any other', according to the psychiatrist, and Elisabet's motives might have been 'infantility', but also 'imagination, sensitivity, perhaps even real intelligence'.[64] The psychiatrist's words suggest a more intensified circularity than Persson's interpretation, since they suggest that the silence proved to be little more than another role. However, the psychiatrist's tone resembles the summing up of a case study, and the added direction that Elisabet is 'pleased with herself' suggests that she may be inaccurate in her interpretations of the situation. Even in the screenplay, therefore, the reader must guess why Elisabet returns to the stage, and from what base. Even more significantly, this speech is absent from the film altogether. Since the only indicator concerning a return to the stage is the shot of Electra, it is perhaps misleading to use the screenplay to determine meaning from the film.

The film and screenplay are separate entities to some extent due to intrinsic differences between the two media, but even more so in this case,[65] since as Keith Bradfield maintains on the back cover '*Persona* . . . is not technically a script, but rather a frame-work for a movie'. The film does not provide the kind of clues offered in the screenplay to the thinking behind the words, for example, directions concerning the characters' minds during the dialogue between Alma and Elisabet's husband or the instance when Elisabet may or (in the film) may not speak to Alma. In the screenplay, it seems more likely that Elisabet tells Alma to go to bed:

You'd better get off to bed, otherwise you'll fall asleep at the table, *says Mrs. Vogler in a calm, clear voice.*[66]

In the film, with the action orchestrated so that Elisabet's face is obscured, the ambiguity is enforced.[67] It is also important to distinguish between Bergman's written reminiscences, Bergman's 'ideas', the screenplay and the film itself.

In general, responses to the ending impose meanings that may not be there, even if not necessarily influenced by the screenplay. Törnqvist interprets along Persson's lines, discussing the 'circular' nature of the film's form: 'In the concluding frames, we see how the fictive characters, Elisabet and Alma, return to their former occupations: those of the actress and nurse respectively.'[68] However, the images of the ending offer very little coherence in terms of a definitive narrative structure.

We do not see Elisabet talking at the beginning or the end, except to say 'nothing', neither are we shown her returning home or acting again directly. Time and space are complicated by the sequence immediately before the ending in which the two women seem to be back in the hospital as nurse and patient, suggesting a number of inconclusive possibilities concerning the narrative. This raises the other question, concerning whether Alma does return to work as a nurse. Alma is depicted wearing a nurse's uniform at the end but, as Sontag asks, 'Where is Alma going when she boards a bus alone toward the close of *Persona*?'[69] In addition, while Alma walks along the beach in her uniform, we see only a distant dark figure boarding the bus.

In the last scenes we see Elisabet folding clothes into a case in a medium close-up straight-on shot. In the previous shot Alma (in casual clothes) watched Elisabet through a net curtain in the doorway, as Elisabet entered the house, and then Alma peeped through a crack in a door the other side of the room, presumably to catch another glimpse of Elisabet in an adjoining room. Elisabet closes the case (we hear it fasten shut), and then walks out to the right of the frame, as the camera pans downwards to focus on the case left lying on the bed. Since this is the last definite view of Elisabet in this setting, it is impossible to say why she should leave the case lying on the bed. There would be a greater sense of continuity and coherence if Elisabet were to go somewhere, and take the case with her.

This is followed by a shot of a door flying open, seemingly by itself, to an extreme long shot across the sea (about two-thirds sky). The camera dollies downwards to Alma walking into the frame, now dressed as a nurse, as she brings in cushions. The downward camera movement seems to link Alma with the case moments ago, and it still remains possible that Elisabet has packed and left Alma's case for her. The door slams loudly behind her, casting her in darkness. A number of brief shots (emphasizing the brisk efficiency that can be attributed to the nurse's role) show her placing the cushions on a bed, followed by a shot of her outside, viewed from inside, as she turns the chairs over onto a table and shots of her bringing in pillows and blankets.

The next sequence shows Alma taking a last look in the mirror, as the image of the intimate moment between herself and Elisabet is superimposed onto her reflection. As the image disappears Alma puts on the nurse's hat. We see a figure that we assume to be her, from the nurse's outfit, walk behind the huge (ship's?) figurehead of a woman, flung back, gazing to the sky. The frame is split vertically here, reminiscent of the composite face of Elisabet/Alma and the shot of Alma half apparent behind the transparent curtain immediately before the mid-way breakdown. The camera progresses towards the figurehead, momentarily hiding Alma(?)'s head, as she puts down a case and bag, and turns to close the door.

Before the door is even shut, there is a cut from the figurehead to the close-up of Electra's face, as she quickly turns, seemingly repeating the shot near the start of the film, since the gesture is the same. This is generally taken to suggest Elisabet's return to the stage. However, it is quick and indeterminate. The (seeming) repetition might even imply circularity, a return to the film's beginnings, backed up by the reflexive final ending of the arc lamps separating. However, although the same gesture is depicted (the same moment in the play perhaps), it is less easy to distinguish the made-up Electra as Elisabet at this stage: it might even be Alma in disguise.

While there might be resistance to the suggestion that it could be Alma, it *is* clear that this is not simply a repeated shot. The earlier shot definitely depicts Elisabet, as does the still placed next to the text in the screenplay's ending, which is taken intriguingly from the film's earlier scene, and not from the ending. It is misleading to claim that this brief glimpse can only suggest that Elisabet returns to the stage (healthy or unhealthy). Once again, the difficulty of interpreting meaning or causes from appearances seems to be deliberately highlighted.

Another interesting aspect of this sequence is the cut from the dwarfing figurehead to the Electra shot. As Alma(?) closes the door on her experiences over the summer, it might appear that she is unable to leave, as Blackwell asserts, the 'sphere of Elisabet's influence', suggested by the swift juxtaposition of images.[70] In the screenplay, while Alma is left alone at the beach house through the winter months, there is a suggestion that she will return to her work and get married, although this does not actually occur within the text, and Alma is still haunted by Elisabet:

> I really do like people a lot. Mostly when they are sick and I can help them. I'm going to marry and have children. *Alma's little conversation is interrupted by Mrs. Vogler's face, filling the picture. A haunting wide-open face, distorted by terror . . .* [71]

It is thus possible to deduce a more definite slant from the screenplay, linking it with Strindberg's play *The Stronger* (1889), in which the silent woman is ultimately more powerful than her gossiping companion. We might also interpret that the talking, and ostensibly stronger, Alma becomes weaker, assuming the problems of her patient. The sick woman Elisabet, regains her speech and returns to her former life. However, despite the fact that it is possible to superimpose such meanings onto the screenplay, it is not explicitly presented in the film.

There is a cut from Electra to a medium long shot of Alma with a bag and suitcase, notably different from the one packed by Elisabet and left on the bed, thus leaving the question of why the camera focused so overtly on this detail unanswered. The camera tracks to Alma's face as she walks along the beach. This is followed by a cut to an extreme low angle of two men[72] (reflexively) up on a crane with a camera, as there is a dolly in to focus on an inverted aerial image of Elisabet apparently lying down. It is possible, as Blackwell argues, that we are seeing Elisabet's new film,[73] suggesting futurity as the film moves back to its beginnings. Once again, this is possible, although no such film is mentioned. It might also be reflexive, in the sense of depicting Liv Ullmann's next film or the shooting of *this* film, but the argument for this is not conclusive. It certainly re-emphasizes the link between the two protagonists' faces, playing on their likeness to each other, and playing with identity by mismatching what the spectator sees with what is seen through the viewfinder. There is then a cut to an extreme long shot of a bus pulling around a corner, and a figure getting on with bags (presumably Alma). The sound of a horn is noticeable at the end of the shot of Alma walking along the beach, continuing through the reflexive shot of the camera, and stopping with the shot of the bus. Blackwell argues that the horn's meaning changes as it may be taken as both the horn of the bus and the horn that is used at the start of a take. It is used again at the start of Bergman's next film *The Hour of the Wolf* (1966). Since the horn begins when Alma walks along the beach, it might also be taken to be the sounds of a foghorn, linking back to Elisabet's dreamlike visit to Alma's room.

The bus drives towards us, and then the camera tilts to the ground. The scene ends with a dissolve to a screen of Alma's/Elisabet's face merging in and out of focus, with the boy placing his hand on the image as before. The screen dissolves to white, against the sound of the opening chaotic music (a cacophony of kettle drums and xylophones among other instruments) and there is a cut to the film leader and arc lamps separating, and then fizzling to darkness. This final reflexivity mirrors the opening, but this time, rather than focusing on projection and the illusion of the film coming to life, here the emphasis is on disintegration and death, as the film comes to an end. It is circular, rather than progressive, in the sense the film returns to nothingness.

Many factors contribute to a sense of closure at the end such as packing, clearing up the house and the departure of the bus. However, other areas are deliberately left hazy. It is not shown explicitly who leaves to go where when, and cause and effect are not addressed. As the ending stands, it is possible to read much of significance, and to formulate stories or meanings from its images. The ending of the film points to itself as a self-conscious mask, and the final sequences appear significantly without words, and in quick succession.

It might be said that *Persona* has continued to be such a magnet for critical discussion because of its enigmas and as a film that represents the height of modernist film-making. Although *Persona* does not take a fixed political stance, it is perhaps more Brechtian in places than is sometimes acknowledged, exploring reflexively the seductive power of performance and the diverse potential of narrative devices. This kind of scrutiny also draws attention to certain political issues such as communication, language and gender as ideological constructs. These issues, as they concern the narration of film, legibility and interpretation, continue in Bergman's next film *The Hour of the Wolf* (1966).

6
Dreams, Fantasies and Nightmare Visions

Larry Gross recalls a crucial shift during the 1960s:

> But it's in 60s European art cinema that we discover the affinities of cinema and dream being explored most thoroughly: Resnais' *Last Year in Marienbad*, Bergman's *Persona*, Buñuel's *Belle de jour*, Antonioni's *Blowup* . . . all movies which give you the uncanny impression of being stories told by madmen . . . In these exploratory masterpieces of the 60s, the use of the dreamlike as a narrative mode – as form as well as content – is a way of making the audience aware of the processes of cinematic representation.[1]

These claims for the films of 1960s art cinema and its affinity with dream are not so unusual in themselves, but they do help to illustrate a more general movement away from films being easily comprehensible. *Persona*, along with other films such as those mentioned above, helped lead the way into new directions. *The Hour of the Wolf* (1966) certainly appears to be 'told by madmen', with its 'use of the dreamlike as a narrative mode'. Significantly though, while *The Hour of the Wolf* is influenced by *Persona* in its blurring of dream and real worlds, it also marks a new step because of its capacity to move on, to convey a person's descent into madness, distorting time and space, and merging dream and reality for its own sake rather than for more self-reflexive purposes. While many of Bergman's films are significant for their use of dream and dreamlike sequences, this chapter takes three key films – *Wild Strawberries* (1957), *The Hour of the Wolf* and *Cries and Whispers* (1972) – to explore an overall transition, from the 1950s to the 1970s, towards greater fluidity.[2]

Bergman claims that the initial dream sequence in *Wild Strawberries* is partly a reconstruction of a dream he once had[3] and that *Cries and Whispers* stems from a dream vision of four women floating in white dresses through a red room in the grey morning light.[4] This suggests that while the dream in *Wild Strawberries* is inserted into the film, *Cries and Whispers* evolves entirely out of a dream vision, implying that it has a more dreamlike nature overall. One possible inference from this is that boundaries between dream and reality tend to be less fixed after the 1960s. Bergman's commentaries in the 'screenplay' or 'story' reveal that in *Cries and Whispers* he was attempting to achieve something on the screen that could not be achieved on the page, the 'natural-real and yet mysterious, in a tension'.[5] It seems that while the desire to integrate external and internal worlds is evident as early as *Wild Strawberries*, it was not until later that transitions between dream and reality could occur more smoothly in film.

Wild Strawberries

Wild Strawberries (1957) was viewed by many as confusing and opaque at the time of its initial showing outside Sweden in 1958, as reflected in Bosley Crowther's warning in the *New York Times*:

> If any of you thought you had trouble understanding what Ingmar Bergman was trying to convey in his beautiful poetic and allegorical Swedish film *The Seventh Seal* wait until you see his *Wild Strawberries* which came to the Beekman yesterday. This one is so thoroughly mystifying that we wonder whether Mr Bergman himself knows what he was trying to say.[6]

Nearly 40 years on, Philip and Kersti French used this quotation to stress how differently they felt about the film, claiming that they were unable to see it as at all 'obscure' or 'unduly problematic' unlike, they proposed, 'a good many Bergman films of the following two decades'.[7]

It is worth taking a closer look at contemporaneous newspaper reviews, to speculate on what might have been 'mystifying' to many British and North American viewers at the time of the initial screenings, bearing in mind that it was before French New Wave and the 'mature' Michelangelo Antonioni trilogy (*L'Avventura*, 1960; *La Notte*, 1961; and *The Eclipse*, 1962). *Wild Strawberries* won the prize at the Berlin Festival of 1958 and opened the 12th Edinburgh Film Festival in August of that year. Two months later, after its première in London in October, Jympson Harman (in the *Evening News*) took *Wild Strawberries* to be 'A New Kind of Film' and, although full of praise, warned that people used to conventional English-speaking movies would find it 'deep' and 'mysterious'.[8]

Pushing the dream sequences to one side momentarily, the overall plot should not have posed too many problems, revolving around the old man Professor Eberhard Isak Borg (Victor Sjöström), travelling to Lund by car to celebrate the 50th anniversary of his doctorate. The message is clear. He needs this extra time to reflect on his life and identity before he dies. The most obvious link is with Victor Sjöström's *The Phantom Carriage* (1920) based on a Selma Lagerlöf novel and starring Sjöström himself as David Holm, the drunken rascal, who has deserted his wife and family and betrayed the trust of Sister Edith, a Salvation Army officer, who is now dying. It is only by her prayers that he is given the chance to review his life and make a fresh start. Bergman has often stated that *Wild Strawberries* was directly influenced by Sjöström's work.[9] It was through his pastor father Erik that Bergman first saw *The Phantom Carriage*, which had been taken up by temperance organizations and religious groups in Sweden. Bergman's regular viewings of the film throughout his lifetime signal his abiding admiration for it.

Swedish filmgoers would thus have been able to recognize some of the narrative elements at the core of *Wild Strawberries*: even if they had not seen *The Phantom Carriage*, there would have been a familiarity with Lagerlöf and Sjöström. However, filmgoers outside Sweden would also have found the overall storyline and moral familiar, considering the similarities with Charles Dickens's *A Christmas Carol*, for example.[10] Indeed, the critic for the *Glasgow Herald* found these aspects to be irritatingly predictable: 'A doubt remains as to whether the moral is not a little trite.'[11]

What really bewildered the critics was the film's use of dream sequences. Isabel Quigly (in the *Daily Mail*) argued that, while the external plot was simple, the underlying plot was complex: 'Dreams, fantasies, memories, conversations' concerning the 'old man's soul'.[12] Overwhelmed by the dream symbolism, some newspaper critics simplified the film, overemphasizing links with *The Seventh Seal* (1956). Ivan Adams (in the *Star*), for example, describes the film as 'doomladen with coffins and personified death speaking the Bergman philosophy from beyond the tomb'.[13] However, the heavy symbolism adopted throughout *The Seventh Seal*, with its allegorical mask, is here reserved mainly for the dream sequences. Viewing *Wild Strawberries* now, it is possible to detect that the dream sequences are drawn from filmic and psychoanalytic conventions, which would have been fairly familiar at the time, if not as easily identifiable as in retrospect. In the initial dream sequence, for instance, specific images from classical surrealist films and German

Expressionism[14] are used.[15] References to Luis Buñuel and Salvador Dali are also detectable in this sequence, along with an intricate relationship with Freudian and post-Freudian theory.

It was not so much the content of the dreams, however, that was causing many of the confusions but the way that dreams, dreamlike scenes and memories were depicted alongside everyday life. Hollis Alpert (the *Saturday Review*) remarked in March 1959: 'The framework for *Wild Strawberries* is decidedly simple . . . But within the frame are fascinating complexities, minglings of dream and reality, of past and present.'[16] This corresponds with some of the initial comments made after that first British showing at Edinburgh in August 1958. The *Scotsman* singles out the film's 'cumbersome shape' and 'frequent lapses into dream sequences'.[17] Bergman's claim that the film arose from the idea of switching between different spaces and different times, intimates that this was a relatively novel idea at the time:[18]

> Then it struck me: supposing I make a film of someone coming along, perfectly realistically, and suddenly opening a door and walking into his childhood? And then opening another door and walking out into reality again? And then walking round the corner of the street and coming into some other period of his life, and everything still alive and going on as before? That was the real starting point for *Wild Strawberries*.[19]

Critics also felt that the dream sequences were conveyed in a new way. For instance, in 'Dream Sequences in Swedish Film' (the *Glasgow Herald*) the film's 'flawless' structure, allocating one quarter of screen time to 'dreams and reconstructions of the past with a dream-like quality', is praised, in contrast to the 'silly' dream sequences in films usually, implying perhaps that dream sequences tended to be cued more obviously.[20] After the later London première, C.A. Lejeune (in the *Observer*) praised the way that *Wild Strawberries* 'mixes dream, memory and actuality so smoothly that one is only aware, at the end of it, of life as a continuing thing that touches, takes, releases and then passes on'.[21]

The style might not have been as unusual to the Swedes as it appears to have been to the English-speaking world. *The Phantom Carriage* was not only similar to *Wild Strawberries* in storyline and in its use of the same star but it also contains, as Philip and Kersti French point out, a 'complicated structure of flashbacks within flashbacks' long before *Wild Strawberries*.[22] As they note, Maureen Turim singles out *The Phantom Carriage* for its 'use of a cinematic means of expression for this ambivalence between states of dreaming, premonition, remembering, and the supernatural'.[23] We might also bear in mind the complex structures of some of Bergman's earlier films: the expressionistic dream sequence within the film within the flashback in *Prison* (1949), for instance, or the intricate use of flashback and symbolism in *Summer Interlude* (1950).

Viewing *Wild Strawberries* now, there seems to be a coherent system of incorporating dreams and dreamlike flashbacks within the main plot. These are introduced with a traditional voice-over and are clearly sig-nalled, for example, the first dream sequence is signalled by the cut from Isak's lit face to his dark body in the foreground of a brightly lit street. His voice-over describes his 'morning walk' in a 'strange part of town' among deserted streets and dilapidated houses. Only gradually through the film do the boundaries between dream and reality slightly merge, for example, in the daydream flashback at Isak's family sum-merhouse. Even here, however, the sequence is clearly introduced with the aid of Isak's voice-over and gentle music. A shot of the house, with closed shutters, in the present-day cold grey winter landscape dissolves to a shot of the same house in midsummer with windows wide open, as the voice-over describes the experience, 'the dear reality of day . . . was transformed into more tangible pictures, which memory presented to my eyes with all the power of actual happenings'. There is a cut to Isak's face as these last words are spoken and the camera tracks in to a close-up. This dissolves to a shot of trees swaying in the breeze, followed by a cut to the clouds accompanied by a brief piano trill, a cut to the wild straw-berry patch and then to Sarah picking the wild strawberries.

Philip and Kersti French see *Wild Strawberries* in the same (revolu-tionary) league as *Hiroshima mon amour* (Alain Resnais, 1959):

> . . . along with Alain Resnais' *Hiroshima mon amour* it [*Wild Strawberries*] created a new relationship in the cinema between external and inter-nal reality, a new concept of cinematic time that Bergman and Resnais were themselves to develop over the next decade and which was to affect permanently the way films have since been made and understood.[24]

Resnais's *Last Year in Marienbad*, perhaps even more perplexing than *Hiroshima mon amour*, came three years after *Wild Strawberries*. It could be said that the 1960s habituated people to being less certain about what was happening in the narrative, and that ten years after *Wild Strawberries* critics were more used to 'foreign' or 'art' cinema, which might explain why they were not as puzzled by *Persona* as might be expected.

Theoretical debates on dream and film

Many theorists, following Surrealist writers of the 1920s,[25] have compared films and dreams theoretically, particularly since the 1970s,
observing that viewing a film bears similarities with dreaming.
Narrative elements sometimes seem to be outside spatial and temporal
laws, and the viewing conditions of the cinema (the darkened room and
sense of isolation) have been said to simulate the state of dreaming.
Much of the work on film and dream has concentrated on the relationship between dream and dreamer and its similarities with the film
image and spectator stemming from the studies of Christian Metz
(1975, 1976)[26] and Jean-Louis Baudry (1976).[27] This was combined with
much of the then current discourse on film and psychoanalysis, and its
interest specifically in 'the spectator'. The conditions of film viewing
allegedly send the spectator back to infancy, like Freud's notions of
infantile wishes that emerge during sleep and bear similarities with the
Lacanian mirror stage, as Nick Browne and Bruce McPherson summarize,
film theory had applied itself to dream theory by looking at 'the "place"
of the filmic spectator from within a psychoanalytic, specifically Lacanian,
idiom'.[28] Around this time, critics began to apply psychoanalysis more
rigorously to specific films, with a combination of close textual analysis
and Freudian and Lacanian analysis. Many also investigated the similarities between film and dream *processes* such as quick editing or overexposed shots to recreate hypnagogic dream states (images occurring
between the stages of being asleep and awake).

The 'Film and Dream' Conference (1978) chose Bergman's films to
investigate similarities between cinema and dream. *Film and Dreams: An
Approach to Bergman*, published as a result of this conference, is concerned with whether film dreams make the spectator respond psychologically and physiologically like a dreamer or whether they resemble
the reviewed dreams of an awakened dreamer. In the first chapter, Vlada
Petric argues that Resnais, Federico Fellini, Buñuel and Bergman are
unique for simulating in the spectator mental and emotional responses
close to those of the dreaming state.[29] Despite the problematic nature of
these hypotheses, the book provides useful perspectives on *Wild
Strawberries*. For instance, Allan Hobson argues that *Persona* uses less
psychoanalytical imagery than *Wild Strawberries*, and thus 'better represents the formal aspects of dreaming than do the explicitly presented
dreams of *Wild Strawberries*'.[30] Marsha Kinder suggests that a shift
towards a more dreamlike texture in Bergman's later films starts with
Through a Glass Darkly when the line between reality and dream begins
to dissolve.[31]

It is not possible to quantify the extent to which films can simulate 'real dreams' in texture. There is nevertheless a clear perception here of a recognizable change in style from *Wild Strawberries* to Bergman's later films, suggesting a greater fluidity between external and internal perceptions and occurrences. After *Persona*, *The Hour of the Wolf* continues to project the psychological inner states of the character.

The Hour of the Wolf

The Hour of the Wolf (1966) remains striking for its depiction of the decaying and fractured mental states of both its male and female protagonists. The painter Johan Borg (Max von Sydow) and his wife Alma (Liv Ullmann) come to stay at their remote island summerhouse. Johan is becoming increasingly insular and insomniac with visions of demons. After a few sunny sequences, we are shown one of Johan's vigils, when he shares his previously private sketchbook with Alma, containing his impressions of the demons that haunt him. Alma is then prompted by a mysterious old woman to read Johan's diary, which recounts encounters with three people while out sketching: his previous mistress, Veronica Vogler; Baron von Merkens, owner of a nearby castle, who invites them to dinner; and Heerbrand, who Johan attacks and knocks to the floor.

Johan and Alma visit the castle. The evening is one of nightmarish humiliation in which the Baron's bizarre family and friends (who bear similarities with Johan's descriptions of his demon drawings) such as Lindhorst and Heerbrand taunt Johan and Alma. Afterwards, Johan does not respond to Alma's pleas to help him. Later, he tells her about an incident when he was punished as a child and about an afternoon when he killed a boy, which is presented in chiaroscuro flashback form. Heerbrand then appears and invites him to the castle to see Veronica Vogler. When Alma asks him to tell her about Veronica, he shoots the gun left with him by Heerbrand in Alma's direction. He returns to the castle, now a weird labyrinth, where his demons torment him as he attempts to make love to Veronica, naked and corpselike, on a cold stone slab at the heart of the labyrinth. She awakens or comes alive and laughs hysterically at him; the demons hanging from the ceiling behind also mock him. Pursued by them, Johan disappears in the forest and Alma, unhurt, follows but never finds him.

Both Robin Wood[32] and Bergman have noted that *The Hour of the Wolf* has often been seen as a regression after *Persona*. However, as they both claim, it is not that simple, bearing in mind *The Hour of the Wolf*'s 'consciously formal and thematic disintegration'.[33] The film attempts, in

Bergman's opinion, to convey a deep-rooted division within him, presumably between external and internal worlds or the unconscious and the conscious, marking an 'unsteady step in the right direction', which *Persona* specifically had given him the conviction to pursue.

T.M.'s (presumably Tom Milne's) immediate response to the film (in *Monthly Film Bulletin*) is telling:

> Although *The Hour of the Wolf* would appear to be altogether less complex than the earlier film (*Persona*), this is largely because Bergman has chosen to offer stylistic signposts as a guide to its flashback geography, and more particularly because the film has such a clear narrative unity in the ineluctable progress of Johan Borg's obsession and self-destruction. Or has it?[34]

Milne is wise to question these assertions, since the 'stylistic signposts' he refers to channel the narrative into extremely murky territory. The white words on the black screen at the beginning of the film indicate some of the film's 'vague' qualities. They claim that the story about to be related is a mixture of Alma's recollections (what Alma 'has told me') and what has been discovered in Johan's diary. The word 'me' adds a further dimension to the story by introducing an implied narrator, significantly not used again.

Alma then begins *her* story, sitting outside her home, at a table in the sunlight. Other sequences – Johan's three visitations while out sketching – stem from the diary, though significantly via Alma, who is reading it. The castle scene seems to evolve out of the diary entries, as a continuation of the fantasy embodied in them. The story of the relationship between Johan and Veronica Vogler also differs depending on the way it is told. Alma reads aloud to Johan from his diary his previous *written* descriptions of the relationship, arguing that it is different to the story that he portrays when *speaking* to her. Neither can be fully truthful; both are equally truthful. At the end of the film, Alma finishes the storytelling, now in a darkened part of the house.

There is not the same play with performance, role or reflexivity as in *Persona*. In *The Hour of the Wolf*, while Alma *says* that she has become like her husband, we do not *see* her become like him, though it becomes impossible to distinguish whose 'story' it is. Three horn sounds accompany the title 'Vargtimmen' ('Hour of the Wolf'), just prior to the first sequence, similar to the horn near the end of *Persona*, preceding the shot of Liv Ullmann in the viewfinder. Significantly, Liv Ullmann, now as Alma,[35] is the first 'character', signalling her reappearance, reflexively, in this new film. However, other than the opening of the film,[36] and the mid-way repetition of the title 'Vargtimmen', the film is not obviously reflexive. With this narrative freedom, there was perhaps less of a need for reflexive devices to distance the viewer. Significantly, the original prologue and epilogue were cut in the finished version, leaving only the dialogue which accompanies the titles (Bergman: 'It was better not to play at any aesthetic games to hold this film at a distance.').[37]

Bergman's horror movie

While during the late 1960s attempts to convey fantasy and dream along-side everyday reality were in some ways peculiar to avant-garde and art-house movies, similar preoccupations, inspired by German Expressionism and the nightmare, were now well established in what had become one of the mainstream film genres: the horror movie. The 1960s marked the start of a period of great richness for horror with, for example, Alfred Hitchcock's *Psycho* (1960), which moved the horror genre from demonic to psycholog-ical terror, and George A. Romero's *The Night of the Living Dead* (1968). This coincided with a re-emergence of writing on the genre. It is not surprising, then, that a film such as *The Hour of the Wolf*, with its portrayal of repressed urges, desires and fears, should bear such a huge debt to this genre, adopt-ing characters, settings and plot developments to help convey the night-mare state. J.P. Telotte's claims exemplify critical discourses on horror and nightmare, which seem to be both tied to, and inspired by, each other:

> Such films typically evoke a dreamlike environment or nightworld in which, as it were our own sleep, we can pleasurably and profitably immerse ourselves . . . .

> The horror film has long been dominated by the sort of monsters, ghouls, and aberrances that might easily be read as embodiments of our repressed urges and instinctual fears.[38]

Similarly, Noël Carroll suggests that 'horror film imagery, like that of the nightmare, incarnates archaic, conflicting impulses'.[39] Psychoanalytical discourse is common to both horror movies and dream. In reading mean-ing from both, film critics, directors and audiences have looked to the unconscious, suggesting that dreams and horror films can be read as the return of the repressed. Alter egos, split personalities, monsters and were-wolves have been read as creatures of the Freudian 'id'. It would seem appropriate to discuss psychoanalysis in relation to horror because horror expresses psychoanalytically significant themes such as repressed sexuality.

The castle's horror is evoked not only by the 'demons' inhabiting it, but also by particular techniques such as subjective camera shots, circular panning shots at the dinner table and swift editing. The castle setting like the 'Terrible Place' in which the victims find themselves in the horror movie,[40] and the (often murderous, incestuous or cannibalistic) 'terrible family' inhabiting it draw on the conventions of Dracula and other vampire films well established by this time. As Wood points out,[41] the Birdman Lindhorst resembles Bela Lugosi's Dracula (*Dracula*, Tod Browning, 1931) and Baron von Merkens recalls Boris Karloff's original Frankenstein's monster (*Frankenstein*, James Whale, 1931). The old woman who peels off her face brings to mind Norman Bates's mother, and the pecking and jabbing Birdman and the corridor full of pigeons suggests Hitchcock's *The Birds* (1963) as well as *Psycho*.

The overall framework bears a resemblance to horror films that begin with the outsider's initiation into the isolated aristocratic 'cannibal' family and end with some form of vengeance. Johan's invitation to the castle by the admiring aristocratic family of demons and his seeming absorption into their world, away from the everyday reality that Alma seems to represent, echoes Jonathan Harker's journeys to Transylvania to improve his prospects, ignoring the entreaties of his bride, in F.W. Murnau's *Nosferatu* (1922). *The Hour of the Wolf* also draws on the werewolf tradition of fission and conflict, traditionally associated with notions of confused sexuality.

Strikingly, when Max von Sydow's Johan[42] storms pompously into the castle pursuing his demons, only to have his face made up and be dressed in a silk gown, it anticipates later horror traditions such as *The Exorcist* (William Friedkin, 1973) and what Carroll describes as the teenage neurotic girl's vacillations between 'fantasies of self-loathing and infantile delusions of grandeur'.[43] As well as being tormented by demons, Johan is the monster himself, 'shooting' his wife. This evokes the werewolf myth implicit in the film's title, of the Shadow killer, the good man transformed during the full moon into a wild animal ready to devour its loved ones:

> Often changeling films, like *The Werewolf of London* or *The Cat People*, eventuate in the monster attacking its lover, suggesting that this subgenre begins in infantile confusions over sexuality and aggression.[44]

Furthermore, the encounter with Johan's ex-lover Veronica, reclining like a statue on a slab of stone, resembles a mixed range of similar encounters in both fairytale and mythology. When Johan kisses the white idealized body, he resembles the prince who awakens Snow White; here the dream becomes nightmare as Veronica is reanimated and laughs hysterically at him from the tomb. Elements from Pygmalion, Dracula and other mythological transformations associated with horror movies resonate throughout the film. Transitional corporeal states are evoked by bodies out of control: Alma is pregnant; Johan is dressed as a woman to confront Veronica and there are the marionettes[45] played by real people in the Birdman's earlier puppet show performance of *The Magic Flute*.[46]

Bergman addresses the subject of Johan being made up by archivist Lindhorst in preparation for Veronica:

> Lindhorst's makeup transforms Johan into a mixture of clown and woman, and then he dresses him in a silk gown, which makes him even more feminine. The white clowns have a multiple, ambiguous symbolism: they are beautiful, cruel, dangerous, balancing on the border between death and destructive sexuality.[47]

The cross-gendering also refers to *Psycho* and the later 'slasher films', where gender confusion is often implied, stemming from issues in childhood.

Johan's demons are either incarnations of Johan's (Alma's) fears, repressed impulses and nightmare visions or distortions of (real) neighbours, contorted in a way to align them with the protagonists' fear and paranoia. To illustrate the hybridization of different character roles, we could say that Alma is both 'Final Girl', the survivor in conventional horror films who 'perceives the full extent of the preceding horror' but does not die,[48] and victim, shot by her monster husband. She is also the bearer of the nightmare, since the visions are conjured up by her words and memories. As Wood asserts, the demons are 'products of neurosis, embodiments of the power of the past over the present',[49] but the question of whose neurosis, of whose past and whose present lingers on.

Johan explains to Alma that the 'hour of the wolf' is the 'worst' time of all. It is the early morning hour when most transitional phases occur like birth, death and nightmares, and 'if we're awake . . . we're afraid'. Folk stories during the Middle Ages used the wolf, werewolf, ogre or wild person as a symbol of the threats to the child outside the boundaries of home.[50] Johan leers like a wolf with blood-like lipstick smeared around his mouth, dripping as he sweats, after lustily kissing Veronica's body. *The Hour of the Wolf* hosts the common Gothic motif of two disparate settings – the home and the forbidden territory (primitive, dark, unknown, castle, labyrinth, tomb and forest). Deviation from the path suggests wantonness, sexual desire and defiance of social law. In contrast to ancient rituals, however, where the initiated would return recuperated, Johan retreats to the dark forest at the end of the film, metaphorically joining the wolves.

Marsha Kinder suggests that *The Hour of the Wolf* 'reworks the werewolf and Little Red Riding Hood myths that imprinted Bergman as a child'.[51] The cannibalism associated with the werewolf and Little Red Riding Hood[52] was clearly on Bergman's mind at the time he made *The Hour of the Wolf*. He claims that 'this cannibal motif, the hour of the wolf, goes back a long way' and that he was planning the film a year before *Persona* when he wrote a script called *The Cannibals*.[53] Kinder cites Bergman's recollections of his magic lantern projections to argue that the colour red unites killer and victim, the conflicting roles assumed by Johan in the course of the film:

> This is where my magic lantern came in . . . Red Riding Hood and the Wolf, and all the others. And the wolf was the devil . . . with a tail and a gaping red mouth . . . .[54]

The fear of cannibalism (devouring, or being devoured by, a parental figure) is at the core of both the werewolf and Little Red Riding Hood stories, and both are linked with emerging sexuality.

When Johan is confronted in the labyrinthine castle by the old woman who makes him kiss her toes (recalling the closet demon who would bite his toes during his childhood punishment), there are overt references to *Little Red Riding Hood*, as Kinder points out;[55] the old woman peels off her face saying, 'I must take my hat off, then I'll hear you better' echoing the grandmother's 'all the better to hear you with' in the Little Red Riding Hood tale. But the symbolism is distorted like a nightmare, creating confusion rather than clarity.

The boy-killing sequence and the childhood punishment

Many devices used in the five-minute-long fishing sequence where Johan kills the boy make it stand out as being dreamlike and nightmarish such as overexposed photography contrasting with the preceding dark sequence, swift editing (over 30 shots) contrasting with the long takes used in the preceding sequences, extreme camera angles and the many images that invite a psychoanalytical reading of Johan's repressed urges, murderous tendencies and issues with sexuality. In addition, there are no words or natural sounds, just frantic music – mechanical sounds that become increasingly like high-pitched buzzing noises – and the boy's cries, initially mute, that eventually pierce through. Johan seems to be 'speaking' rapidly at one point, 'shouting out' mute words, as is often the case in nightmares.

While the bleached out photography mirrors the first dream sequence in *Wild Strawberries*, there is no introductory voice-over here to cue the ensuing sequence as a dream. The over-exposure also recalls Frost's sequence in *Sawdust and Tinsel* (1953), which – though introduced as a 'real' story of the past – is conveyed in a half-dream/nightmare, half-flashback style to emphasize excruciating humiliation. The boy-killing sequence is also signalled as a past event; Johan introduces it by saying that he was out fishing one day, on a coast where he and Alma had once visited. These words and the expressionist style thus cue the flashback-dream in a similar way to the sequence in *Sawdust and Tinsel*, making it stand out in quite a traditional way as something other than 'real'. Moreover, as Petric asserts, the contrast between the light and dark sequences increases as Johan's 'psychic trauma becomes more intense';[56] the function of light is most dramatic in climaxes such as when Johan 'kills' his wife and when he runs out of the house. Like the sequence in *Sawdust and Tinsel*, the location of the boy-killing sequence next to the sea, and the painfully bright light[57] associated with it, helps to convey deep psychological issues that relate to the male protagonist.

Also, the presence of the easel on the rocks in front of Johan links this sequence with the 'visions' in Johan's diary of the dreamlike visitations by Baron Von Merkens, Veronica Vogler and Heerbrand, who all appear when Johan is out sketching with the easel similarly situated in the foreground of the frame. This again helps to signal the sequence as a nightmare.

In addition to these factors the narrative has strong psychosexual elements to it, indicating repressed urges usually associated via psychoanalysis with the dreamworld. It is possible to read this sequence, for instance, as one of repressed homosexuality.[58] Wood suggests that the sequence can be best interpreted as the attempt to repress homosexual tendencies, with the fishing rod and its position having phallic overtones and Johan's clumsy attempts to reel in symbolizing denial.[59] In a number of shots the two brightly lit, half-naked male bodies resemble each other.

Such connotations also emphasize the film's connections with the horror genre. Like the werewolf or Mr Hyde, homosexuals are often represented to suggest the 'other', as Harry M. Benshoff points out: 'Both movie monsters and homosexuals have existed chiefly in shadowy closets, and when they do emerge from these proscribed places into the sunlit world, they cause panic and fear.'[60] In this sequence, homosexual suggestions are combined with Oedipal references and parental/child struggles that are also inherent in wolf mythology. In *The Wolf Man* (George Waggner, 1941), tensions between father and son result in the father beating the son to death with a silver cane in 'a paroxysm of oedipal anxiety'.[61] Certainly, sexual imagery common to Freudian dream symbolism figures highly in the sequence. The boy's attack seems to convey castration anxiety, as Stig Björkman suggests,[62] as does his inspection of Johan's drawings, the fishing rod and the three fishes (all Freudian phallic symbols). As Björkman goes on to assert, the boy, by 'indolently lying' on the beach watching Johan's actions, is a challenge of a sexual nature,[63] but the scene could also be construed as an erotic invitation.

Whether or not the sequence signals the stifling of homosexual desire, it certainly suggests Johan's fears of creative and sexual inadequacy and an attempt to demolish the past and the father who exerted power over him. The sequence ends with the shot of the boy's body lurking beneath the sea's surface, a shot that is repeated after the sequence of Johan's encounter with Veronica in the centre of the labyrinthine castle, suggesting that the attempt to obliterate memories is unsuccessful.

Bergman claims that when he made the film, the boy-killing sequence was a realistic expression of Johan's manic fear of being bitten. The boy is one of his demons, Bergman argues:

> Johan Borg couldn't make up his mind whether he'd killed a boy who really existed or whether it had only happened in his imagination. The boundary between dream and reality had been blurred.[64]

Although not signalled as a dream, the content and style of the boy-killing sequence make it stand out as a nightmare vision. However, any signposting is complicated by the blurring between this sequence and the story Johan tells Alma immediately before, concerning his childhood punishment of being locked in the cupboard by his father, and the fear of the little man living in there who could 'gnaw the toes off naughty children'. In the sequence with the boy Johan kills the demon, who has bitten him. The boy is of a similar age to Johan when he was punished; the boy bites his ankles, as the demon in the cupboard does. But the links with the previous sequence also suggest that Johan's role is not so clear. As Kinder asserts, he 'identifies both with the brutalised child and with the closeted demon – a pattern which exactly fits the sado-masochistic dynamic in the homosexual male, as delineated by Freud'.[65] There is so little light when Johan begins his story about his childhood punishment that we can only just see the window behind them, making the words work on the imagination like the beach story in *Persona*. Not only is there no flashback-style narration here, but it is a voice in virtual darkness. Bergman claims that while he had initially intended to show the man in the cupboard, he was still too involved in the experience.[66]

Empathy with Johan's fear as the music intensifies and he rubs his head[67] is significantly undercut by the close-up of Alma desperately trying to keep awake for him, despite his oblivion. There is a cut from this close-up to the sequence with the boy,[68] and at the end of this sequence, it dissolves back to Alma still listening, making it unclear whose hallucinations are being represented.[69] The blurring between these two key sequences helps to convey the nightmares and hallucinations of a deteriorating mind, making it unclear where reality ends and fantasy begins. The shattering of clear signposting systems and individual subjects for identification indicates the kinds of confusions at stake across the film as a whole.

Johan's diary

Stylistically, the diary sequences also seem to represent something beyond the 'real', for example, the extreme camera angles during the Baron's visit and the dazzling light during Veronica's visit. In contrast, the earlier parts of this sequence (from the visit of the old lady[70] who tells Alma to look at the diary through to the opening of it) tend to use conventional continuity editing such as the match-on-action as Alma passes through the front door to the garden. The cuts between close-ups and extreme close-ups of the old woman and Alma are reminiscent of the symbolism employed in Bergman's earlier films such as the knight's encounter with Death in *The Seventh Seal*, David's encounter with the man with the umbrella in *It Rains on our Love* (1946) and Isak's encounter with his aged mother in *Wild Strawberries*. However, the fact that Alma does not speak and that the old lady's voice is completely muffled by the winds when she tells Alma the crucial information about the diary under the bed makes it similar to Bergman's later work such as *Cries and Whispers*. That these sequences are just as easily attributable to Alma as to Johan is suggested by the cuts back to close-ups of Alma reading after each visitation. These close-ups become more extreme as the story intensifies, for example, after the scene with Veronica.

While the cuts to Alma, and the different dates for each visit, signal that the scenes are not continuous, the use of the same clothing (Johan wears the same black polo-necked jumper in all of the three visits) helps to fuse the scenes together. This continues up to when Johan arrives home wearing the same jumper, just as Alma has finished reading the diary. Johan's dishevelled appearance suggests that he has just been in the incident with Heerbrand, but this defies temporal–spatial conventions. Defying these further, Johan tells Alma that they have just been invited to the castle.

Philip Strick claims that it is possible to deduce what is 'real' and 'unreal' in *The Hour of the Wolf*, suggesting that the scenes where the couple are together might be taken as 'real', the castle scenes as 'distorted reality' and all the scenes in Johan's diary and the murder of the boy as 'totally unreal'.[71] There does seem to be a sense of a gradual disorientation in the film, perhaps aided by the movement from graphically lighter sequences at the beginning to darker sequences at the end. The sequence with the boy, the castle sequences and the forest episode at the end all use particular technical effects to help convey an altered state. However, as we have seen, the film neither has a straightforward plot that 'drops off' at signalled moments into another realm nor gradually descends to an altered state, and even the opening home scenes in which the couple are together are less coherent than they might initially appear.

These first few sequences are structured so that Alma tells part of their story, followed by a set of 'glimpses' of their times together, which amount to blurred reminiscences of an anonymous 'narrator' from Alma's recollections and Johan's diary. The couple's arrival by boat stems from Alma's story, suggesting her viewpoint, retrospectively. There are no words in this sequence, anticipating the format used in the latter half of the film, where words and images belong to separate sequences. Furthermore, the sharp chiaroscuro effect of this sequence, its coastal location and the presence of Johan pressing the oar into the water also anticipate the nightmarish sexual tensions of the boy-killing scene.

The couple speak in the next sequence (Johan drawing Alma), registering a formula of alternate sequences – with and without words – that will continue throughout the film. This scene was not referred to in Alma's story. The final sequence, of Johan returning home from drawing to find Alma hanging out the sheets on the washing line, is significant for its sudden shift from a happy to a nightmarish mood. The sequence complies with the greater format also, since there are again no words in this sequence. Although this scene is not directly referred to in Alma's story, it does convey the feeling (expressed in her story) that Johan is growing restless, in the way that he walks off after Alma tries to kiss him. Another pattern is also emerging – the length of each sequence is decreasing each time[72] – which, together with the alternation between words and images, adds a sense of constructedness to what might otherwise be perceived as naturalistic.

Furthermore, there is a strange bright light on Alma's face before it appears in close-up through the sheet, creating a bleached out look like the boy-killing sequence. The flapping sheets strongly resemble birds' wings, and when one flapping sheet obscures Johan's face, it mirrors the flapping pigeons in the castle sequence in the second half of the film. Significantly this sequence occurs at a later point in the screenplay, described in Johan's diary only, *after* the scene with Heerbrand:

> I could still feel the blow in my right hand when I got home. Alma was outside hanging up the wash. She came toward me with a smile and put her arms around my neck and kissed me. I broke away and went inside. I lay on the bed and turned my face to the wall.[73]

This might also help to explain why cause and effect is so confused in the film; there is no explanation for Johan's strange return and odd mood, until perhaps later when Alma reads the diary. But then, as we have seen, there is the sense that time is once again distorted, because the diary scenes and Johan's return, seem to be continuous in time.

Thus, many of the sequences in *The Hour of the Wolf* echo and mirror each other, drawing on symbolic and psychoanalytic registers. Motifs and conventions materialize in unexpected contexts, and sequences interconnect in ways that make it difficult to distinguish between dream and everyday reality. While there are references to certain horror and fairytale motifs and conventions, many of these are twisted and confused in ways that make them less easily comprehensible. Distinct settings are used, but it is not clear how or why the character arrives at these; temporal and spatial clues are denied. The demons seem to spread beyond the castle. The film ends with Alma alone claiming that she has shared Johan's visions of demons, making it unclear how much of what has been seen is subjective, whose nightmare it has been and who plays the roles of the monster and victim.

Cries and Whispers

In some ways, *Cries and Whispers* (1972) appears to have a relatively straightforward narrative that 'drops off' into other levels. It is likely that the flashback sequences relate something that has actually happened to the sisters, or refers in a symbolic way to important aspects of their characters. The sequences certainly do not work in the same way as the expressionistic flashback-dream of Johan with the boy, for example, in *The Hour of the Wolf*. However, as mentioned earlier, *Cries and*

Whispers evolved out of Bergman's dream vision, and this is felt in the way that chronological time does not seem to be of great importance. The remembrances and the present day occurrences, together with the cries and whispers, hold an equal presence within the house. *Cries and Whispers* uses a stylized system of colours to create atmosphere, with the effect of creating a form of expressionism quite different from the elongated shadows, chiaroscuro lighting and distorted angles in *The Hour of the Wolf*.

Agnes's 'resurrection', however, stands out[74] for being the only sequence in *Cries and Whispers* that cannot be described in terms of an actual happening and that has been singled out by critics as the most dreamlike. Bergman's analysis is interesting because it is fundamental to the issue of interpretation and meaning that has become apparent in his work:

> How tired I am of hearing that imagination must always be held responsible to the intellect! . . . Does Agnes perhaps only seem to be dead? Is she a ghost? . . . No, I hadn't thought of making a ghost film . . . Agnes' death has been caught up halfway out into the void. I can't see that there's anything odd about that. Yes, by Christ there is! This situation has never been known, either in reality or at the movies.[75]

This sequence begins with Anna fetching Maria and Karin because she hears someone calling out. We hear the voice of the dead Agnes ask Anna if she can see Karin and Maria in turn. Karin will not comfort Agnes, but Maria tries to, until she rushes off in horror as Agnes's hands pull her downwards by the head. Anna herself says that she will sit with Agnes, and the sequence ends with the pietà style image of Agnes lying across Anna's arms.

Some critics have suggested that the sequence is not only dreamlike but an actual dream, and in particular Anna's dream or wish-fulfilment. This is supported by the fact that Anna is in the first and last shot of the sequence. It is also supported by certain aspects of the way that it is introduced. The fade to red from the close-up of Anna's face signals that this next sequence will relate to Anna specifically. The cries that resemble baby's cries link Agnes's death with the death of Anna's own daughter, as it fades from red to a close-up of Anna behind the bars of her baby's crib. Other effects make this sequence dreamlike, including the expressionistic tint to the sharp blue and black colour of the living room. Anna walks with a somnambulist's gait, slowly entering a room, where we eventually see Maria and Karin standing motionless against doorways as if in a trance. Anna whispers to Maria, 'Can't you hear . . . someone is crying?' and the camera tracks to the left as Anna walks over to Maria.

There is a close-up of Maria's face as she mouths indistinguishable words. The same is true of Karin who remains silent while Anna's breathing grows increasingly fevered. These nightmarish scenes, where the characters are unable to speak, recall parts of *The Hour of the Wolf* such as the boy-killing sequence. There is also the suggestion that Anna and Agnes each provide the lost and longed for mother/child the other lacks. This is visualized earlier in the cut from the crib where Anna remembers her (now dead) daughter to the sequence where Agnes remembers her dead mother. The two scenes are also linked by the non-diegetic piano music of Chopin's mazurka that plays as Anna prays for her daughter and Agnes remembers her mother wandering in the park.

Peter Harcourt refers to the sequence simply as Anna's dream: 'Each of the sisters is allowed one flashback in the film; while Anna, almost as if she has no memory relevant to this story, is allowed a dream.'[76] However, as Deborah Thomas argues, while we can see this sequence as Anna's dream or 'wish-fulfilment', its 'reality status' is more complicated.[77] Thomas asserts that it is also a direct consequence of Karin and Maria's ability to touch each other, just as their inability to sustain closeness is a direct consequence of their inability to relate to Agnes in her greatest need.[78] This suggests that the sequence is a representation of the way that the sisters are towards Agnes in relation to Anna, emphasizing Anna's ability to be close to another human being. Thomas also suggests that the resurrection sequence 'involves a collaborative descent into death, (and then into the unconscious) on the part of all four women'.[79]

Egil Törnqvist claims that this is one of the most dreamlike passages in the film and also draws attention to the subjectivity of the sequence on the part of Anna, pointing out that her emotional experience of the dead woman is conveyed through a subjective zoom in on Agnes's face. He notes that Agnes wears a baby's hood, merging her with Anna's daughter.[80] However, like Thomas, he also interprets the resurrection scene as representing a shared vision. He compares the sequence with the ghosts of the Milkmaid and the Consul in *The Ghost Sonata*,[81] who are 'people whose death has been "caught up"', thus recalling Bergman's claims that Agnes's death has been 'caught up halfway out into the void'.

This sequence thus attracts diverse readings. During the televised *Masterclass* on *Cries and Whispers*, led by Terence Davies, one of the students asserts that it is a 'wishful dream' (on the part of Anna) and Davies responds, 'Yes, but not shot like a dream – shot as if it were real.'[82] Certainly, the camera and editing techniques are not as extreme as those used in the more obviously dreamlike sequences of *The Hour of the Wolf*. Although the group do not go on to discuss how a dream might be shot, they do review some of the unusual techniques used during this sequence which seem to pertain to dreaming. One of these is the exaggeration of space used between the room where Agnes lies and the room where Maria and Karin are waiting. Davies points out how far the women have to go to get to the room where Agnes's body is, bearing in mind that it was just 'a tiny hall'. This effect is actually only exaggerated during Maria's walk to the room. This is achieved by the camera's backward tracking as she walks towards the camera, past Karin, cut with a medium shot of her black silhouetted profile walking slowly in front of a large window. She stops as she reaches the vertical middle bar of this window and turns. There is a cut to an extreme close-up of Anna opening the door, which then cuts back to Maria beginning to walk again in front of the second large window, past Anna waiting by the door of Agnes's room. This is dreamlike and bears some resemblance to the castle sequence in *The Hour of the Wolf*, when Johan runs through the long hallway on his way to find Veronica, disappearing behind several archways and reappearing in front of numerous windows. However, here the impact is not that of hasty disorientation, but a gradual build up of fear as Maria approaches the room of the corpse. The shots convey real time, with Maria's hesitations extending the terror. Similarly, when Maria runs out of Agnes's room terrified the camera is, as one of the Masterclass students asserts, 'just a bit slow to catch up with her', exaggerating her feeling of entrapment. Here, the dream/nightmare *seems* to belong to Maria, who we identify with momentarily.

The medium of film perhaps lends itself more readily to the creation of an ambiguous atmosphere than the 'story' (screenplay). For example, while in the film the camera remains on Anna's face throughout the unusual conversation between her and Agnes, with Agnes's voice off-screen, suggesting that it is all a figment of Anna's imagination,[83] the words in the screenplay state that Agnes actually speaks and that Anna sees her lips move. The sequence with Maria begins in the same way, and as soon as we see Agnes's body, the voice disappears. The initial ambiguity is maintained, very precisely, so that Agnes's sentence ends just before the camera focuses on her face. When Agnes's hands unexpectedly enter the frame and pull Maria's head downwards to kiss her, it is a shock to the viewer. The camera withdraws as Agnes's hands pull Maria's head. When Anna finally closes the door of Agnes's room on the two sisters, there is a cut to a medium long shot of them standing in black, one slightly in front of the other, as the cello music starts up. Two extreme close-ups of each of the sisters reveal them to be vacant and motionless, like stone, literally petrified. Karin, with eyes wide open looks down and tries to speak, mirroring her inability to speak at the start of this sequence. While Maria and Karin stand paralyzed, there is a cut to the high angled shot of the pietà pose, with Agnes cradled in Anna's arms. Petric asserts that the film replaces Karin's claim in the screenplay that the whole thing is only a dream with non-verbal images that convey 'the paralysis of a dream' felt by Maria and Karin, and similar to the effect created when Maria rushes out of the room.[84]

Törnqvist claims that there are other sequences that are 'almost as dreamlike' as Agnes's continued life after death, citing Karin's self-mutilation, Joakim's suicide attempt and the Chaplain's self reproaches.[85] He argues that while conventional cues to dreams are rarely used, the sequences are difficult to accept at face value since they seem to portray a more subjective form of reality, blotting out the borderlines between dream and reality.

However, unlike *The Hour of the Wolf*, the shots are generally 'naturalistic' and the overall atmosphere is unusual. Bergman's diary notes leading up to the writing of the screenplay give a picture of how the ideas developed. Bergman toys with the idea of Agnes dying at the beginning of the film, and yet not being dead.[86] Later, he reflects that his ideas (which may not even amount to a film) 'consist of this poem: a human being dies but, as in a nightmare, gets stuck halfway through and pleads for tenderness, mercy, deliverance, something'.[87] Already there is the idea that while two others will act with the 'dead' Agnes, it is only a third person who saves her by gently rocking her, 'going with her part of the way'.[88] He also writes that it is important that he is not derailed into a boring 'elaborate description', but must remain with the 'concrete fluid dream that was unfolding'.[89] Thus, the events are almost secondary to the images such as the white dresses, the red room and the number of sisters. This seems to recall the early sequences in *The Hour of the Wolf*, the 'glimpses' of the couple's life together, that mark an important new step in Bergman's work.

Transitional states of life and death

While certain episodes such as the sequence of Agnes's resurrection just described, can be seen as dreamlike, the whole film has an illusory, internal atmosphere to it. Bergman's reflections at the start of the written 'story' of *Cries and Whispers* indicate that the film came about in an evolutionary way, growing from images reappearing in the mind:

> What it most resembles is a dark flowing stream: faces, movements, voices, gestures, exclamations, light and shade, moods, dreams. Nothing fixed, nothing really tangible other than for the moment,

and then only an illusory moment. A dream, a longing, or perhaps an expectation . . . .[90]

As Törnqvist notes,[91] another effect used to help convey the mood is the re-positioning of the bed from the corner of the main living room at the beginning to another separate room adjoining it after Agnes dies, further emphasized by the exaggerated space between the two rooms in the sequence discussed. The expressive and dreamlike atmosphere is also reinforced by the way that Agnes dies so quickly and so quietly, and the simple device of the light coming into the room and then going out once she is dead.[92] These elements are attempts to comment on the huge, and paradoxically narrow, line between life and death, with the resurrection itself suggesting an in-between existence. The borderline between the binary oppositions of life and death is made more fluid, and allusions to dream in the film act as an analogy for this liminal state.

Like *The Hour of the Wolf*, *Cries and Whispers* employs the fade-out and in between episodes, to suggest a switch between time zones. Here in a striking red, expressive perhaps of something raw to the individual, each fade registers the introduction of significant material on the four women. Each woman has a fade-out followed by a flashback. The device adds to the sense that, while every episode has occurred at some point of time in the past, it is ever present in the imagination and within the spirit of the house. This is a poetical concept that is common in the plays of August Strindberg. For instance, the multiple realities in *The Ghost Sonata* (1907) and *A Dream Play* (1902), with their fragile distinctions between life, death, spirits and visions, permeate *Cries and Whispers*. The film is set during the same period as Strindberg, Henrik Ibsen and Anton Chekhov were writing, and its narrative is reminiscent of Chekhov's *Three Sisters* (1901) and *The Cherry Orchard* (1903). The theatre's substantial influence on Bergman is also implied by the camera's focus on the doll's house during the opening sequences of the film, recalling Ibsen's 1879 play.[93]

The colour red also dominates the furnishings of the house: the walls, the carpets and some of the curtains. Bergman explains in the screenplay that to him the red is 'internal', and representative of the 'inside of the soul' or the 'moist membrane in shades of red'.[94] The last comment seems to relate to the womb[95] and thus also adds to the paradox of the use of red to signify both the soul (death) and the womb (birth). Once again, the device seems to stress the narrow line between life and death, drawing attention to the slim strand that makes a human alive.[96] This is supported by (what are possibly) baby's cries and whispers accompanying the fades to red, suggesting alienation felt by someone on the brink of life/death. As Törnqvist asserts, the pietà pose at the end of the resurrection sequence is a 'complex fusion of death and birth'.[97] It also identifies Agnes with Anna's daughter as well as Christ.

Like *The Hour of the Wolf*, *Cries and Whispers* borrows much of its symbolism from traditions of fairytale. There are overt similarities with Cinderella and the ugly sisters, for instance, and the striking juxtapositions of red (Maria's gown, the draperies) and white (the other gowns, the sheets) throughout the film mirror the pricking of the finger in *Sleeping Beauty* and the three drops of blood on the snow/milk in *Snow White*. Furthermore, Karin's blood-smeared mouth evokes the wolf motif discussed earlier, drawing on cannibalistic relationships between parent and child. As well as being an innocent victim (of the cancer witch), the lost child of the fairytale (like those depicted in the magic lantern show of *Hansel and Gretel* in Agnes's flashback) and the 'lamb' implied by the sacrificial pieta pose, Agnes is also a wolf. Propped up in bed in a bonnet, uncannily reminiscent of the wolf dressed as grandmother, she grasps onto Anna in an attempt to bring her down into death. This image of the corpse rising has to be seen as truly horrific.

The tradition of Swedish painting

The paintings of Edvard Munch are particularly relevant to *Cries and Whispers* in the way that they express atmosphere via a similar stylization of colour. Peter Harcourt analyses the 'psychology of colour' in his discussion about Bergman as an expressionist.[98] He asserts that while the black figures turned away from each other in Munch's *Death in the Sick Room* (1893) convey loneliness, the most expressive element is the red floor. This leads on to the question of whether colour, in itself, can be associated with a certain meaning. He concludes that the red women in *The Dance of Life* (1899) seem to express passion, as is also the case with *Jealousy* (1895) and *Virginia Creeper* (ca. 1900). In general though, as is the case with *Cries and Whispers*, the colour red suggests raw emotion.[99]

This connection with Munch can be traced back to *Wild Strawberries*. Philip and Kersti French see resonances in the shot where Isak enters the summerhouse and stands to the right of the frame, detached and alienated, as the family prepare breakfast inside:

> This shot draws on the series of Munch paintings from the 1890s (which Strindberg was reviewing in Paris) in which the foreground figure has his or her back to the other people, as though they are manifestly on, or in, his or her mind. The figure is lonely, agonised, detached, and we read the painting starting from the foreground.[100]

The shot is certainly reminiscent of Munch's *Jealousy*, by way of its distraught male figure in equivalent dark coat standing in the foreground to the right of the canvas, with Eve in a red dress tempting Adam in the background.

Philip and Kersti French describe how Munch 'takes over almost entirely' in the earlier part of the second 'return-to-childhood dream', when Isak stands outside excluded from the togetherness of his brother and Sara.[101] This is similar, as French suggests, to the painting (1893) and woodcut (1895) *Moonlight*. There is another recollection of *Jealousy* when he sees his wife's infidelity. What is interesting here is that the Munch style developing in *Wild Strawberries* to denote dreamlike sequences[102] is later employed in *Cries and Whispers* to create a dreamlike tone across the whole film.

Music also shapes the tone such as when Maria and Karin touch each other. Their words are reduced to inaudible whispers, and natural sound is replaced by the non-diegetic Bach's unaccompanied cello piece reminiscent of the 1960s trilogy. Various meanings can be interpreted from this sequence: Törnqvist sees it as a communion, whereby the warm, lofty music for one instrument resembles the human voice,[103] whereas Harcourt infers that these stylized devices symbolize the impossibility of sustaining this illusory closeness.[104] The music is a fragment of the saraband from Bach's suite for cello in C minor. Retrospectively, connections can be made with Bergman's final film *Saraband* (2003) in which the 'saraband' comes to symbolize illusions of closeness between father and daughter (Karin).

The film's ending, involving a flashback from Agnes's diary of a perfect day with her sisters and Anna in the garden, is similar to the final vision in *Wild Strawberries* in the way that it offers a moment of paradisaic existence in the women's lifetime. It is similar to this final vision because of the ambivalence over whether it is a real moment or a wished-for one. As Thomas asserts, it is just as much Anna's visualization as Agnes's.[105] The sequence significantly begins with a dissolve from the candle (of life) in front of Anna to Agnes, who fills the screen with her wide white umbrella, like an enormous flower, her perfect white hat and white dress. It is a heavenly vision in this sense, suggesting perhaps, as the final words claim that 'the cries and whispers died away'. This is similar to the ending of Strindberg's *The Ghost Sonata*, where there is a paradisaic vision of the hereafter. Here, it is the humanistic equivalent suggesting perhaps that Agnes is now at peace and the house can rest. Rather than the cries being wiped away by God as in Revelations, here they are silenced by this vision of 'perfection' on earth.

The problem with taking this illusory ending as a happy reminiscence of a perfect day is that it does not compensate for the great weight of misery embodied in the rest of the film. However, despite the irony that Maria and Karin are not able to sustain this closeness with any of the women present, the scene does occur, at least in film-time, at the end. Harcourt argues that the sequence is devoid of time with its close-up of Agnes's face as she rocks on the swing, looking wide-eyed at the camera.[106] But it is also a reflexive moment recalling the fresh-faced defiant stare by the same actress 20 years before in *Summer with Monika*. Here, in maturity, the character values the happiness of the moment, 'come what may, this is happiness for a few minutes'. As Davies argues, all the time we have longed to go outside, and the ending is just the right moment for this last, light and tranquil scene to be placed. The extent to which the sequence suggests a humanist resolution, however, remains ambivalent due to the knowledge we have gained of the transient love of the sisters and the way that Anna is alienated in these shots.

This ambivalence is explored further in the next (concluding) chapter, which explores the many layers of *Fanny and Alexander* (1982). While the film projects a fluidity between fantasy and reality, its style, by comparison with *The Hour of the Wolf* and *Cries and Whispers*, seems conventional and illusionist. These areas will be teased out, before going on to address similar elements concerning the mask and identity, retrospectively.

7
Conclusion: Celebrating the Illusion

Fanny and Alexander (1982)[1] celebrates masquerade. It has a showy confidence, reminiscent of Bergman's films of the late 1950s (*Wild Strawberries*, 1956; *The Seventh Seal*, 1956; *The Face*, 1958), but its rich glossiness of colour and extreme duration make it stand out as an epic. Framed within a prologue and an epilogue, and with its division into five acts, it is structured like a conventional theatre drama, as a tribute to Bergman's career in the theatre. Its production for television (the television version lasting over five hours) gives it a less conclusive feel than a conventional film.

The large maze-like Ekdahl home with its elaborately rich décor making it an icon of Swedish upper-middle-class culture at the start of the twentieth century, allows for a sense of nostalgia for Bergman's childhood and the world of his beloved grandmother. This illusory, dreamlike realm of the child (of Fanny and Alexander) contrasts with the austere Lutheran household of the bishop Edvard Vergérus,[2] and tensions between Alexander and the bishop (his step-father) are reminiscent of Bergman's with his own father. The cruel bishop's scratching away at Alexander's fabrications to find 'truth', for example, recalls Bergman's father's attacks on Bergman's own 'lies' during childhood and can be taken as a metaphor for attacks on artistic creation.[3]

The narrative is propelled by the journeys of Emilie and her children, Fanny and Alexander, re-discovering good (the Ekdahls) after evil (the bishop). Fairytale conventions[4] are employed throughout and help convey the bishop's world such as Alexander being locked in the attic by his ogre-like step-father; lightning striking through the bars on Fanny and Alexander's windows and the evil maid with blistered hands plotting against the children.

117

However, *Fanny and Alexander* needs revisiting in terms of tone. Many critical responses to the film have judged it on the basis of it representing a return to humanism, dismissive of the depth and austerity of many of Bergman's other films. This is a reductive, and unsatisfactory, reading of *Fanny and Alexander*. While it may be a testament to Bergman's childhood world, to the dreams of his childhood and to his career in the worlds of film and theatre, there is also a sense of nausea at the adult male Ekdahls's luxuriation in illusions. In contrast to the binary oppositions of good and evil represented by the Ekdahls and the bishop, respectively, there is a celebration of fluidity throughout the film that advocates a sense of life as a series of illusions. However, the film's style by comparison with films such as *Persona* (1965), *The Hour of the Wolf* (1966), *A Passion* (1968) or *Cries and Whispers* (1972), is transparent or illusionist, complying generally with classical continuity. Illusion is undoubtedly one of the film's central concerns, but the film's relationship with this concept is not easily defined and is sometimes contradictory.

Multiple realities

> Uncle Isak . . . he says that we're surrounded by realities, one outside the other. He says that the world is teeming with phantoms and spirits and ghosts, souls, spooks, angels and devils . . .[5]
> (Act V 'Demons', the puppet master Aron to Alexander)

Against patriarchal control (represented by the bishop, the Church as institution and the adult male Ekdahls) Isak Jacobi, the kind-hearted Jew, offers a more fluid way of perceiving his surroundings. His vision of a world in which there is no fixed boundary between fantasy and reality can be taken as a key to the film as a whole.

Isak is able to rescue Fanny and Alexander from the bishop by casting an illusion of them lying on the bedroom floor. After sneaking the children into the trunk he buys from the bishop and covering them in a black blanket, Isak allows Edvard to look inside the trunk. Although Edvard suspects Isak, he is unable to see the children in there. When Edvard goes to check that they are still upstairs, Isak manages to transfer what is either a mirror image of the children or, as Jesse Kalin suggests,[6] a couple of life-size puppets onto the floor of the bedroom above. Isak does this by concentrating his powers to replicate their image from their exact position in the trunk. This act recalls the conjuring tricks associated with Isak's role as shopkeeper of fantastical large-scale marionettes, and refers to the illusions of the theatre and cinema. Emilie's order to the bishop not to touch the children halts the bishop's physical cruelty, but it also suggests that what the bishop sees is an optical illusion – a visual projection that would disintegrate at the touch.

However, there are other ways of reading this sequence. Emilie's order not to touch can also make the vision ghost-like, suggesting a less explicable form of reality. The peculiar order echoes Christ's *'noli me tangere'* to Mary Magdalen at the sepulchre,[7] and is thus indicative of a spiritual vision. Downstairs, Isak seems to hold the vision with extreme effort, a white glow surrounds him and he drops to the floor exhausted after the bishop leaves the room upstairs. In this sense, the illusion differs from Aron's trickeries as puppet master, for example, and resembles the breathing corpse-like statue Aron later shows to Alexander as an example of something that he hates because of its inexplicable nature.

The visions throughout *Fanny and Alexander* create a blurring of reality and fantasy that might recall films like *Persona*, *The Hour of the Wolf* and *Cries and Whispers*. However, in this later film, while the illusion is not 'explained' as such, a clear sense of time and space, and cause and effect remains. Visions appear as part of the ongoing diegesis, propelling the narrative forward in a linear way. The bishop is shown looking at the children lying on the floor, revealing to us what Edvard (thinks he) sees. Although not filmed literally from his point of view, we can see that there is a level of subjectivity here. The sequence can be explained as part of the overall narrative and does not jar with the film's verisimilitude: it is clear that somehow Isak has projected this image, at least to the extent that Edvard thinks that he sees it. It enables Isak to leave with the children safely inside the trunk. Thus, while the act itself is inexplicable, playing on the theme of multiple realities, stylistically temporal–spatial relationships are not upset, and the sequence works using a conventional cause and effect relationship. In this sense, the film can be seen as illusionist, conforming with classical continuity much more than *Persona* or *The Hour of the Wolf*, for example.

Similar processes are working when Fanny and Alexander see the ghost of their father, Oscar, which can be linked back to the magic lantern sequence in Act I and to theatrical references to *Hamlet*.[8] The vision appears at the end of Act II 'The Ghost'. Told to leave the table after their father's funeral (having witnessed the new-found intimacy between their mother and the bishop) Fanny and Alexander pass the orchestra that is playing in front of the statue. This recalls the Prologue where Alexander sees the statue's arm move upwards, and is perhaps a sign of an impending vision emphasized by the holding of the shot on the orchestra and statue after they have walked by. There is a cut to a shot (and the tune) of a moving mechanical toy, followed by a cut to a screen, where slides of a fairytale are being projected by Alexander through the magic lantern, reminiscent of the one shown in Act I.[9] The statue, the mechanical toy, the magic lantern projection and the music which runs to the end of the projection all act as pointers to what will follow.

When the projection and music finish, harpsichord music is heard and Fanny asks Alexander (whose head has fallen into his hands), 'Did you hear it?' Fanny gets up, walks towards the camera as it tracks back, stares incredulously, then runs to wake up Alexander. There is also a link with the dreamworld in the suggestion that Alexander is asleep as the ghost appears. There is a cut from the two children at the door to their view of the room, with their father off-centre (scarcely noticeable on first viewing) in a white suit, playing the harpsichord. This is followed by a cut to a close-up of Alexander. The camera tilts down to Fanny. There is a cut to a close-up of Oscar, one hand on his chin, the other playing a few harpsichord keys. He looks up, staring directly at the camera. This cuts to a close-up of Alexander, held for a few seconds. There is a cut to a close-up of Oscar, finally linking the ghost with Alexander. There follows a fade to black.

Thus, while the sequence is shot naturalistically suggesting a blending of different forms of reality stemming from preceding Bergman films, the magic lantern fantasy directly feeds into the episode with the ghost. It is cued in an overt way, along with the mechanical toy and the music box tune, to evoke the fantasy world. In general, the film takes a specific viewpoint on the ghosts; they are visions of those who have a particular visionary insight like the children and their grandmother Helena Ekdahl, who also sees visions of Oscar later in the film.

The title of this act refers at first to the part Oscar plays as Hamlet's father's ghost as well as to his actual role as ghost in the film. Both Fanny and Alexander are very involved in the play rehearsals and know the story of *Hamlet*. This is an overt pointer to the way that art and life can feed off each other. It thus recalls the art/life dichotomy evident in *Summer Interlude* (1950), but here the vision of the ghost offers a further layer, or a merging of the two to form an in-between phase, as in *Cries and Whispers*. Oscar says on his deathbed that he will play the role of ghost better when dead than he has done in life. Such links thus help to point to the concept that the vision may stem in part from the imaginative force behind the magic lantern and *Hamlet*.

Fanny and Alexander might be seen as a useful key to unlock other more equivocal Bergman films. Indeed, the film has come to be perceived (often problematically) as being not only about Bergman's work, but also about

Bergman himself. It has been frequently pointed out that there are striking similarities between Alexander and Bergman as a child. Indeed, Bergman has aligned himself with Alexander as both 'seer' and embellisher of the truth, claiming that 'Jof[10] and Alexander are in turn related to the child Bergman'.[11] Furthermore, the movement of the female statue's arm stems from Bergman's own childhood[12] and Alexander's projection of the magic lantern slides clearly refers to Bergman's childhood awe at his own power of artistry.[13] It is thus worth reconsidering the sequence where Oscar's ghost appears to Fanny and Alexander in terms of point of view. In this sense, certainly, the sequence is not only about the fuelling of artistic power by childhood fantasy, but specifically relates to Bergman as film director or 'author' of *this* film. The question of authorial vision, therefore, also depends in part on the extent to which the sequence is subject to Alexander's viewpoint. Marilyn Johns Blackwell argues:

> We share the first-person created mental events of the character (Alexander) and thus come to identify with his experience of the mergence of fantasy and reality: a mergence between spectator and spectacle ensues, privileged by a subjective camera that employs frequent panning and point-of-view shots. Bergman seems to have abandoned the multiple viewpoints of *Persona* and *Cries and Whispers*. Even though the film is named for both the boy and his sister, it is his viewpoint that is privileged while Fanny is relegated to a supporting role.[14]

Other theorists such as Egil Törnqvist concur with this final point, 'Fanny's part in the film is rather small compared with Alexander's'.[15] Blackwell concludes that in this sequence, as in the film as a whole, 'imagination' and 'narrative authority' is 'largely gendered as male'[16] albeit a prepubescent boy.[17] It is true that the final cut from the close-up of Alexander to the close-up of Oscar establishes a relationship between Alexander and his father's ghost; from then on Alexander alone sees his father's ghost, twice more in the apartment and once in Isak's shop. However, it is Fanny who first sees the developing relationship between their mother and the bishop. She is also first 'seer' in respect of the father's ghost, and initially there is a cut from the two of them rather than just from Alexander. It is too extreme to argue that the relay of "point-of-view shots" between father and son establishes 'Alexander's authority of vision and excludes Fanny from that imaginative power'.[18] Indeed, as Blackwell asserts, certain components 'problematise the film's coherent male point of view' such as Helena's visions of Oscar's ghost, the episode of stealing the children (to which Emilie is also party) and the later mergence of Alexander with Ismael.[19] A number of other sequences can be added to this. For example, when Alexander is being punished at the bishop's house, Fanny actively denies that Alexander has lied and there are close-ups of her looking on in horror at his caning, and a close-up of her turning from the bishop in disgust when he attempts to pat her cheek afterwards. While there is less attention to her literal point of view, there is a clear alertness to her mental viewpoint.

However, it is significant that the film has been seen as privileging Alexander's (or the child Bergman's) viewpoint. A number of factors combine to perpetuate the impression that the film is on the whole coherent and that it is essentially about Bergman and his childhood. It is an impression that Bergman has sometimes helped to perpetuate, for example, in citing his own words from *The Magic Lantern* to conclude his comments on *Fanny and Alexander*, and in summary of *Images*, illustrating his childhood's influence on his film-making:

> It was difficult for me to differentiate between what existed in my imagination and what was real. If I made the effort, perhaps I could make the reality remain real, but then, for instance, there were always the ghosts and the visions. What was I supposed to do with them? And the fairy tales, were they real or not?[20]

The positioning of this citation at the close of *Images* helps to enforce the argument that the boundaries of the real are the main focus for Bergman's work. However, along with many critical interpretations of the film, it also enforces the idea that *Fanny and Alexander* is about Bergman's childhood meandering between different realms of reality via the less bounded forces of the child's mind. Perhaps it is. But this further emphasizes a particular (male/authorial) viewpoint. There is a suggestion that Bergman has the imaginative visions of his childhood to thank for much of his adult work in film and theatre, and that in a circular fashion much of his childhood visions were stimulated by fantasies such as the theatre, the magic lantern and fairytale. These kinds of claims are made repeatedly throughout *Images*. I do not dispute them. However, seeing the film solely in this way is what leads to assumptions that the film is essentially grounded in Bergman's own experiences. It also leads to problematic perceptions of the film as unequivocally 'humanist'.

Fanny and Alexander depicts visions of ghosts or dream visions alongside everyday reality; the sequences with these visions are specifically signposted and designated to a number of visionaries – Helena, Fanny, Isak, Emilie – and, most frequently, to Alexander. Visions appear within the 'natural' surroundings, and are undisputedly seen whether with real or subjective vision. For example, when ghosts of the bishop's dead children appear to Alexander in the attic and attack him for suggesting that the bishop murdered them, we can make sense of the sequence in terms of cause and effect; Alexander is haunted by fears projected onto him by the bishop. The attic is an apt setting for these visions.

There is a sharp contrast with films like *Persona* and *The Hour of the Wolf* where nightmare and reality mingle with alarming confusion. Whereas Johan's diary in *The Hour of the Wolf* opens up further layers of reality indistinguishable from each other, in *Fanny and Alexander* different layers are clearly cued. For example, when Isak tells Alexander the story about life as a journey towards the end of the film, conventional flashback-style systems are adopted to signpost the story's visualization.

Isak's philosophy of a number of realities 'one outside the other' forms the basis for *Fanny and Alexander*, confirming that its themes and ideas stem from Bergman's preceding works such as: *Persona*, *The Hour of the Wolf*, *A Passion* and *Cries and Whispers*. *Fanny and Alexander*'s naturalistic representation of dreams and visions differs from the more conventional flashback systems of a film like *Wild Strawberries* or the heavily symbolic visions in *The Seventh Seal* (the appearance of Death on the beach, for example). In its naturalism, perhaps, *Fanny and Alexander* could be seen as less conventional than a film like *Cries and Whispers* that employs specific techniques to evoke different realms of reality in the sequence of Agnes's resurrection. However, there is a systematic approach and a sense of coherency in the formulation of sequences within *Fanny and Alexander*, reminiscent of the pre-trilogy films. There is a coherent sense of what is happening, compliant within the verisimilitude of the fairytale-like settings.

Stylistically, in this sense, the film is humanist. Gabriel Pearson and Eric Rhode offer useful definitions, in terms of film style. Looking at New Wave works (Jean-Luc Godard's *Breathless*, 1959, and François Truffaut's *Shoot the Pianist*, 1960), they summarize what might loosely be termed modernist components:

> They break the rules of construction; sequences are barely connected; moods veer violently and without explanation. Like a cat teasing a ball of wool, the thread of a tale may be arbitrarily picked up, played with, and just as easily dropped.[21]

While these stylistic definitions clearly do not apply to *Fanny and Alexander*, making it in their sense 'humanist', the film's vision of multiple realities might be said to belong to the opposite camp (existentialism) in which 'at our present state of knowledge we can no longer believe in a stable reality'.[22]

Pearson and Rhode take Luigi Pirandello's play *Henry IV* as an example of a work that, despite its probing questions concerning reality and illusion, remains 'idealist humanism' because of its sense of form:[23] 'The most challenging question for a humanist – as to whether a central reality exists or not, or whether there is only illusion and therefore an art which can only be illusion imitating illusion – remains unasked.'[24] If this is the central question being asked in a film like *Persona*, then it might be said that stylistically such a question is consciously contained, rather than unasked, in *Fanny and Alexander*. As Pearson and Rhode clarify:

> The humanist assumes that (to use Sartre's image) experience is an onion from which one peels off layers and layers of illusion to expose a small white nub of reality at the centre. But if we shift to an existentialist view, we conceive of experience as an unending series of appearances, each of which is equally 'real'.[25]

Such a philosophy of infinite realities is clearly communicated in *Fanny and Alexander* which, while humanist in terms of its allegiance to form and in the extent to which it is a coherent reflection of Bergman's childhood world, significantly endorses post-humanist preoccupations. The question of what is uncovered once humanism has been abandoned is very relevant to *Fanny and Alexander*.

The mask and multiplicity

Unlike *Persona*, *Fanny and Alexander* permits a world in which meaning can reliably be found in expressive faces such as Alexander's excitement with his magic lantern, Fanny's joy at Christmas time, her horror at the bishop's cruelty and the bishop's terror when Emilie leaves him. Significance can also be found in the synchronous events that form the vast tapestry of interrelated themes and motifs, seeming to suggest an underlying truth to be discovered. In sharp contrast, however, the extensive references to the theatre and role-playing foreground the concept of a series of selves, each as real as the other.

Fanny and Alexander opens with a dissolve into the top part of a theatre building only gradually revealed to be a toy theatre, rather than a real theatre. As the camera tracks downwards to the gentle non-diegetic theme music, into the sliced stage, the backdrops rise. The first reveals an acropolis scene, with red stage curtains very obviously in view. This backdrop is then raised to reveal another, of trees and figures in red and white dresses reminiscent of *Cries and Whispers*. The second backdrop rises to reveal its puppet master Alexander, hand on chin staring through the back of his model theatre. He lifts his characters, places them on stage, before realistic-looking stage lights. This is again a direct reference to Bergman, not only as a stage and film director, but also to his childhood's influence on these careers.

Fanny and Alexander explores the transference from the 'small' make-believe world of the child to the institutionalized theatre world of the adult. A visual parallel is made between Alexander's puppet theatre at the start of the 'Prolog' and the real theatre at the heart of the city, across the road from the Ekdahl apartment, in the scene opening Act I 'The Ekdahl Family Celebrates Christmas'. This sequence begins with shots of fast flowing water and buildings on the edge of town. As a man lights torches alongside a building, a church bell chimes four times, transforming into lower chimes and a darker sky to stress that time has passed. The camera focuses on the top of the theatre, as the church rears almost threateningly behind. The real theatre resembles the puppet theatre physically, as the camera tilts downwards, to the sounds of orchestral trumpets setting up. There is a seamless cut to the inside of the building, down the grand chandelier at its centre, past the arched ceiling of the stage and the gilt-edged red curtain to the orchestra below. The movement ends with the camera suspended from above looking down on the audience, against the sounds of excited talking. The camera action closely mirrors that on Alexander's theatre, imitating the sliced section of the puppet theatre.

There is a further dimension to this parallel. The positioning of the church steeple at the start of the sequence connects with the stage performance of the nativity style mystery play, recalling links between religious ritual and theatre explored in films like *Summer Interlude* (1950), *The Seventh Seal* (1956), *Winter Light* (1962) and *The Rite* (1969). It is significant that the archrivals of church and theatre should also be conveyed as parallel palaces of illusions and dream visions.

The Ekdahl family is completely absorbed in the world of theatre until the death of Oscar, who is the theatre manager as well as Emilie's husband and Fanny and Alexander's father. The Ekdahl family apartment stands opposite the theatre, and the whole family is involved in the productions. The first shot of the apartment is from the outside at Christmas, showing it lit up like a theatre, with the red curtains of the living room resembling those of both the city theatre and Alexander's theatre. The reunification of the family at the end is signified by the reformation of the theatre. However, as will be discussed later, it is hard to see Emily's return as unambiguously positive.

There are clues to suggest that *Fanny and Alexander* upholds the idea that the theatre, like the cinema, is a space for illusions that are healthy and valuable (a concept formulated in *Summer Interlude*, for example) and that life has parallels with the theatre. Neither of these concepts is revolutionary, particularly in the realm of theatre, where the Shakespearian notion that all the world is a stage has become somewhat clichéd. However, it can be argued that *Fanny and Alexander* pushes these concepts further, suggesting that all is masquerade and a number of 'truths' are possible.

After Oscar's death, Emilie decides to forego the opulent lifestyle represented by the Ekdahls and opt for a life with the bishop, which *appears* to offer harsh reality and truth. In her leaving speech (in Act III) to the members of the theatre company after their performance in *Twelfth Night*, Emilie states that she is tired of the lies of the theatre world and seeks a life of truth. Before she speaks, a metal safety curtain slowly rattles down to the stage floor sealing her and the other actors off from the auditorium. Her deep red dress, gold neckband and crown (matching the red and gold apartment and the theatre) and her heavily made-up face connote the falsities that she speaks of:

> We draw the theatre over our heads like a mantle of security. The dressing rooms are bright and warm, the stage enfolds us with kindly shadows. Playwrights tell us what to say and think (*cuts to view the clown*). We laugh and cry and rage (*another character takes off a wig*) . . . We mostly playact . . . So I pass my life in a wonderful self-deception . . . I don't know what I really am, as I never bother to find out the truth.

The terms 'self-deception', 'really am' and 'truth' recall classical notions of truth and falsity in relation to the mask. After the speech, the actors leave the stage in ones and twos, each with a parting line. The actors' performances are also foregrounded in other parts of the film, for example, their stock responses when they pay their respects to Emilie after Oscar's death. This would link with what Emilie has said about being told how to act and how to feel. During Emilie's speech, parts of the set and stage are carried offstage and the actors take off their costumes. After the speech, Alexander starts to perform the opening speech from *Twelfth Night* before his mother tells him to stop playing the fool. The next act opens with the sequence where the bishop interrogates Alexander for fabricating stories about being sold to the circus. However, Emilie eventually rejects the bishop's world and returns to the world of the theatre. Juxtaposed in montage with the bishop punishing Alexander for saying that he murdered his late wife and children, Emilie discusses with Helena her blindness at falling for the bishop's performance: 'I'm an actress, I should have seen through his pretence.'

At the end of Act III, prior to their marriage at the start of Act IV, the bishop says that Emilie and the children must come to his house without possessions and renounce the theatre, suggesting the traditional associations of the theatre with luxury, falsity and depravity. Emilie tells him:

> Sometimes I have wondered whether there was something radically wrong with my feelings. I could not understand why nothing really hurt, why I never felt really happy . . . My God is different, Edvard. He is like myself, fluid and boundless and intangible, both in his cruelty and his tenderness. I am an actress; I am used to wearing masks. My God wears a thousand masks. He has never shown me his real face, just as I am incapable of showing God my real face. Through you I shall learn to know God's being.

At the end of Act V, at the end of their marriage, and just before the bishop dies, he says to Emilie, 'you once said that you were always changing masks, so that finally you didn't know who you were . . . I have only one mask. But it is branded into my flesh'. Thus, Edvard says that he has a single mask, implying a fixed sense of identity. It transpires that Emilie's experiences of fluidity have an authenticity lacking in the bishop's fixed notion of human identity and truth. There is a materiality in the bishop's household and in his regulated lifestyle that is just as constructed and theatrical as the Ekdahl apartment.

We can thus see a transition from the philosophical standpoint represented in Emilie's speech of seeing theatrical performance as false (echoing the truth/falsity dichotomy in *Summer Interlude*) to perceiving everything as a performance or set of constructs. This transition mirrors philosophical developments related to performativity, stemming back to J.L. Austin's *How to Do Things with Words* written in 1962.[26] Austin decided to focus on speech acts 'issued in ordinary circumstances' (everyday performatives),[27] arguing that utterances in conventional acts (rituals, ceremonies) and those in the theatre or poetry are in a peculiar way 'hollow' or 'void'. This coincided with a more general anti-theatrical prejudice in philosophy up until that point akin to Emilie's speech. In the theatre, Austin argued, language is used 'not seriously', but is 'parasitic' on its normal use; the words cited are mere 'etiolations of language'.[28] This philosophy has subsequently been extended and modified, since in everyday life there is also a sense of citation. There is theatricality in every word that is spoken; words are merely repeated or cited rather than created or chosen. It was Jacques Derrida who first pointed out that all performative utterances have a general citationality or iterability.[29] Andrew Parker and Eve Kosofsky Sedgwick distinguish between the two philosophical standpoints:

> Where Austin, then, seemed intent on separating the actor's citational practices from ordinary speech-act performances, Derrida regarded both as structured by a generalised iterability, a pervasive theatricality common to stage and world alike.[30]

These developments are extremely valuable because they have enabled a powerful appreciation of the ways that identities are also constructed repeatedly through a network of citational processes.

Each of Emilie's different performances is shown to be as real as the next, and the concept of multiplicity seems to be synonymous with the adult females in the film. To Helena, for instance, everyday life is a performance. In Act I, she talks of her previous affair with Isak as if it were a play; he unbuttoned her, 'then the curtain was drawn aside and there stood my dear husband'. She addresses the camera as if it is her husband, spreading her arms out as if to an audience, claiming, 'it was just like a farce by Feydeau'. Her melodramatic descriptions enforce her claim: 'He rushed to get his pistol, with me clinging to his leg.' After this – looking in the mirror, standing in front of Isak – she says that she must wash, repaint her face and put on her stays and silk dress: 'A weepy lovesick woman turns into a self-possessed grandmother – We play our parts.' Similarly, in Act IV, 'Summer's Events', Helena discusses in what she terms as one of her 'monologues', addressed to the vision of her dead son Oscar, the roles she has played through life. She enjoyed being a mother, she states, and being an actress but when she was pregnant she did not care for the theatre, '. . . for that matter everything is acting'. Moreover, the set is like that of a play, depicted in long shot with three walls and the floor in view, placing us in the proscenium arch. Some widespread interpretations of the film need to be challenged to enforce these claims about multiplicity in relation to identity and gender performance.

Reviewing the tone of *Fanny and Alexander*

Fanny and Alexander has been seen as a warm, optimistic and magical film. This perception has been encouraged to some extent by its reception as a testament film, rounding off Bergman's career. In 1982, upon completion of *Fanny and Alexander*, Bergman announced his official retirement from film-making, and has since claimed (in 1988), 'my decision to give up the movie camera was undramatic and grew out of my work on *Fanny and Alexander*'.[31] Bergman's direction of a number of films after *Fanny and Alexander* – *After the Rehearsal* (1984), *The Blessed Ones* (1986), *Karin's Face* (1986), *In the Presence of a Clown* (1997)[32] – did little to shake the perception of *Fanny and Alexander* as Bergman's last major film. We might take Peter Cowie's representation as a classic example, '*Fanny and Alexander* amounts to a kind of climax in the career of Ingmar Bergman – a fairy tale that has cost $6 million and contains some sixty speaking parts, plus around 1,200 extras'.[33] Some of the responses might have been slightly different had it been known that a further film *Saraband* (2003), the television movie written and directed by Bergman, would be marketed as 'Bergman's last feature'.

When shooting first began in 1981, *Fanny and Alexander* was regarded as a homecoming for Bergman who, as Frank Gado points out, had not directed a play or a film in his native land for five years except for the Fårö documentary.[34] *Fanny and Alexander* appears to be a film of celebration, reflection, reminiscences, warmth and great richness. This also fits with Bergman's account of the genesis of the film, recounted by a number of critics, of it being a positive response to a friend, Kjell Grede (a filmmaker once married to Bibi Andersson), who asked Bergman why he rarely put any of his usual cheerful vitality into his films.[35] Bergman's original intentions written before he made the film also reflected this:

> I want to depict finally, the joy that I carry within me, in spite of everything, and which I so seldom and so feebly have given attention to in my work . . . a life, luminous and happy. . . .[36]

Alongside these conceptions lies the history behind the film. The location is based on Bergman's grandmother's home,[37] and several members of Bergman's family appear in the film, as Gado notes.[38] These factors tie in with the sense that it is a celebration of family togetherness. Robert E. Lauder describes it as a 'culmination' representing the victory of the warm Isak over the stern bishop of no human warmth. It is a film of 'human interpersonal relations'.[39]

Thus, the 'happy' scenes seem to contain a genuine confidence in a return to unashamed humanism. Many critics take the film to be a celebration of human togetherness and family love. For example, to Peter Harcourt, *Fanny and Alexander* registers a return to an earlier period of film-making marked by humanist concerns. In Harcourt's case, along with many other critical responses to the film, humanism suggests something very specific. The term is used to signify optimism and films that contain moments of cultural communion and exchange, where characters share emotions and 'feel something in common with one another, whether from a divine or a merely secular point-of-view'.[40] Harcourt's thesis is that there is a gradual transition, though not in a simple, linear way, from Bergman's early films which deal with apparent theological preoccupations to a phase of more humanist concerns and on to a 'nihilist refusal of the possibilities of meaningful human interaction'. He compares what he terms the 'humanist' *Wild Strawberries* with the 'modernist' *A Passion*.[41] In this perspective, Harcourt argues, *Fanny and Alexander* represents a step back or a re-think:

> . . . he can recover from what is arguably the most nihilistic film he has ever made, *From the Life of the Marionettes* (*Aus dem Leben der Marionetten*, 1980), a film made in Germany, to achieve for his faithful followers the most lavish film production that Bergman has ever designed for the film theatres, his ultimately 'humanist' farewell to feature filmmaking – *Fanny and Alexander* (*Fanny och Alexander*, 1982).[42]

Significantly, critics who disliked the film soon after its release saw it in a similar light to Harcourt; they disliked it for similar reasons. Charles B. Ketcham, for instance, saw it as superficial compared with Bergman's previous explorations, and described it as a 'radical break from the mainstream of Bergman's art'.[43] Ketcham's problem with the film was that while it acknowledged themes dealt with before, these themes, he argued, were all caricatured to the point of fantasy.

Pauline Kael saw the film as a final ploy to warm audiences with 'lovingly placed gingerbreading': 'They can come out of the movie beaming with pleasure at the thought of Ingmar Bergman's finally achieving harmony with himself.'[44] She criticized the film's shallow characters: 'Nobody is religious, nobody is in any way spiritual; in fact Alexander's idealised family is so hearty and indulgent it's gross.'[45]

Gado also takes the view that *Fanny and Alexander* was a move away from preceding pessimism and opaqueness: '*Fanny and Alexander* was to be a very different film . . . A celebration of life, it would recreate the world of Bergman's childhood.'[46] Gado points out that the Swedes have a special nostalgia for the decades before World War I in which the two Oscars reigned,[47] enhanced, I would imagine, by Sweden's rapid twentieth-century transformation from agrarian to urban society. However, as Gado has argued, by suggesting that we see *Fanny and Alexander* as 'two films',[48] the film can be seen in a very different light.

Gado discusses the psychosexual tensions of the film by making comparisons with *Hamlet*. He also argues convincingly that the reason why Alexander will not go to his father's bedside when he is dying is his guilt for 'having wished his father were out of the way so he could have his mother all to himself (just as he will later wish his stepfather's death into occurring)'.[49] There must also be some truth in what Gado goes on to argue that the basis of Alexander's hatred of Vergérus is sexual:

> In one respect, the Bishop represents a surrogate self to be hated and punished for acting out Alexander's desires. More obviously, he is also the other half of a split father image – not the emasculated Oscar who makes the son feel guilty but the overpowering sexual rival who makes him feel impotent.[50]

But added to this is a further layer: Emilie directly denounces the link with *Hamlet* and tells Alexander not to play Hamlet; she is not Gertrude and Edvard is not the evil uncle Claudius. Whether she protests too much is open to debate, but Shakespeare's play is nevertheless a very conscious, conspicuous reference, rather than a discreet parallel.

Gado stresses that Oedipal tensions within the family relationships pivoting around Emilie, particularly between Alexander and the two 'fathers', are far too strong to be glossed over:[51]

> Clearly Bergman's fascination is with the psychosexual anguish expressed through the nuclear dream; the rest is a conjurer's trick performed both for his own diversion and to enlist an audience's sentimental approval.[52]

While Gado is surely right about the psychosexual relationships, it is possible to contest his further suggestion that the 'rest' (the Epilogue) is merely for Bergman's 'diversion' and to 'enlist an audience's sentimental approach':

> The dramatic incoherence becomes especially obtrusive in the final scenes, where Bergman's message of hope responds to no argument

... How – and to whom – does it matter that Maj ... will sell fash-
ions (instead of cakes as Gustav has intended)?[53]

It matters tremendously, in the sense that it is a sign that Maj is acting
of her own free will. Indeed, the women's positions within the psychosexual drama, which are borne out very strongly in the final scenes, tie in
with, rather than contradict (as Gado suggests) the rest of the film. Gado
argues that 'the most egregious disjunction is that none of these concluding developments bears on the overpowering drama of self-discovery
at the centre of *Fanny and Alexander*'.[54] However, an alternative reading
would be that there is no self-discovery at the centre and that the ending
is an integral part of the film rather than simply being there for the effect
of 'palliating' the film's horror for the audience.[55] The ending has a real
bearing on the meaning of the preceding psychological drama.

Gustav Adolf's rambling post-dinner speech in the Epilogue, celebrating the double christenings of his and Maj's daughter (Helena Viktoria)
and Emilie's and the bishop's daughter (Aurora), is saturated with
utopian illusion: 'Our little world has closed around us in security, wis-
dom and order after a time of horror and confusion.' Encircling the
table, reaching the children, thus drawing attention in the Epilogue to
the world of the children, Gustav Adolf states:

> We might as well ignore the big things. We must live in the little world
> (*Alexander looks up*) and make the best of it. Suddenly death strikes, and
> the abyss opens ... But let us dismiss all that unpleasantness ... We
> must be able to grasp the world and reality that we can complain of its
> monotony with a clear conscience ... Let's be happy ... take pleasure
> in the little world. Good food, smiles, blossoming trees, waltzes ....

Thus, Gustav Adolf concludes that the Ekdahls exist to make the most
of the pleasures in the world rather than 'to see through it'. The terrors
in the world are *known*, but the Ekdahl household represents a safe
haven, similar to the safety of the theatre, where happiness can be
established, even if illusory, for a short time. Gustav Adolf's argument is
not so much that one should forget the terrors absolutely, but that – in
light of them – happiness should be treasured all the more. This echoes
the humanist philosophy that human love and togetherness can pre-
vail, even if short-lived. The narrative structure of the film suggests a
journey, similar to many Bergman films, which could be seen to uphold
this philosophy. Emilie leaves behind the ogre-like bishop and returns
to what could be seen as a 'happy ending' and a conscious acceptance

of illusions such as those suggested in Gustav Adolf's speech and in Emilie's return to the theatre.

On the surface, a number of parallels can be made between the narrative structure of *Fanny and Alexander* and many of Bergman's earlier films. The most obvious example would be *Summer Interlude* where the female performer returns to the world of the stage, having achieved self-discovery, to conform to a healthy compromise between two binaries, to a conscious wearing of a mask balanced with her real life. A similar relationship between two fixed notions of art and life can also be seen in many of Bergman's 1940s films such as *A Ship Bound for India* (1947). We saw challenges to this in *Summer with Monika* (1952) and a more obvious resistance in *Persona*, which draws attention to the performance of gender, offering little sense of a resolution. While in some respects *Fanny and Alexander* clings onto a traditional, illusionist style, there is arguably no self-discovery, and unlike Marie in *Summer Interlude*, Emilie actually becomes the stage manager. While the post-dinner speech advocates a return to the world of illusion, this is quite clearly Gustav Adolf's personal perspective rather than that of the other characters (in whom the films invests empathy): Emilie, Helena, Fanny and Alexander or Isak, for example.

Törnqvist points out that the name Ekdahl has been synonymous with people consoling themselves with illusions about life since the Ekdals in Henrik Ibsen's *The Wild Duck* (1884). The additional 'h' in Bergman's film indicates the Ekdahls's upper middle-class status. Törnqvist observes the similarity between Gustav Adolf's statement, 'rob a man of his subterfuges and he goes mad and begins hitting out' and the view expressed by Relling in Ibsen's play, 'if you deprive an average man of his illusions you simultaneously steal his happiness'.[56] Törnqvist's observations are very suggestive because the use of the name Ekdahl thus helps to distance us from them. Gustav Adolf's particular reliance on illusions – rooted in patriarchically conceived ideologies – is not a reliance we are directed to share.

What is most striking about the (just under eight minute) post-dinner speech sequence is the fact that it consists of one speech, told from beginning to end, and that Gustav Adolf is the only speaker. While the purpose of the speech is to mark the birth of the two girls, no one apart from Gustav Adolf has control of the word in this sequence. *Fanny and Alexander* frequently flaunts the conventions of patriarchy, where men have control over the word during ritual. Previously there has been the marriage[57] of Emilie and the bishop and Oscar's very public funeral (contrary to his requests). We might see Fanny and Alexander's responses to this – Alexander's muttering of swear words as they are forced to join the funeral procession and Fanny's knowing smile – as active disavowals or repudiations of these conventions.[58] In the post-christening speech, the filming itself might be seen as a disavowal or renunciation of the religious convention of naming the girls and fixing their identities.

There is an overwhelming abundance of artifice in this sequence. Gustav Adolf refers to the fruit trees in blossom but what we see are flowers and blossoms hung up inside, and within a space that is clearly constructed. The didactic element of Gustav Adolf's speech, expressed in a flippant tone provokes discomfort: 'We must live in the little world . . . let us dismiss all that unpleasantness.'

Camera and character movements in this sequence revolve around the round table, which mirrors the theme of circularity and orderliness in the sequence. While the use of a round table could indicate equality, the camera undercuts this by foregrounding Gustav Adolf's desire for hierarchical and masculine control. The sequence begins with an extreme high angle shot of the baby girls, heads towards the bottom of the frame, their pink cradles appearing like two ovals. The first camera movement is a pan upwards to include most of the large round table smothered in pink flowers. The overwhelming use of pink artifice works as a forceful signifier of gender, suggesting that the truth of gender is being undercut.[59]

The small group of male musicians are visible in the background, signalling as diegetic the waltz music that has continued since the opening of the shot. While the cooks join the table, as part of Gustav Adolf's patronizing observance of equality at such occasions, hierarchy is perhaps all the more enforced by the fact that it is only the chief cooks that are seated, while the maids are standing behind.

The next shot is on the 180 degree line from the opposite side of the table, behind the small male orchestra sitting in a circle, the bald head of the flautist in the position of the babies' cradles previously. The shot mirrors the previous shot by the camera position and movement, as it tracks forward and zooms into the table. These two shots, which are of a similar length (about 20 seconds), set up the sense of order and symmetry emblematic of the whole sequence. In addition to the visual symmetry, the music of the second shot echoes the first, so that another round of the waltz (itself a circular rhythm) starts up again, giving the effect of having returned to the same point as the second shot begins. In this shot the word 'EPILOG' appears on screen, which rounds off the film by mirroring the 'PROLOG' at the start.

Gustav Adolf interrupts this symmetrical pattern by standing and then slamming his hands on the table, shouting. He stops the music and the hum of talking at once. The camera also stops moving and maintains a static extreme long shot of Gustav Adolf as he addresses the family.

A series of intricate cross-cutting follows, indicating Gustav Adolf's desire for control over the members of his family and household. As he addresses those present individually, there is a cut to a medium close-up of the characters introduced, as though the members are only made significant by his word. While there is the illusion of patriarchal control, the order prioritizes the female members, beginning with Helena, the matriarchal figure. His power is also undercut by the responses of the characters; Isak's look of weariness, Helena's knowing glance ('I see you raise an eyebrow mother'), Emilie's fond but derisive looks and Gustav Adolf's statement that his daughter is laughing at him. Added to this is the comical cut from Gustav Adolf's extravagant address to the actors, 'if only I could kiss you all' to the shot of the old actor awakening in horror from his slumbers.

The symmetry and sense of control continues as Gustav Adolf's main speech begins, and he starts to walk to the left and around the table, with the camera tracking after him. This movement is mirrored in the latter half of the speech, when he encircles the table again the same way round, as if completing the spider's web. When the camera begins to track around the table for the second time, the look on Isak's face is almost that of disgust, suggesting that he is beyond the oppressive patriarchy. There is also a sense of resistance to Gustav Adolf's illusions of power when he pauses behind certain characters, particularly the children, as he stands hands out, having reached the far side of the table. Ridicule mounts up each time he looks over his daughter's cradle and the beak of the ornate stork on its side seems to peck at his face.

In contrast to the diegetic waltz music, which introduces Gustav Adolf's speech, played by *male* players, the music which starts up as Gustav Adolf holds his 'little empress' in his arms at the end of his speech is that of the non-diegetic music box, symbol of illusionist happiness since early Bergman, for example, *It Rains on our Love* (1946). It is also used in the film to indicate the beginning of a more fantastical sequence, for example, the statue's arm movement or visions of Oscar's ghost. While the music from the male musicians might be taken as 'real', the non-diegetic music box tune suggests authorial comment, indicative of the constructions of gender that we have seen in the pink décor. The final sound of this shot is a baby squeaking, as if a small female voice finally responds. The following ten-second static shot that marks the end of this sequence represents the large family photograph, with matriarchal Helena in the middle, Maj and Emilie on either side with their babies. This is accompanied by loud baby cries, as the photograph fades into sepia tone. As the cries die away, the music box tune alone remains, followed by silence as the shot of the photograph is held. There is thus a sense of a need to capture and maintain the moment. The sequence fore-grounds the constructed elements of male dominance. It begins with the babies and ends with the static shot of the family photograph, the grand-mother at the centre as a means to undercut traditional power relations.

Cries and Whispers was strongly criticized in the 1970s for depicting, in Joan Mellen's terms, women whose 'lives lack meaning because they are rooted in biology and an inability to choose a style of life independent of the female sexual role'.[60] Constance Penley even went so far as to crit-icize what she saw as the film's near morbid interest in the suffering of women, with fixed female character types from victim to temptress to earth mother[61] existing within a 'coven of witches'.[62] Varda Burstyn has a point, however, in suggesting that these views mistake 'a portrayal of women's oppression for its justification' when the film offers a 'powerful condemnation' of patriarchy rather than a reinforcement of sexism.[63] What annoyed critics so much initially about *Cries and Whispers* was its refusal to offer any hope for change. In this sense, *Fanny and Alexander* can be seen to contrast with the earlier film's bleak attitude.

The women obtain a freedom in the final sequences of *Fanny and Alexander*, which is not provided in *Cries and Whispers*. Significant scenes include the brief episode where Emilie warns Rosa, the new maid, about Gustav Adolf, and the following incident where Gustav Adolf's wife Alma, treats him like a boy, offering him beer and sandwiches in bed. While Gustav Adolf rambles on about his lovely wife and mistress and family togetherness, Emilie and Alma discuss Alma's escape to the country to see Emilie later in the week. Gustav Adolf is deaf to their calm whisperings. This is followed by the sequence where his mistress (Maj) and his daughter (Petra) reveal to Emilie their fear of remaining under his control; they want to go to Stockholm to help in a new milliner's shop. Significantly, Helena's confirmation that this can be arranged demonstrates that she has control.

The women make their own decisions, perhaps explaining why Emilie does not go with Gustav Adolf and Carl earlier but waits to escape from the bishop in her own time. It is also significant that Emilie selects the next play, Strindberg's *A Dream Play*, in which, she suggests, there are roles for them both.[64] *A Dream Play* is a modernist text that explores the con-cept of fluidity, despite being by 'that abominable misogynist' (Helena). The preface of the play which Helena reads aloud to Alexander at the close of the film is immediately relevant to *Fanny and Alexander*:

Everything can happen, everything is possible and probable. Time and place do not exist, on an insignificant basis of reality, the imagination spins, weaving new patterns: a mixture of memories, experience, free fancies, incongruities and improvisations.

Fanny and Alexander can now be seen as a contrast to *Hamlet* rather than a parallel; 'Gertrude' survives. Moreover, it was a daring endeavour to put on a Strindberg play at the time *Fanny and Alexander* is set, since it was declared unstageable on publication in 1902.[65] Emilie will take over the control of the theatre and Helena is the head of the Ekdahl household. Emilie laughs, 'Now it's up to us, isn't it?' but Helena's 'Do you think so?' indicates that the balance is still precarious. Helena encourages Emilie in her desire to take over the control of the theatre again, and to ignore Gustav Adolf: 'It's your theatre . . . Time we made clear to our second-rate Napoleon that he's facing his Waterloo.'[66] Thus, after Gustav Adolf's speech, the final sequences revolve around the women's words, actions and decisions.

There is a telepathy running through the film that also contrasts with the male public speeches. Fanny and Alexander try to make the bishop die by chanting in their locked bedroom. Helena at the start of the film seems to know that something awful is wrong with Oscar that others cannot see. Similarly, Emilie rushes back to the children in fear that Alexander may have made something up that will aggravate the bishop, just at the exact moment when Alexander is being punished for his stories.

Such telepathy culminates in the figure of Ismael who is able to merge with other people, flowing into their thoughts, appearing to conjure the bishop's death by projecting Alexander's hatred and desires, saying 'perhaps we're the same person . . . perhaps we flow into each other'. Ismael can also be seen as representing fluidity in terms of transgressing gender and sexual boundaries. Ismael is referred to as 'my brother' by Aron, wears male clothing, but is played by an actress, Stina Ekblad, with shaved eyebrows, speaking in a distinctly female voice. Törnqvist observes that this hybrid nature extends to Ismael's speech, which is Finno-Swedish.[67] Ismael's androgyny represents a fluidity of identity and echoes the words of Strindberg's preface, just after the passage Helena reads aloud, 'the characters split, double, multiply, evaporate, condense, disperse, assemble'.[68] As Blackwell asserts, 'Ishmael's androgyny points to Bergman's perception of the restrictedness of sex roles and, specifically, to the great human potential that lies beyond genderedness.'[69]

As Ismael states that perhaps s/he *is* Alexander, the aunt in Edvard's house knocks over the lamp that sets off the fire which eventually kills the bishop. This is made possible because Emilie has seized the opportunity of popping sleeping pills in the bishop's drink, in the hope of merely sending him to sleep while she escapes. The cross-cutting between the sequence with Alexander and Ismael and events at the bishop's house emphasize the sense of a number of events coinciding to create a resolution. In this sense, in contrast to what has been said in relation to the concept of truth, there is a kind of Jungian synchronicity at work,[70] a selection of meaningful coincidences accumulating to result in a resolving 'good'. This would suggest that essentialism has not been completely abandoned in *Fanny and Alexander*, and that certain elements have a sense of significance, even though other aspects of the film clearly challenge this outlook.

After *Fanny and Alexander*

It is now possible to re-view *Fanny and Alexander* in light of *Saraband* (2003), marketed definitively as Bergman's 'last feature', helping to give this study of *Fanny and Alexander* a more long-term perspective. While *Saraband* also concerns the trials and tribulations of family life, it forgoes the confidence of style and gloss celebrated by *Fanny and Alexander*. *Saraband* is certainly no lavish saga but rather a much more condensed personal drama, in the vein of Bergman's earlier 'chamber films'. *Saraband* is retrospective: Liv Ullmann's character (Marianne) returns to stay for a short while with her ex-husband Jonas (Erland Josephson) visualizing a return to *Scenes from a Marriage* (1973). *Saraband* also signifies Bergman's return to film-making at the age of 85, as the words on the (Tartan) DVD cover stress, marketing 'Bergman' as indefatigable auteur.

Saraband and the 'making of' *Saraband* connect formally. While DVDs often contain behind the scenes footage, the 'Behind *Saraband*: 45 minute on-set documentary' is particularly fitting, in light of Bergman's lifelong preoccupations. It calls attention to the fact that most of the scenes are constructed in the studio. The tricks are carefully unveiled, as we are shown the meticulous detail necessary to create the church interior, the autumnal leaves in the 'outside' wood setting and Julia Dufvenius's performance (as Karin, daughter of Johan's widowed son Henrik) when she learns to fall and roll down the steep bank. Beautiful 'exterior' shots are faked as part of the construction of a Swedish landscape associated with Bergman as director. This construction self-consciously exposes both the magician conjuring illusions that 'Bergman' has come to embody and the artisanal skill and collaboration involved in the art of cinematography.

Connections between the film and the documentary are made explicitly. *Saraband*, for instance, is dedicated to Ingrid, Bergman's late wife (recollecting *Through a Glass Darkly*'s dedication to his then wife, Kabi). There is a moment in the documentary when Bergman discusses the 'core' of *Saraband*. Sitting round a table with his friends and colleagues, Bergman recounts the story of speaking with Erland (Josephson) about the loss of his wife. The idea that death is the end, so comforting to Bergman in his earlier years, had become torturous to him since Ingrid's death. He could not face the idea of never seeing her again. Erland advised him that it is best to hold onto the vision of seeing her again, if this is what he wants. This relates to the concept of illusion in *Saraband* (and *Fanny and Alexander*); 'illusion' is to be understood not in terms of a fantasy or falsity, but as a layer, a way of seeing or a vision that a person is able to hold onto as 'true' as anything. It is this kind of illusion that the fifth saraband represents to Henrik, as the part of Bach's cello suites that his daughter Karin is able to play. When he asks Karin to play it, as a 'perfect ending', it is an illusion (for him) to hold onto.

What is probably most arresting about the documentary sequence, however, is the reactions of the woman sitting next to Bergman, her face captured in extreme close-up, as she nods in an affirming way through Bergman's story, holding back tears, sympathizing presumably with his loss. Like *Persona*, when the camera focuses on Elisabet listening to Alma's story, the response of the listener is focused on. As in *Persona*, the audience creates its own cinematography. This construction of the 'personal' element of *Saraband* is crucial. Bergman is shown to maintain a close relationship with his actors, as 'true auteur' explaining the film the way he sees it.

The documentary thus works alongside the film as a reflexive device, helping to draw attention to key narrative and thematic concerns. It is reminiscent of the reflexive devices explored nearly 40 years before when *Persona* first drew attention to itself as modernist mask. However, the construction is here set apart as a separate documentary, functioning also, as it does on the DVD for *Fanny and Alexander*, for example, as a marketing tool for the 'Bergman' brand. That the mask of auteur should be sold so unashamedly is hardly surprising, particularly bearing in mind Erik Hedling's claim that the continued existence of the Swedish film industry is solely thanks to auteurism:

> Without the auteur, by tradition a necessary predicament for applying concepts of high art to film, there would certainly be no governmental support for domestically produced films, and hardly any film can survive without part of its funding coming from the state.[71]

Representations of old Bergman as unrelenting auteur permeate the media. In *Saraband* Jonas says that he has lived long enough to learn all his answers. In Marie Nyeröd's documentary series, *Ingmar Bergman Complete* (2004), despite the wealth of new footage of his life on the island of Fårö, his friendships and long career, Bergman remains inflexibly faithful to the stories that he has told throughout his life in the media, suggesting that Bergman has also learnt his answers, as citational stock phrases.

Saraband is not a light film. Incestuous undertones between Karin and her father culminate in them sharing a bed one night. By the end of the film, Karin has made her decision to leave home to attend a school for young orchestral musicians in Hamburg rather than become a soloist as her father Henrik wishes. Father and son (Jonas and Henrik) continue to show bitterness towards each other. *Saraband* is framed at the start and finish with scenes of Marianne speaking to camera at a desk with a mass of family photographs, against the sound of Bach music. These framing sequences mirror those with Ullmann in *The Hour of the Wolf*. Bach has become synonymous with Bergman's films (echoing, for example, the incest scene on the boat in *Through a Glass Darkly*). The photographs recall a number of films from *A Passion* to *Karin's Face*, the short film about Bergman's mother. *Saraband* is, less ambivalently than *Fanny and Alexander*, the woman's (Marianne's) story, where the female characters make decisions. At the end of *Saraband*, Marianne talks about a connection she has made with her daughter, who is mentally ill. They touched, and this physical closeness represents a light for her. This offers a small ray of optimism, but no sense of a resolution to round off either the narrative or Bergman's career, in the way that *Fanny and Alexander* seemed to for so many when it was first released.

It is possible that the concept of *Saraband* as Bergman's 'final feature' makes it easier to challenge the perception of *Fanny and Alexander* as simply a humanist farewell and final testament to Bergman's life and career in film and the theatre. The disharmonies are expressed much less ambiguously in *Saraband*. Having abandoned the ironic gloss, *Saraband* does not need to be Bergman's 'last feature' in the way that viewers wanted *Fanny and Alexander* to be.

The necessary illusion

Fanny and Alexander, with its many references to masks and the paranormal, seems to offer a coherent, transparent reflection on Bergman's preceding films. Furthermore, its ornate 'confidence', reminiscent of *Wild Strawberries*, *The Seventh Seal* and *The Face*, seems to offer a celebration of

Bergman's more illusionist film-making. However, as we have seen, it is not the straightforward allegorical film that it appears; its relationship with illusion is not only complex and chaotic, but also contradictory.

Isak's philosophy of multiple layers of reality forms the basis for *Fanny and Alexander*. Its ghost visions suggest layers of reality – phases between life and death or dream and reality – reminiscent of *Cries and Whispers*, and the blurring of reality and fantasy also recalls *Persona*, *A Passion* and *The Hour of the Wolf*. Furthermore, *Fanny and Alexander*'s naturalist filming of these visions alongside other realities is distinguishable from the devices used in pre-trilogy films such as the flashback systems of *Wild Strawberries* or the heavily symbolic visions of *The Seventh Seal*. In terms of style, though, compared with *Persona* and *The Hour of the Wolf*'s rejection of temporal-spatial, cause and effect coherency, *Fanny and Alexander* is relatively illusionist, transparent and humanist.

However, *Fanny and Alexander*'s complexities suggest that the claims that it is (simply) a return to humanism need to be carefully scrutinized and contested. The grand christening finale needs to be looked at with some scepticism. It is not an unproblematic celebration of human togetherness and exchange, of the kind seen in the moment of cultural communion between the characters having lunch with Isak Borg in *Wild Strawberries*. It also differs from *Wild Strawberries'* final dream vision of Isak's parents denoting Isak's harmony with himself and the final celestial vision in *The Seventh Seal*. In *Fanny and Alexander*, there is a strong level of discomfort with the adult male Ekdahls's dependence on their necessary illusions.

Fanny and Alexander clearly celebrates masquerade and the fantasies afforded by the theatre, cinema and television, offering a very different take on illusion from the truth/falsity binaries of *Summer Interlude*. In *Fanny and Alexander*, references to the theatre suggest a series of selves, each as 'real' as the other, thus moving on from 'the necessary illusion' – fantasies and dreams are necessary to endure harsh realities – to the concept that *all* is necessarily masquerade. *Fanny and Alexander* is not unequivocally a feminist text and it is certainly not a postmodernist text, but it is possible to argue that it is beginning to create a space within which key aspects of both feminism and postmodernist concepts concerning identity can be discussed.

Many different aspects of illusion are drawn on in *Fanny and Alexander*, and it is in respect of identity that some of the most important areas of the film come to light. We have seen that *Summer with Monika* begins to explore the performance of gender, a concept that is pursued further in films like *The Silence* and *Persona*. *Fanny and Alexander* ends with the concept of multiple identities, roles and selves, an outlook that corresponds with feminist theorists such as Elizabeth Grosz:

> Perspectives cannot simply be identified with appearance, underlying which there is an abiding and stable reality. Rather, there are only perspectives, only appearances, only interpretations. There is nothing beyond the multiplicity of perspectives, positions, bodily forces; no anchor in the real.[72]

Fixed notions of identity are deconstructed in *Fanny and Alexander* in favour of a multiplicity of perspectives. Any allusions to an abiding reality or truth are certainly destabilized, if not (finally) abandoned. Rather than the self-discovery that rounds off *Summer Interlude*, there is an acceptance in *Fanny and Alexander* of indeterminism, instability and the disruption of fixity as being positive. Paradoxically, the film generally conveys these deliberations in an illusionist style, suggestive of Bergman's earlier film-making. This homage to conventional form explores clearly and lucidly the prospect of infinite realities and multiple truths.

Notes

1—Introduction

1. Quotations of dialogue are taken from the subtitles unless otherwise stated. Distinctions will be made between these and translations in the screenplays.
2. Ingmar Bergman, *The Magic Lantern: An Autobiography*, translated by Joan Tate (London: Hamish Hamilton, 1988). Originally published in Stockholm: Norstedts Förlag, 1987.
3. Bergman, *Images: My Life in Film*, translated by Marianne Ruuth (London: Faber and Faber, 1995). Originally published in Stockholm: Norstedts, 1990.
4. At 24 frames per second, a film of 100 minutes is in total darkness for 40 minutes.
5. Stig Björkman, Torsten Manns and Jonas Sima, *Bergman on Bergman: Interviews with Ingmar Bergman*, translated by Paul Britten Austin (New York: Da Capo Press, 1993). (Originally published in 1970. First translated into English by Paul Britten Austin, New York: Simon & Schuster, 1973) p. 6.
6. Ibid., p. 8.
7. *Ingmar Bergman – The Magic Lantern*, produced by Mark Lucas, directed and edited by Jane Thorburn, *An After Image Production*, Channel Four Television, 1988.
8. *Ingmar Bergman – The Director*, produced by Alan Horrox, directed by Michael Winterbottom, a Thames Television Production for Channel Four in association with Swedish Television 2, Svensk Filmindustri, Die Zeit TV GMBH, TPI Trebitsh Produktion International GMBH, 1988.
9. It should be noted that there are similarities between these interests in illusion and those of the leading Swedish scholar Maaret Koskinen. Her doctoral thesis *Spel och speglingar. En studie i Ingmar Bergmans filmiska estetik* (Stockholm: Norstedts, 1993) broadly translated as *The Mirror and the Play within the Play* centres on the cinematic aesthetics of Bergman's work. Her second book on Bergman, also published in Swedish, *Ingmar Bergman: "Allting föreställer, ingenting är". Filmen och teatern – en tvärestetisk studie* (Stockholm: Nya Doxa, 2001) translated as *Everything Represents, Nothing Is: Ingmar Bergman and Interartiality*, is a study of Bergman's films and theatre productions from a comparative, 'interartial' perspective. I am extremely grateful for Koskinen's helpful feedback on a draft proposal for this study.
10. Lloyd Michaels, ed., *Ingmar Bergman's 'Persona'* (Cambridge & New York: Cambridge University Press, 2000) pp. 1–23.
11. Ibid., p. 18.
12. Ibid., p. 19.
13. Significantly, the Swedish title *Kvinnodröm* translates literally as 'Woman's Dream' and it was released in the United States under the title *Dreams*.
14. Arthur Knight, quoted in David Bordwell, *Narration in the Fiction Film* (University of Wisconsin Press, 1985) p. 231.

15. The distinction was not always so clear in criticism in (non-English-speaking) Europe, where art films were not so distinguished from the norm.

16. This is particularly the case in Chapter 4, as part of an analysis of stylistic shifts from *The Seventh Seal* to *Through a Glass Darkly*, and in Chapter 6 to help define contemporary spectatorial difficulties with the formal integration of dream and reality in *Wild Strawberries*.

17. While a further investigation into the way that Bergman's work was received in Sweden would lead the study slightly off focus here, it would clearly be a worthwhile exercise in another study. Erik Hedling's article illustrates the political complexities at stake with the reception of Bergman's films in Sweden: 'Initially, Bergman's films were often – though certainly not always – met with outright malice in Sweden, particularly within literary circles or within the late 1960s new Marxist intelligentsia.' Erik Hedling, 'Bergman and the Welfare State', *Film International*, Issue 19, Vol. 4, No. 1 (2006) p. 56.

18. David Thomson, *A Biographical Dictionary of Film* (London: André Deutsch, 1995). Originally published as *A Biographical Dictionary of the Cinema* (Martin Secker and Warburg, 1975).

19. For an interesting study on Bergman from a postmodern perspective, cf. Marc Gervais, *Ingmar Bergman: Magician and Prophet* (Montreal and Kingston: McGill-Queen's University Press, 2000).

2—The Mask and Identity: *Summer Interlude*'s legacy

1. A. David Napier, *Masks, Transformation and Paradox* (London: University of California Press, 1986) p. xxiii.

2. John Mack, 'About Face', in *Masks: The Art of Expression*, ed. by John Mack (London: British Museum Press, 1994) p. 24.

3. Napier (p. 33) asserts that while the proverb 'nothing to do with Dionysus' denotes the difference between Dionysian abandon and the intellectual tone of Greek theatre, it also suggests that the connection was made even then.

4. Ian Jenkins, 'Face Value: The Mask in Greece and Rome', in Mack, p. 156.

5. The processions of singing and dancing in Medieval European 'Carnival' are rooted in religious celebrations, generally marking a transitional phase of death and rebirth, a cyclical renewal of destruction (Winter) and regeneration (Spring). Cf. Mikhail Bakhtin, *Rabelais and His World*, translated by H. Iswolsky (Bloomington: Indiana University Press, 1984) and Claudia Manera, 'Carnivalesque Disruptions and Political Theatre: Plays by Dario Fo, Franca Rame, and Caryl Churchill' (unpublished doctoral thesis, University of Reading, September 1999) pp. 34–8. The Christmas mummer plays, still performed using masks in various parts of Britain, also involved ritualistic representations of death and rebirth.

6. Elin Diamond, *Unmaking Mimesis: Essays on Feminism and Theatre* (London and New York: Routledge, 1997) p. 44.

7. The use of masks for rites and performances is still widespread in non-Western cultures. In African and Oriental cultures, for example, masks are used not just as objects, but can be painted on the face.

8. Note that the literal translation of the Swedish title *Sommarlek* is 'Summer Games'. The sense of playing (before the rigours of 'adulthood' set in) is less explicit in the term 'interlude'.

9. These distinctions are teased out in Napier, p. 8.
10. This is generally the meaning which has been used in discussion of film stars to distinguish between actor and the 'appearance' of the actor manifest in the different roles played. Cf. Richard Dyer, *Stars* (British Film Institute, 1979).
11. Cf. Christopher F. Monte, *Beneath the Mask: An Introduction to Theories of Personality* (Saunders College, USA: The Dryden Press, fourth edn, 1991) p. 7.
12. Carl Jung, 'The Relations between the Ego and the Unconscious', *The Collected Works of C.G. Jung*, Vol. 77 (Princeton, NJ: Princeton University Press, 1953 and 1966) p. 158.
13. Jung, 'Two Essays in Analytical Psychology', in ibid., p. 192.
14. R.D. Laing, *The Divided Self* (Baltimore: Penguin, 1959) p. 95.
15. Monte, p. 451.
16. Abraham H. Maslow, *The Farther Reaches of Human Nature* (New York: Viking, 1971) p. 65.
17. Similarly, staging Molière's *Don Juan* (Hof Theatre, Salzburg, 1983) Bergman changed the first act by introducing Don Juan, the renowned rake, in a dressing gown, scratching his fleas and tugging at his hair. His falsity is signalled when he later dons an elaborate costume and make-up for the seduction. Cf. Paisley Livingston, *Ingmar Bergman and the Rituals of Art* (Ithaca and London: Cornell University Press, 1982) p. 36.
18. Bergman claims, 'Maj-Britt Nilsson was wonderful. She really kept the two roles, the older and the younger, quite distinct'. Stig Björkman, Torsten Manns and Jonas Sima, *Bergman on Bergman: Interviews with Ingmar Bergman*, translated by Paul Britten Austin (New York: Da Capo Press, 1993). Originally published in 1970. First translated into English by Paul Britten Austin, New York: Simon & Schuster, 1973, p. 54.
19. Cf. Monte, p. 429.
20. Ibid., pp. 657–8.
21. In Japanese 'Kabuki' theatre and South Indian 'KathaKali' theatre, the actor absorbs the mask as it is painted on.
22. The comment made by Marie's colleague in the dressing room – 'We're 28 – us aunts' [my translation] – contradicts Gado's suggestion that she is over 30.
23. Frank Gado, *The Passion of Ingmar Bergman* (Durham: Duke University Press, 1986) p. 146.
24. Henrik's aunt is played by Mimi Pollack, seen in the later flashback aptly playing chess with the priest in a pre-echo of *The Seventh Seal* (1956). She is a cross between Death in this later film and the Man with the Umbrella in *It Rains on Our Love* (1946).
25. Note the death mask in *The Seventh Seal* (1956) as it hangs from the tree as Jof sings to Mia, and from the wagon during the wild strawberries 'communion'.
26. *Bergman on Bergman*, p. 64.
27. These preoccupations with art and life recall the Pygmalion myth, *Metamorphoses*, Book X, lines 245–97. (cf. London: Penguin Books, 1955, p. 244) and reworkings of the myth such as Pirandello's *Diana and Tuda*, translated by Marta Abba (London: Samuel French, 1950).
28. In the cartoon sequence, where Marie and Henrik's drawings come alive, the fat man (theatre manager) squashes the boy in the cap (Henrik) and then pulls down the blind.

29. Cf. Monte, pp. 618–19.
30. *Coppélia*, the ballet, is partly based on E.T.A. Hoffmann's *The Sandman*. Cf. J.M. Cohen, ed., *Tales from E.T.A. Hoffmann*, illustrated by Gavarni (London: The Bodley Head, 1951).
31. This is reminiscent of Michael Powell and Emeric Pressburger's *The Red Shoes* (1948), the adaptation of the Hans Christian Andersen fairytale about a ballerina forced by the Svengali-like impresario to make a choice between dancing and love. Like *Summer Interlude*, it also contains extensive ballet sequences.
32. In E.T.A. Hoffmann's tale, Coppélius attempts to cast a spell to bring Coppélia, his clockwork doll, to life by stealing Franz's soul (Franz has fallen for the ideal doll, forsaking his real lover Swanhilda). Swanhilda, disguised as 'Coppélia', having sneaked into Coppélius's apartment, emerges from the box she has hidden in and dances with fearsome life and energy, smashing all the toys. When Franz awakens from his duped state he is dragged away by Swanhilda, leaving Coppélius with his lifeless broken doll. While such a reference might allude to notions of the constructedness of femininity as a patriarchal construct, these ideas are not significantly pursued throughout the film to make them of central interest here. To enforce this point, note the Lyon Opera Ballet's production of *Coppélia*, for example, which deals much more overtly with these ideas, ending with not one but hundreds of 'Coppélias' breaking out of the rigid body. 'Summer Dance' Series, BBC 2, 1994, RM Arts.
33. In *The Seventh Seal*, Jof and Mia play clowns to warn against 'the black man waiting on the shore', and Death bears the features of a white clown.
34. Robin Wood, *Ingmar Bergman* (London: Studio Vista, 1969) p. 39.
35. The Swedish title includes 'gycklare' ('clown'). The verb 'gyckla' means 'to joke', 'jeer at' or 'ridicule', suggesting that the clown is both the maker and the butt of the joke.
36. Bergman claims that it was the first film he bought for his collection, and '*Sawdust and Tinsel* was intended as a conscious reply'. Cf. *Bergman on Bergman*, p. 82.
37. The original scene takes place in a quarry, but allegedly a shoreline was the 'perfect location' for glaring sunshine. Cf. Peter Cowie, *Ingmar Bergman: A Critical Biography* (London: Martin Secker and Warburg, paperback edn, 1992) p. 113.
38. Cf. *Bergman on Bergman*, p. 87: 'I think I've already told you that for me bright sunshine is charged with anxiety – I wanted everything to be as white as possible; hard, dead and white. Merciless in some way.'
39. A negative was made up from the print, and then a print from that negative. This process was repeated persistently until the graininess of the image disappeared, leaving only the stark contrast of black and white. Cf. Cowie, p. 115.
40. Ibid., p. 114.
41. It is also significant that Bergman should use a Christian reference here, at a moment of humiliation: 'If I've objected strongly to Christianity, it has been because Christianity is deeply branded by a very virulent humiliation motif.' Cf. *Bergman on Bergman*, p. 81.

42. Napier asserts that the stage was seen as antithetical to the Christian world view. Cf. Napier, p. 5. In the (Catholic) Corpus Christi plays disguise was kept to a minimum, and masks were associated with devils.

43. Les Riens are citizens of Ascona, the Swiss town where in *The Face* Albert Emanuel Vogler's Magnetic Theatre once worked 'genuine miracles', and there are parallels between the performers and Vogler, echoed in the name of one of them, Albert Emanuel Sebastian Fisher.

44. Although in *Bergman on Bergman*, p. 240, when describing *The Rite* Bergman refers to Dionys*ius* (my emphasis), the details of the rite seems to relate more to Dionys*us*.

45. Because of the representations of Dionysus's life, also known as Bacchus, he is known as god of wine, who loosens care and inspires music and poetry.

46. Ingmar Bergman, *Images: My Life in Film* (London: Faber and Faber, 1995) p. 175.

47. This Christian ritual is the central act of Christian worship, in which bread and wine are consecrated and consumed as Christ's body and blood to be a memorial of his sacrifice on the cross.

48. Including on some occasions goat sacrifice, or even 'Omophagia' using human victims. Priests imitated the eating of raw flesh.

49. Such rites were linked with the myths of the god. One story tells of Dionysus as an unborn child being rescued from the ashes by his father Zeus, after Hera has jealously consumed Dionysus's mother with lightning. Zeus places the unborn child in his thigh until he is born. As such, in a similar way to Christ, Dionysus appears as god of vegetation, a suffering god, who dies and comes to life again. Another variation on the story is that of Dionysus Zagreus. In this myth, Hera orders the Titans to devour the baby Dionysus, but Athene takes his heart to Zeus, who then burns the Titans. Out of the ashes springs a new race of men with some divine nature. Zeus swallows his son's heart, and Dionysus Zagreus is born.

50. *Bergman on Bergman*, p. 242.

51. Livingston, p. 161.

52. Peter Cowie, *Ingmar Bergman: A Motion Monograph 2/6* (Loughton, Essex: Motion, December 1961) p. 10. I would suggest that his later view is more accurate: 'She [Marie] becomes the portal figure in the drama; the men in *Summer Interlude* are subordinate to her psychological importance.' Cowie (1991) p. 85.

53. *Bergman on Bergman*, p. 54.

54. Ibid., p. 54.

55. An evil power has transformed a group of young maidens into swans, who resume their human form every night. On receiving a crossbow for his 21st birthday, Prince Siegfried pursues the swans to their lake. He catches sight of Odette, the swan princess, as woman and falls in love with her. He decides to announce their betrothal at his 21st birthday ball; this public declaration would break the spell and free Odette from her swan existence. However, when the sorcerer Von Rothbart discovers the plan, he transforms his wicked daughter Odile into Odette's double. Siegfried is taken in, and pledges his love to the imposter. She ridicules him and departs with her father. It is too late, and he has now doomed Odette to her spell for life. They meet up at the lake, where the two of them drown themselves.

3—Female Defiance: Dreams of Another World in *Summer with Monika* and the Early Films

A shorter version of this chapter was published: Laura Hübner, 'Her Defiant Stare: Dreams of Another World in *Summer with Monika*', *Studies in European Cinema*, Vol. 2, Issue 2 (2005) pp. 103–13.

1. As will become clear later in this chapter, Bergman did not always both write and direct these early films, as he tended to do after the 1940s.
2. This particular reading would also complement Marilyn Johns Blackwell's proposal that 'in the pre-trilogy works, not surprisingly the imaginer is male, while in the post-1960 films it is female, with the exception of Johan Borg and Alexander'. Johan Borg is the protagonist in *The Hour of the Wolf* (1966) and Alexander is the boy in *Fanny and Alexander* (1982). Marilyn Johns Blackwell, *Gender and Representation in the Films of Ingmar Bergman* (Columbia: Camden House, 1997) p. 197. However, the suggestion, through the rest of this chapter, that Monika's dreams are central, begins to question this kind of pre/post-trilogy distinction.
3. Cf. Jacques Lacan, 'The Mirror Stage', in *Écrits: A Selection*, translated by A. Sheridan (London: Tavistock, 1977) pp. 1–7.
4. Laura Mulvey, 'Visual Pleasure and Narrative Cinema', *Screen*, Vol. 16, No. 3 (1975) p. 13.
5. Douglas Pye, 'Movies and Point of View', *Movie*, Vol. 36 (2000) p. 9.
6. It was also known as *Man with an Umbrella*.
7. It was released outside Sweden as *Land of Desire/Frustration*.
8. Blackwell, p. 6.
9. Like Carné's films, the location of many of Bergman's early films is a port which, while foregrounding the possibility of escape, is also intensely restricting if access to foreign shores is denied (compare the claustrophobia of *Le Jour se lève*, 1939).
10. All of Bergman's films of the 1940s contain the simplicity underlying the concept of the good protagonist/s, set apart from the corruption of others, that tends to be associated with Italian neo-realism as outlined by Peter Bondanella, *Italian Cinema from Neo-Realism to the Present* (New York: Frederick Ungar Publishing Company, 1983) p. 38.
11. Cf. Stig Björkman, Torsten Manns and Jonas Sima, *Bergman on Bergman: Interviews with Ingmar Bergman*, translated by Paul Britten Austin (New York: Da Capo Press, 1993). Originally published in 1970. First translated into English by Paul Britten Austin, New York: Simon & Schuster, 1973, pp. 32–3.
12. Geoffrey Nowell-Smith, *Visconti* (New York: The Viking Press, 1973) p. 32.
13. *Bergman on Bergman*, p. 33.
14. Ibid., p. 33.
15. In this specific sense, they resemble the femme fatales of more mainstream films of the period such as *Detour* (Edgar G. Ulmer, 1945) or *The Lady from Shanghai* (Orson Welles, 1948).
16. *Bergman on Bergman*, p. 78.
17. Paul Britten Austin, *The Swedes: How They Live and Work* (Devon: David and Charles, 1970) pp. 12–13.

18. Peter Cowie, *Ingmar Bergman: A Critical Biography* (London: Martin Secker & Warburg, 1992) p. 87.
19. However, the delay in Marie's transition is due to the fact that her summer affair with Henrik is cut short by his death, rather than resolved.
20. Robin Wood, *Ingmar Bergman* (London: Studio Vista, 1969) p. 35.
21. This is reminiscent of *A Ship Bound for India*, suggesting that the previous generation, probably alluding to the generation of Bergman's parents, did not (have the opportunity for) escape.
22. Blackwell, p. 197.
23. Jessica Benjamin, *The Bonds of Love* (New York: Pantheon, 1988) p. 5f. Cited in Blackwell, p. 6.
24. Jörn Donner, *The Personal Vision of Ingmar Bergman*, translated by Holger Lundbergh (Bloomington and London: Indiana University Press, 1966) p. 86.
25. Brian McIlroy, *World Cinema 2: Sweden* (London: Flick Books, 1986) p. 72.
26. Bergman directed *The Wild Duck* at the Royal Dramatic Theatre in Stockholm, March 1972.
27. Bergman wrote the music into his screenplays. (Cowie, p. 104). According to Erik Nordgren, the regular composer for Bergman's films, on the journey out to the archipelago, Bergman added the 'music concrète', later broadcast on Danish radio, as he stood 'with two kettle drum sticks and hammered on the piano strings'.
28. Being both figure for identification and object is not necessarily a paradoxical situation, as Jackie Stacey argues ('Desperately Seeking Difference', in *The Sexual Subject: A Screen Reader in Sexuality*, London and NW: Routledge, 1992, p. 256) discussing *Desperately Seeking Susan* and *All About Eve*: 'The rigid distinction between *either* desire *or* identification, so characteristic of psychoanalytic film theory, fails to address the construction of desires which involves a specific interplay of both processes.'
29. Cf. for example, *Bergman on Bergman*, pp. 74–6, discussing their affair, claiming 'I was no little infatuated with Harriet'.
30. Donner, p. 104.
31. The train motif is used similarly in other Bergman films of this time. For instance, *Thirst* depicts a couple's train journey back home to Scandinavia after their holiday in Basle. Chosen as a romantic alternative to flying, the train journey proves to be a lengthy confinement within a claustrophobic compartment, highlighting the great void between the couple.
32. Melvyn Bragg, *The Seventh Seal*, BFI Film Classics (London: British Film Institute, 1993) p. 15.
33. Ibid., p. 15.
34. Ibid., p. 17.
35. Cowie, p. 102.
36. Jim Hillier cites these examples: 'Bergmanorama', in *Godard on Godard* (originally published in *Cahiers*, Vol. 85, July 1958) pp. 75–80, and a review of *Summer with Monika* (originally published in *Arts*, 680, July 1958) pp. 84–5. François Truffaut, 'Bergman's Opus', in *The Films in My Life* (originally published in 1958) pp. 253–7. 'L'Ame au ventre', a review of *Summer Interlude* (*Sommarlek*), *Cahiers*, 84, June 1958, pp. 45–7. Jim Hillier, ed., *Cahiers du Cinéma, The 1950s: Neo-Realism, Hollywood, New Wave* (London: Routledge, 1985) p. 175.
37. Hillier, ed., p. 175.

38. Fereydoun Hoveyda, 'La Première personne du pluriel' ('The First Person Plural'), *Cahiers du Cinema*, 97 (July 1959). Translated by Liz Heron in Hillier, p. 54.
39. Wood, p. 41.
40. Cowie, p. 104.
41. Donner, p. 86.
42. Philip Mosley, *Ingmar Bergman: The Cinema as Mistress* (London/Boston: Marion Boyars, 1981) p. 53.
43. Wood, pp. 42–3.
44. *Bergman on Bergman*, p. 75.

4—Religion, Truth and Symbolism from The *Seventh Seal* to *The Silence*

1. When asked by Stig Björkman if the trilogy was already planned as he made each film, Bergman claimed: 'Not until all three were finished ... It must have been Vilgot Sjöman who first pointed it out to me.' Stig Björkman, Torsten Manns and Jonas Sima, *Bergman on Bergman: Interviews with Ingmar Bergman*, translated by Paul Britten Austin (New York: Da Capo Press, 1993). Originally published in 1970. First translated into English by Paul Britten Austin, New York: Simon & Schuster, 1973, p. 172.
2. Revelations 8:1.
3. Egil Törnqvist, *Between Stage and Screen: Ingmar Bergman Directs* (Amsterdam University Press, 1995) p. 98.
4. Bergman, cited in Steene, ed., *Focus on 'The Seventh Seal'* (Englewood Cliffs, NJ: Prentice-Hall, 1972) pp. 70–1.
5. William Barrett, *Irrational Man*, pp. 24–5, quoted in Charles B. Ketcham, *The Influence of Existentialism on Ingmar Bergman* (Lewiston/Queenston: The Edwin Mellen Press, 1986) p. 59.
6. Note that Bergman claims: 'Then came existentialism – Sartre and Camus. Above all Sartre. Camus came later, with a sort of refined existentialism. I came into contact with it in the theatre, among other things in connection with my production of *Caligula* with Anders Ek at the Gothenburg City Theatre in 1946. But its inner and social contexts largely left me cold.' *Bergman on Bergman*, pp. 12–13.
7. Jean-Paul Sartre, *Existentialism and Humanism* (reprinted in London: Methuen, 2000, original lecture delivered in Paris in 1945) p. 28.
8. Cf. Melvyn Bragg, *The Seventh Seal*, BFI Film Classics (London: British Film Institute, 1993) p. 49.
9. Ketcham, p. 59.
10. Peter Cowie, *Ingmar Bergman* (London: Martin Secker and Warburg, 1982) cited in Bragg, p. 28. The later performance, which was critically acclaimed, was directed 16 September of that year, at the Royal Dramatic Theatre, Stockholm, by Bengt Ekerot, a member of the 40-talisterna, accomplished stage director and Death in the later film.
11. This mirroring is much stronger in the film than in the later published screenplay, where, for example, the knight alone shows compassion to the witch. Ingmar Bergman, *Four Screenplays of Ingmar Bergman*, translated by

Lars Malmström and David Kushner (New York: Simon and Schuster, 1960) p. 147.

12. Törnqvist, p. 100.
13. Ibid., p. 101.
14. Bergman also claimed: 'We decided to make death as a clown ... at the circus, the white clown always frightened us.' G. William Jones, ed., *Talking with Ingmar Bergman* (Dallas: Southern Methodist University Press, 1983) p. 32.
15. The archangel Michael will conquer the dragon (the Devil) and, after the Day of Judgement, God will dwell among humanity. He 'shall wipe away all tears from their eyes, and there shall be no more death, neither sorrow, nor crying, neither shall there be any more pain: for the former things are passed away'. Revelations 21:4.
16. The final vision of Borg's parents across the bay mirrors the student's vision of a paradisiacal Isle of the Dead at the end of August Strindberg's *The Ghost Sonata*.
17. The film is based on a medieval legend and folk song called 'Töre of Vänge's daughters' about the rape and murder of a virgin, Karin, while she is on her way to church. Ulla Isaksson wrote the screenplay.
18. Bergman quoted in Review of *The Four Screenplays of Ingmar Bergman*, *Saturday Review*, 23 December 1961.
19. Birgitta Steene, *Ingmar Bergman* (NY: Twayne Publishers, 1968) p. 65.
20. In the screenplay, the machine's silhouette is described as resembling a giant insect.
21. Robin Wood, *Ingmar Bergman* (London: Studio Vista, 1969) p. 107.
22. Ibid., p. 109.
23. Bergman in Vilgot Sjöman, *Dagbok med Ingmar Bergman* (Stockholm: Norstedts, 1963), a diary kept while Sjöman observed Bergman's shooting of *Winter Light*. Excerpts (English translation) in Göran Palm and Lars Bäckström, *Sweden Writes* (Stockholm: The Swedish Institute, 1965) p. 28.
24. John Coleman, 'Bergman Minus', *New Statesman*, 16 November 1962.
25. *Bergman on Bergman*, pp. 167–8.
26. Tony French, 'Suffering into Ideology: *Through a Glass Darkly*', *CineAction*, Vol. 34 (June 1994) p. 72.
27. Ketcham, p. 127.
28. At an awards interview in Dallas, Bergman again said that he regretted the *deus ex machina* ending of *Through a Glass Darkly*. 'I felt the film stops when the helicopter goes away with the mad girl. But I felt the people needed to have an explanation, to have some sort of contact, to have some moment of something else. So I wrote that last scene, that is *terrible* to me today.' Jones, ed., p. 67.
29. Arthur Gibson, *The Silence of God: Creative Response to the Films of Ingmar Bergman* (NY and London: Harper and Row Publishers, 1964) p. 93.
30. Steene, p. 103.
31. The literal translation 'The Communicants' might seem more apt.
32. Christ's Passion was four hours, according to the sexton.
33. Wood traces visual evidence of alienation from traditional beliefs and customs. As Tomas prepares to leave the schoolroom, a plough horse is led past his large, smart car. The bells of Frostnäs Church are rung by machinery. Electric light has replaced the candles. When one of Märta's pupils tells Tomas that he refuses to be confirmed, a flashy American style comic is

noticeable in the scene. As Tomas and Märta drive to Frostnäs Church, the car is held up at the level crossing by a train pulling huge industrial containers (Wood, p. 111).

34. Ketcham, p. 167.
35. Wood, p. 112.
36. Steene, p. 103.
37. Wood, p. 122.
38. Gibson, p. 102.
39. Ibid., p. 114.
40. Bergman cited in Jones, ed., p. 58.
41. Robert E. Lauder, *God, Death, Art and Love: The Philosophical Vision of Ingmar Bergman* (New Jersey: Paulist Press, 1989) p. 72.
42. Ingmar Bergman, *Images: My Life in Film*, translated by Marianne Ruuth (London: Faber and Faber, 1995) p. 271.
43. When Ester and the concierge are unable to communicate in each other's languages, for instance, and the latter knows no French or German, Ester uses her hands to gesture a refill. The first word that Ester learns in the language is 'casi' for 'hand' emphasizing the importance of touch.
44. *Smiles of a Summer Night* is not a film considered in any depth here because, while religious questions are touched on in the film, they are, arguably, not its major concern.
45. Leslie Mallory, 'The Man who Must Make Films', *Evening Standard*, 5 February 1958.
46. Lennart Nilsson's 'The Screen: I am a Conjuror – Visions at the Box Office' in the American journal *Time*, 14 March 1960, acknowledges the earlier discovery of Bergman in Europe and goes on to claim: 'In the last four years the films of Ingmar Bergman ... almost unknown outside Sweden before 1956, have captured an impressive amount of screentime in more than a dozen countries ... they have carried off the top prizes at the big film festivals and set the turnstiles twirling on the commercial circuits as no Scandinavian film has done since Garbo was a girl.' On 16 March 1960, in 'Sweden Making American publicity', *Variety* claimed that Bergman had 'emerged as the foremost international film-maker'. He had made the front cover of *Time* the week before, and his life and accomplishments had been recorded in *Life*, *Esquire, Saturday Review, Mademoiselle, New York Times, Sunday Magazine*, a three part series in *New York Tribune* and numerous feature articles in other publications.
47. The narrative draws on conventions of journeys of faith reminiscent of, to use British examples, John Bunyan's *The Pilgrim's Progress* or Geoffrey Chaucer's *The Canterbury Tales* with the anti-clericalism of, for example, William Langland's *Piers the Plowman*. The dialogue and characters echo medieval morality plays such as *Everyman*. Törnqvist cites (p. 96) contemporary novels for the historical/epic but modern theme such as Harry Martinson, *Aniara* (1956), Eyvind Johson's *Return to Ithaca* (1953) and Pär Lagerkvist's *Barabbas* (1950). Contemporaneous newspaper reviews made connections with Strindberg's plays such as *Folk Sagas* or *To Damascus*. Birgitta Steene cites George Bernanos's *The Diary of a Country Priest* and the various editions of *Faust*. Links can be made with the 'fortyists', existentialist literature and poetry. *Cahiers du Cinéma* (May 1958) p. 45 ff quotes Kafka,

to make links between Bergman and poetry, roughly translating as 'the chords of the modern poet's lyre are the immense bands of celluloid'.

48. Bragg, p. 19.
49. Hollis Alpert, 'Style is the Director', *Saturday Review*, 23 December 1961.
50. Dilys Powell, Review of *The Seventh Seal*, *Sunday Times*, 9 March 1958.
51. 'The Heart of the Matter – in Medieval Dress – Finest film Sweden has ever made', *Manchester Guardian*, 8 March 1958.
52. Programme for the Academy Cinema where the film was screened in London.
53. William Whitebait, Review of *The Seventh Seal*, *New Statesman*, 8 March 1958.
54. Isabel Quigly, 'Cardboard Pastoral', *Spectator*, 14 March 1958.
55. Ibid.
56. Lloyd Michaels, *The Phantom of the Cinema in Modern Film* (State University of New York Press, 1998) p. 4. Furthermore, as Murray Smith asserts, in order to identify the spectator evaluates characters on the basis of the values they embody. Murray Smith, *Engaging Characters: Fiction, Emotion and the Cinema* (Oxford University Press, 1995) p. 75.
57. Nina Hibbin, 'Ingmar Bergman's *The Seventh Seal* – Y for Shocking', *Daily Worker*, 8 March 1958.
58. Bergman's earlier films clearly differed in terms of style, but Bergman was most generally known for his films of the late 1950s.
59. Penelope Gilliat comments, 'Bergman is still sowing his wild strawberries, and symbolic devices abound'. Penelope Gilliat, Review of *The Virgin Spring*, *Observer*, 4 June 1961. Burgo Partridge asserts, 'Mr Ingmar Bergman's latest film is even more of a parody of *The Magician* [*The Face*] than *The Magician* was of *The Seventh Seal*.' Burgo Partridge, 'Cold Comfort on the Farm', *Time & Tide*, 8 June 1961. The three films were associated together.
60. Note that *So Close to Life* won three prizes at Cannes (May 1958), *Wild Strawberries* won the Golden Bear at Berlin Festival (June 1958) and *The Virgin Spring* won the Academy Award 'Best Foreign Film' (April 1961).
61. Partridge describes, 'the same morbid preoccupation with darkness and dirt and dumbness and evil and sin, the same Hansel and Gretel woods, the same tautly staring faces belonging to the same actors and actresses ... There is one part of his message, and a private personal part, that is not getting through'.
62. *Wild Strawberries* is not a main film in the chain of descent from popularity. However, the film is interested in the characters as individuals only so far as they say something about Isak. Sarah represents the Sarah he once loved (both played by Bibi Andersson). The two lads represent Isak and his brother, as contenders for Sarah's love, and as opposite poles of religion and science.
63. *Towne International Little Cinema*, 16 January 1962.
64. Certain Bergman films that preceded these late 1950s films such as *Waiting Women* focus on a small set of characters. The style was nevertheless heavily schematic with its convoluted flashbacks, themes and motifs.
65. Review of *Through a Glass Darkly*, *Time*, November 1962.
66. W.J. Weatherby, 'Ingmar Bergman's Mirror', *Guardian*, 12 January 1961.
67. John Coleman, 'Bergman Minus', *New Statesman*, 16 November 1962.
68. Ketcham, p. 117.
69. Arthur Knight, Review of *Through a Glass Darkly*, *Saturday Review*, 17 March 1962.

70. Lennart Nilsson 'The Screen: I am a Conjuror – Visions at the Box Office', *Time*, 14 March 1960.
71. 'Darkly', Review of *Through a Glass Darkly*, *The Times*, 16 November 1962.
72. There are inconsistencies within this; the actor who played the hotel caretaker could not learn the language, so made up his own. *Bergman on Bergman*, p. 176.
73. Ibid., p. 184. It is interesting to compare this with an earlier Bergman film *Thirst* (1949), where the couple pass through Berlin just after the war, and starving people are begging at their windows for food. In this film, time and place are very significant.
74. Ibid., p. 185.
75. Note the film's dedication to the Swedish-Estonian pianist Kabi Lareta (Bergman's wife at the time).
76. French, p. 71.
77. *Bergman on Bergman*, p. 181.
78. Ibid., p. 168.
79. Ibid., p. 168. Contemporary newspaper critics also made this connection; *Time* noted 'something reminiscent of Strindberg'.
80. *Strindberg Plays: One*, translated by Michael Meyer (London: Methuen's World Dramatists, 1987) p. 101.
81. Wood, p. 123.
82. Ketcham, p. 211.
83. In retrospect, the comical interlude *Now about These Women* (1964) filmed between *The Silence* and *Persona* would reflexively make these points justifiable, not only with the provocative title, but also with the parody of the critic. A note to the audience, 'these fireworks are not to be read symbolically' follows the thunderous explosion of fireworks accidentally set off around the mansion, resulting in a surreal display into the starry night. The film can be seen as a parody, displaying dissatisfaction with the way that people have been reading the films.

5—*Persona*: Cinema as Mask

1. Birgitta Steene, 'Bergman's *Persona* through a Native Landscape', Lloyd Michaels, ed., *Ingmar Bergman's Persona* (Cambridge University Press, 2000) pp. 38 and 40.
2. Cf., for example, Robin Wood's monograph, *Ingmar Bergman* (London: Studio Vista, 1969) pp. 151–3.
3. Ingmar Bergman, *Images: My Life in Film* (London: Faber and Faber, 1995) p. 54. This theme is also emphasized in the screenplay: 'Alma: I can't bear to hear Karl-Henrik's voice on the telephone. He sounds so artificial. You hear your own voice and ... And you think "Don't I sound false!"', *Persona* and *Shame*, translated by Keith Bradfield (London: Calder & Boyars, 1972) p. 73.
4. Ibid., pp. 59–60.
5. Thomas Elsaesser, 'Reflection and Reality', *Monogram*, Vol. 2 (Summer 1971) p. 7.
6. Marilyn Johns Blackwell, *Persona: The Transcendent Image* (Urbana & Chicago: University of Illinois Press, 1986) p. 2. Barthes's phrase is also applied later by Lloyd Michaels in his introduction to *Persona* in Michaels, ed., p. 18.

7. Peter Wollen, 'Godard and Counter Cinema: *Vent d'Est*', *Afterimage*, Vol. 4 (Autumn 1972) reprinted in Bill Nicholls, ed., *Movies and Methods* (Berkeley: University of California Press, 1976).

8. Penelope Houston, 'It's that Bergman again', in *Spectator*, 29 September 1967.

9. Egil Törnqvist, *Between Stage and Screen: Ingmar Bergman Directs* (Amsterdam University Press, 1995) p. 142.

10. Stig Björkman, Torsten Manns and Jonas Sima, *Bergman on Bergman: Interviews with Ingmar Bergman*, translated by Paul Britten Austin (New York: Da Capo Press, 1993). (Originally published in 1970. First translated into English by Paul Britten Austin, New York: Simon & Schuster, 1973) p. 210.

11. Ibid., p. 59.

12. Ibid., p. 210.

13. Susan Sontag, 'Bergman's Persona', *Styles of Radical Will* (London: Secker & Warburg, 1969) p. 136.

14. Elsaesser, p. 2.

15. Wollen, p. 501.

16. Ibid., p. 502. Brechtian modernism can also be seen in the work of a number of others (such as the collaborative films of Jean-Marie Straub and Danielle Huillet), cf. Martin Walsh, *The Brechtian Aspect of Radical Cinema*, ed. by Keith M. Griffiths (London: BFI Publishing, 1981).

17. Allen, p. 9.

18. Wollen, p. 506.

19. Ibid., p. 506.

20. Elsaesser, p. 8.

21. The narrative is also confused in terms of time and space when there is an abrupt return to Alma dressed as nurse in the hospital immediately *before* the ending of the film at the summerhouse.

22. Sontag claims, 'what counts as new cinema can be recognised ... by the "felt presence of the camera"' (Sontag, p. 139).

23. Cf., for example, Bruce Kawin, 'Mindscreen: Bergman, Godard and First Person Film', *Film and Dreams: An Approach to Bergman*, ed. by Vlada Petric (New York: Redgrave Press, 1981) p. 125: 'At this moment and for the first time, all the masks are off'. Blackwell (p. 79) suggests that when the film 'skips, cracks and burns' the surface of the intimacy 'has begun to crack', the intensity 'too much to bear'. Sontag (p. 140) asserts, 'Bergman's intention ... is the romantic opposite of Brecht's intention of alienating the audience ....'

24. Blackwell, p. 79.

25. Christopher Orr, in Michaels, ed., p. 101.

26. Elsaesser, p. 2.

27. Ibid., p. 3.

28. Sontag, cf. pp. 126–8.

29. Wood, 'Persona Revisited', *CineAction*, Vol. 34 (1994) pp. 59–67. Reprinted, slightly revised, in *Sexual Politics and Narrative Film: Hollywood and Beyond* (New York and Chichester, West Sussex: Columbia University Press, 1998), Part V: 'Women-Oppression and Transgression', pp. 248–61.

30. Note that Wood's 1969 monograph on Bergman is dedicated: 'To Göran Persson, who taught me to think about Bergman.'

31. Göran Persson, 'Bergman's *Persona*: Rites of Spring as a Chamber Play', *CineAction*, Vol. 40 (1996) p. 22. It is interesting that Persson should use

Jungian terms ('individuation') and preoccupations ('rite') here. Jungian psychoanalysis has tended to be applied to Bergman's films (more than Freudian psychoanalysis has), perhaps due to the films' concerns with the mask and the collective unconscious.

32. Persson, p. 23.
33. In fact, the female Oedipus complex (the term 'Electra complex' was soon deemed to be inappropriate by Freud) marks the stage where the girl gives up her wish for a penis and replaces this with a wish for a child, 'and *with that purpose in view* she takes her father as a love object'. Unlike the boy, the girl castration complex prepares for the Oedipus complex, which becomes a 'haven of refuge', and modifies the development of a 'super ego', so that it cannot attain strength and independence. See Sigmund Freud, *The Essentials of Psychoanalysis: The Definitive Collection of Sigmund Freud's Writing*, selected with an introduction and commentaries by Anna Freud (Middlesex: Penguin Books Limited, 1986) p. 409.
34. Wood, 1994, pp. 65–7.
35. World Classics, *Sophocles: Antigone, Oedipus the King, Electra* (Oxford University Press, 1989) p. 134. Sophocles wrote *Electra* in 409 BC.
36. Persson, p. 26.
37. In the screenplay, the situation more closely resembles Wood's interpretation that Alma and Elisabet merge so that Alma is a mask for Elisabet's voice. (*Persona* and *Shame*, p. 91; Elisabet is dressed in Alma's nurse's uniform, pp. 95–7; Alma's repeated monologue about having the baby is spoken in the first person, p. 97; 'Alma hears this voice, speaking on and on through her own mouth, and she stops and tries to avoid Elisabet's eyes.')
38. David Boyd, *Film and the Interpretative Process: A Study of* Blowup, Rashomon, Citizen Kane, 8½, Verigo, Persona (New York: Peter Lang Publishing, 1989) p. 180.
39. This bi-focal shift of vision between seeing the actress and the character relates to the 'spiral' of subjectivity that draws us into *Persona*. John Orr expounds: 'Here resemblance has the double focus, the relationship of subject to subject on screen, and the relationship of star to spectator in the act of viewing ... We see her [Elisabet] for an instant as stage star in the fixed mask of make-up and costume, the mute icon as pure enigma, before she is transformed into sick patient, pale and plain, dethroned. Sister Alma ... is also the one who becomes starstruck by her. So it begins, the vicious spiral of imitation and desire.' John Orr, 'The Screen as Split Subject 1: *Persona's* Legacy', *Contemporary Cinema* (Edinburgh University Press, 1998) p. 72.
40. Richard Allen, *Projecting Illusion: Film Spectatorship and the Impression of Reality* (Cambridge University Press, 1995) p. 129.
41. Christopher Orr in Michaels, ed., p. 94.
42. Erik Hedling, 'Bergman and the Welfare State', *Film International*, Issue 19, Vol. 4, No. 1 (2006) p. 57.
43. Gwendolyn Audrey Foster, 'Feminist Theory and the Performance of Lesbian Desire in *Persona*', in Michaels, ed., p. 132.
44. Various feminist theorists strongly criticized Bergman's sexual politics, for example, Joan Mellen's 'Bergman and Women', in Joan Mellen, *Women and their Sexuality in the New Film* (New York: Horizon Press, 1973) pp. 106–27. This work will be explored further later.

45. Cf. Foster, p. 138 for a more comprehensive discussion of this area.
46. It is *'our* little boy' (my emphasis) in the screenplay, suggesting more of a merging of roles than the film version implies. *Persona* and *Shame*, p. 87.
47. I am resistant to Boyd's argument so far as interpreting Alma love-making to Elisabet's husband as the 'cause' (i.e., sexual triangle) *expected* for their conflict, *belatedly* produced, because this seems like speculation and is no more justified than a different reading. Boyd, p. 181.
48. Lucy Fischer, 'The Lives of Performers: The Actress as Signifier', *Shot/Countershot: Film Tradition and Women's Cinema* (Basingstoke & London: Macmillan Education, 1989 and Princeton, NJ: Princeton University Press, 1989) p. 74.
49. Bergman, p. 54.
50. Cf. Wollen, p. 502.
51. Sontag, p. 144.
52. *Bergman on Bergman*, p. 209.
53. Ibid., p. 209.
54. Cf. Wollen, pp. 503–504.
55. Note that white frames are also used in *The Silence*.
56. Törnqvist, p. 138.
57. *Bergman on Bergman*, p. 199.
58. Persson, p. 23.
59. Note that the boy in *The Silence* also reads Mikhail Lermontov's *A Hero of Our Time* (1840/41).
60. *Bergman on Bergman*, pp. 198–9.
61. Ibid., p. 199.
62. Ibid., p. 199.
63. Persson, p. 31.
64. *Persona* and *Shame*, p. 99.
65. In general the screenplays from the 1950s bear a closer resemblance to the films, whereas after *Persona*, with films such as *The Hour of the Wolf* (1966) or *A Passion* (1968), they tend to be 'story' drafts without dialogue that are to be interpreted by the actors and during production.
66. *Persona and Shame*, p. 59.
67. Similar evolutions are possible between the page and the theatrical stage.
68. Törnqvist, p. 142.
69. Sontag, p. 133.
70. Blackwell, p. 112.
71. *Persona and Shame*, pp. 100–101.
72. Blackwell (p. 113) states that this is Bergman and Sven Nykvist, which seems to be accurate.
73. Ibid., p. 113.

6—Dreams, Fantasies and Nightmare Visions

1. Larry Gross, 'Too Late the Hero: Stanley Kubrick', *Sight and Sound*, Vol. 9, Issue 9 (September 1999) p. 23 (front cover caption '"Eyes Wide Shut": In Your Dreams').
2. Robert T. Eberwein's *Film and the Dream Screen: A Sleep and a Forgetting* (Princeton University Press, 1984) develops a systematic taxonomy of dreams

in film: (1) dreams in films identified as belonging to particular characters, cued by: voice-over, fade, dissolve, superimposition, transition from shot of sleeper; (2) films that manifest 'actual dream screens' of characters, (*Sherlock, Jr., Spellbound, The Temptations of Dr. Antonio, Persona*); (3) films in which cues are withheld or disguised (*8½, Fireworks, City of Women*) or that disclose at the end that they are entirely oneiric structures (*Dead of Night, Belle de Jour, The Discreet Charm of the Bourgeoisie*). Cf. also Eberwein, 'The Filmic Dream and Point of View', *Literature/Film Quarterly*, Vol. 8, No. 3 (1980) pp. 197–203, which praises conventional dream sequences that employ a mixture of subjective shots and objective shots of the dreamer rather than purely subjective shots (*The Lady in the Lake*, 1946).

3. Bergman claims this many times. For example, Bergman, *Images*, translated by Marianne Ruuth (London: Faber and Faber, 1995) p. 22.

4. Cf. *Images*, p. 83. Also, *Four Stories by Ingmar Bergman: The Touch, Cries and Whispers, Hour of the Wolf, A Passion*, translated by Alan Blair (London: Marion Boyars, 1977) p. 63.

5. *Four Stories by Ingmar Bergman*, p. 85. *Cries and Whispers* was originally published in the *New Yorker Magazine*, 1972.

6. Bosley Crowther, Review of *Wild Strawberries*, *New York Times*, 2 June 1959.

7. Philip and Kersti French, *Wild Strawberries*, (London: BFI Publishing, 1995) pp. 62–3.

8. Jympson Harman, 'A New Kind of Film', *Evening News*, 23 October 1958.

9. Cf. for example, Stig Björkman, Torsten Manns and Jonas Sima, *Bergman on Bergman: Interviews with Ingmar Bergman*, translated by Paul Britten Austin (New York: Da Capo Press, 1993) pp. 26, 136.

10. Philip and Kersti French cite letters written by Selma Lagerlöf, 'for years I have carried around in my head a plan to write one of those Christmas stories that Dickens used to write', and a week later, 'if only I could finish my Christmas Carol …'. *Du lär att bli fri: Selma Lagerlöf skriver till Sophie Elkan*, ed. by Ying Toijer-Nillsson (Stockholm: Banners, 1992) pp. 381–2, quoted in French, p. 44.

11. 'Dream Sequences in Swedish Film', *Glasgow Herald*, 25 August 1958.

12. Isabel Quigly, *Daily Mail*, 24 October 1958.

13. Ivan Adams, 'Other Bergman', *Star*, 23 October 1958.

14. Examples of the tradition of cinematic dreams from the German silent movies include, for example, Robert Wiene's *The Cabinet of Dr. Caligari* (1919) and G.W. Pabst's *Secrets of a Soul* (1926).

15. Cf. Allan Hobson and Jacob Zelinger's extended analysis on this in Vlada Petric (ed.) *Film and Dreams: An Approach to Bergman* (New York: Redgrave Publishing Company, 1981) Chapters 4 and 5. Significantly, Hobson claims, 'the imagery is absolutely straightforward in its symbolism', p. 78.

16. Hollis Alpert, 'The Other Bergman', *Saturday Review*, 21 March 1959.

17. 'Melancholy Swedish Journey', *Scotsman*, 25 August 1958.

18. In 'avant-garde' cinema, this idea was more commonplace. See, for example, Maya Deren's *Meshes of the Afternoon* (1943).

19. *Bergman on Bergman*, p. 133.

20. 'Dream Sequences in Swedish Film', *Glasgow Herald*, 25 August 1958.

21. Anthony Lejeune, ed., *The C. A. Lejeune Film Reader* (Manchester: Carcanet, 1991) p. 299.

22. French, p. 43.
23. Maureen Turim, *Flashbacks in Film* (New York and London: Routledge, 1989) pp. 94–8, quoted in French, p. 44.
24. French, p. 69.
25. See, for example, Paul Hammond, ed., *The Shadow and its Shadow: Surrealist Writing on the Cinema* (London: Polygon, 1991).
26. Using similar terms to Baudry (see below), Metz explored the spectator's regressive relationship to filmic representations. Christian Metz, 'The Fiction Film and its Spectators: A Metapsychological Study', translated by Alfred Guzzetti, *New Literary History 8*, August 1976, p. 85.
27. Some of the theory drew on Plato's myth of the cave in *The Republic*, concerning prisoners who, chained to walls within a cave, experienced the world as shadows. Baudry and Frank D. McConnell extended Plato's allegory to consider film viewers. Jean-Louis Baudry, 'The Apparatus' translated by Jean Andrews and Bertrand Augst in *Camera Obscura 1* (Fall 1976) pp. 107–13. Frank D. McConnell, *The Spoken Seen: Film and the Romantic Imagination* (Baltimore: Johns Hopkins University Press, 1975) pp. 88–91.
28. Nick Browne and Bruce McPherson, 'Dream and Photography in a Psychoanalytic film*: Secrets of a Soul*', *Dreamworks*, Vol. 1, No. 1 (Spring 1980) p. 35. *Dreamworks* aimed to assemble latest thinking on dream processes from anthropology, philosophy, psychology and religion. This first (and last) issue, focused on psychoanalysis and the physiological similarities between film and dream processes.
29. Petric, 'Film and Dreams: A Theoretical-Historical Survey', in Petric (ed.).
30. Allan Hobson, 'Dream Images and Substrate: Bergman's Films and the Physiology of Sleep', in Petric (ed.) p. 94. By 1966, observation and dream reports were combined with studies of automated brain processes. Hobson even goes so far as to link *Persona* with Bergman's experiences of vertigo.
31. Marsha Kinder, 'The Penetrating Dream Style of Ingmar Bergman', in Petric (ed.) pp. 57–72.
32. Robin Wood, *Ingmar Bergman* (London: Studio Vista, 1969) p. 159.
33. *Images*, p. 28.
34. T.M. (Tom Milne?), Review of *The Hour of the Wolf*, *Monthly Film Bulletin* (BFI), Vol. 35, No. 415 (August 1968) p. 151.
35. Note the use of the same name as the nurse in *Persona*, perhaps a reminder of interchangeable roles highlighted in *Persona*. Veronica's surname 'Vogler' also echoes Elizabeth Vogler in *Persona*, played by Liv Ullmann, as well as Herr Vogler, the magician, in *The Face*. The name 'Johan Borg' also recalls Isak Borg in *Wild Strawberries*, linking the protagonists' absorption into dream in both films.
36. Banging and voices open the film, with footsteps, laughter and voices as the credits go up, followed by hammering and the 'director's' (Bergman's?) voice shouting 'Silence! Camera!' and then, after the written words 'Svensk Filmindustri', 'Ooyah!'.
37. *Bergman on Bergman*, p. 212.
38. J.P. Telotte, *Dreams of Darkness: Fantasy and the Films of Val Lewton* (Urbana and Chicago: University of Illinois Press, 1985) pp. 1, 5.
39. Noël Carroll, 'Nightmare and the Horror Film: The Symbolic Biology of Fantastic Beings', *Film Quarterly*, Vol. XXXIV, No. 3 (Spring 1981) p. 18.

40. Cf. Carol J. Clover, 'Her Body, Himself: Gender in the Slasher Film', *Fantasy and the Cinema*, ed. by James Donald (London: BFI, 1989) p. 101.
41. Wood, pp. 159–60. Significantly, Wood was writing prolifically about the horror movie, and specifically about Hitchcock as well as about Bergman, during this time.
42. Five years later Sydow would play the Exorcist for the possessed teenage girl. Sydow's persona was similarly adapted in Hollywood for his portrayal of Christ in *The Greatest Story Ever Told* (George Stevens, 1965) seven years after *The Seventh Seal* and *Wild Strawberries*, where his character serves petrol to Isak at what is sometimes taken as 'The Stations of the Cross'.
43. Carroll, p. 19.
44. Ibid., p. 22.
45. The marionette is also a key feature of the horror genre, and critical discourses have made the link with Freud's writings on 'The Uncanny'. Cf. Sigmund Freud, 'The "Uncanny"' in *Art and Literature*, Pelican Freud Library, Vol. 14 (Harmondsworth: Penguin, 1985). Marionettes also figure in a number of Bergman's later films, for example, *From the Life of the Marionettes* (1980) and *Fanny and Alexander* (1982).
46. Bergman directed a film version of Mozart's opera *The Magic Flute* in 1975.
47. *Images*, pp. 35–8.
48. Ibid., p. 106.
49. Wood, p. 165.
50. The lusty wolf in oral, literary, visual and filmic traditions, emerging usually at night and during winter, is an apt symbol for the dangerous, uncivilized or unrepressed side of (human) nature. Associated with fertility and phallic symbolism, it represents birth as well as death. The werewolf – the man who becomes half wolf during the full moon – embodies some of these conflicts.
51. Marsha Kinder, '*From the Life of the Marionettes* to *The Devil's Wanton*: Bergman's creative transformation of a recurring nightmare', *Film Quarterly*, Vol. XXXIV, No. 3 (Spring 1981) p. 28. Significantly, this is juxtaposed with Carroll's article (discussed earlier) on horror and the nightmare.
52. In many versions of the story, the wolf forces the child to eat the grandmother's flesh and drink her blood in a distorted transubstantiation ritual registering the coming of age, but also acting as a warning to deter children from talking to strangers. Variations of *Little Red Riding Hood* can be found in ancient Egyptian, Greek, Roman, Celtic, Teutonic and Native American mythologies, diluted variants of the cannibalism exist in Western stories today.
53. *Bergman on Bergman*, p. 215.
54. Ingmar Bergman, 'Introduction', *The Four Screenplays of Ingmar Bergman*, translated by Lars Malmstrom and David Kushner (New York: Simon and Schuster, 1960) p. xiv. Quoted in Kinder, in *Film Quarterly*, Vol. XXXIV, No. 3 (Spring 1981) p. 28.
55. Kinder, 1981, p. 30.
56. Petric, 'Bergman's Cinematic Treatment of Psychopathic Phenomena', Petric (ed.) p. 158.
57. Note Bergman's claims when discussing *Sawdust and Tinsel* (1953) that his nightmares are bathed in extreme sunlight, 'for me bright sunshine is charged with anxiety', *Bergman on Bergman*, p. 87.

58. This would also relate to Johan's physical attack on Heerbrand in the diary sequence. Heerbrand seems to be the embodiment of one of the drawings Johan introduces to Alma as 'practically harmless ... I think he's homosexual', and who reappears after Johan's story of the boy, and brings him the gun with which he tries to 'kill' Alma.
59. Wood, pp. 165–6.
60. Harry M. Benshof, *Monsters in the Closet: Homosexuality and the Horror Film* (Manchester University Press, 1997) p. 2.
61. Ibid., p. 2.
62. *Bergman on Bergman*, p. 117.
63. Ibid., p. 117.
64. Ibid., p. 220.
65. Kinder, 1981, p. 29.
66. *Bergman on Bergman*, p. 220. Bergman states it was only in *Fanny and Alexander* that he was able to depict the punishment of the young boy in a rational, objective way. *Images*, p. 41.
67. The story refers to Bergman's childhood experiences of being locked in the closet. Cf. Ingmar Bergman, *The Magic Lantern*, translated by Joan Tate (London: Hamish Hamilton, 1988) pp. 8–9. It is cited again in *Images*, pp. 38–41.
68. In the screenplay, there is another story between the story of the punishment and the boy-killing sequence. *Four Stories*, p. 116.
69. The sequence relates to the Freudian notion of dream being an infantile wish, incorporating material from the 'day's residue'.
70. *Summer Interlude* is brought to mind with the diary, and when Alma pulls up the blind at the start of the sequence, suggesting that what follows will be dreamlike. Agnes also pulls up the blind at the start of *Cries and Whispers*.
71. Philip Strick, 'The Hour of the Wolf – Two Views', *Ingmar Bergman: Essays in Criticism*, ed. by Stuart M. Kaminsky (with Joseph F. Hill) (London, Oxford & New York: Oxford University Press, 1975) pp. 275–6.
72. The first sequence is nearly five minutes, the boat sequence is just under three minutes, Johan drawing Alma is just over one minute, his return home is only about 40 seconds.
73. *Four Stories*, p. 103.
74. The other flashbacks in the film are signposted in quite a conventional way with systematic fade-outs (albeit to a striking red) from close-ups on each of the sisters to a significant episode in each of their pasts. While it is possible to question whether they are flashbacks or dreams, for instance, the device itself is unproblematic.
75. *Four Stories*, p. 86.
76. Peter Harcourt 'Ingmar Bergman's "Cries and Whispers": A Discussion', *Queen's Quarterly*, Summer Issue, Vol. LXXXI, No. 2 (1974) p. 250.
77. Deborah Rose Thomas, 'The Color Films of Ingmar Bergman', MA Thesis, Warwick University, September 1978, p. 41.
78. Ibid., p. 44.
79. Ibid., p. 44.
80. Egil Törnqvist, *Between Stage and Screen*, (Amsterdam: Amsterdam University Press, 1995) p. 158.
81. Törnqvist observes a link between *Cries and Whispers* and *The Ghost Sonata*. Anna and the milkmaid both represent altruistic nurturing love and a

willingness to serve. Bergman cast the same actress (Kari Sylwan) in both parts. Törnqvist, p. 147.

82. Terence Davies, *Masterclass: Cries and Whispers*, produced and directed by Mamoun Hassan, presented by Davies with students of the National Film and Television School, Channel Four, 1990.

83. A similar technique is used when Karin goes in and speaks to Agnes.

84. Petric, pp. 164–71.

85. Törnqvist, p. 146.

86. *Images*, p. 96.

87. Ibid., p. 97.

88. Ibid., p. 97.

89. Ibid., p. 101.

90. *Four Stories*, p. 59.

91. Törnqvist, p. 158.

92. In the documentary *Ingmar Bergman – The Magic Lantern*, Bergman claims that this light happened by chance. Produced by Mark Lucas, directed and edited by Jane Thorburn, *An After Image Production*, Channel Four Television, 1988.

93. In 1981, Bergman would direct a double bill of *A Doll's House* and *Miss Julie* (Strindberg) at Residenzteater, Munich, with his play *Scenes from a Marriage* at a theatre across the street on the same night. Furthermore, while Bergman directed plays by Strindberg, Ibsen and Chekhov many times on stage, it is significant that these were particularly part of his schedule around the filming of *Cries and Whispers*. He directed *Three Sisters* in 1978 (Residenzteater, Munich) and *The Ghost Sonata* in 1973 (Royal Dramatic Theatre, Stockholm), and he tackled *A Dream Play* several times over this period: 1963 (television production), 1970 (Royal Dramatic Theatre, Stockholm) and 1977 (Residenzteater, Munich). Bergman's major homage to this play is *Fanny and Alexander* (1982) which refers to *A Dream Play*.

94. *Four Stories*, p. 60.

95. Agnes shows symptoms of cancer of the womb.

96. As P. Adams Sitney argues, the liminal zone between life and death is also suggested in the dawn opening. 'Color and Myth in *Cries and Whispers*', *Film Criticism*, Vol. 13, No. 3 (Spring 1989) p. 39.

97. Törnqvist, p. 156.

98. Peter Harcourt, 'Ingmar Bergman's *Cries and Whispers*', *Queen's Quarterly*, Summer Issue, Vol. LXXXI, No. 2 (1974), pp. 247–57.

99. Ibid., p. 249. Derek Jarman, *Chroma* (London: Century Random House, 1994) p. 32, unpacks the different elements of passion associated with red (love, sex, emotion and death). Also, the splashes of red (Karin's coat, the London bus) against the 'grey' city in the opening sequence of *The Touch* (1971) might be taken to connote both the death of Karin's mother and the passionate affair to come.

100. French, pp. 54–7.

101. Ibid., p. 55.

102. Note also allusions to Swedish artist Carl Larsson, in the dreamlike idyll of the first flashback to Isak's summerhome in the 1890s. As French asserts, Larsson was known for advocating the 'apparent domestic bliss' of his country household at Sundborn in the province of Dalarna, and created the 'national dream' for the perfect furnishing of homes. French, pp. 52–3.

103. Törnqvist, p. 151.
104. Harcourt, p. 254.
105. Thomas, p. 40.
106. Harcourt, p. 256.

7— Conclusion: Celebrating the Illusion

1. It is the longer version of *Fanny and Alexander* meant for television (326 minutes) that will be considered here, rather than the shorter theatrical release for cinema transmission. Bergman claims that he was forced to cut out 'vital parts' for the theatrical release, 'I knew with each cut I reduced the quality of my work.' Ingmar Bergman, *Images: My Life in Film* (London: Faber and Faber, 1995) p. 380.
2. Vergérus is the name given to the perfunctory health official in *The Face* (1958), while Elis Vergérus is the successful architect who catalogues with scientific precision photographs of people in *A Passion* (1968). Andreas Vergérus (Max von Sydow) is the rational businessman husband who contrasts with the more passionate, physical American archaeologist David Kovac (Elliott Gould) in *The Touch* (1970).
3. The lie about being sold to the circus comes directly from Bergman's experience, and his father's disciplining of him is very similar to that of Alexander's by the bishop. Cf. *Images*, p. 11.
4. Bergman's words at a press conference in 1980 also connote the fairytale world, describing the film as 'a huge tapestry filled with masses of color and people, houses and forests, mysterious haunts of caves and grottoes, secrets and night skies', Peter Cowie, *Ingmar Bergman: A Critical Biography* (London: Martin Secker and Warburg, paperback edn, 1992) p. 338. In *Images*, p. 360, Bergman refers to the '2 godfathers' of the film. The first was an illustration from E.T.A. Hoffmann's *The Nutcracker* of two children quivering close together one Christmas Eve, giving him the idea of beginning *Fanny and Alexander* with a Christmas celebration (recalling the reference to E.T.A. Hoffmann's tale of *Coppélia* in *Summer Interlude*). The second was Charles Dickens, with the bishop and his home, the Jew in his boutique of fantasies and the children as victims. *Images*, p. 362.
5. This philosophy is reminiscent of Eva in *Autumn Sonata* (1977) who believes that her son lives beyond the grave, but very close: 'Everything exists side by side, one thing penetrating the other ... In that way there must also be countless realities, not only the reality we perceive with our blunt senses, but a tumult of realities arching above and around each other, inside and outside ... There are no limits.'
6. Jesse Kalin, *The Films of Ingmar Bergman* (Cambridge University Press, 2003) p. 171.
7. John 20:17.
8. Like *Hamlet*, to which the film pays direct tribute, the issue of whether the ghost is 'real' or not is a potentially worthwhile area to pursue.
9. The earlier magic lantern sequence occurs significantly when Alexander is unable to sleep, and he narrates the fairytale that has been boxed with his new present, while projecting the slides before the other children. The story concerns a poor young girl, Arabella, whose mother is dead, and whose

father is 'carousing with loose women'. As Alexander reads, 'What is that terrifying white figure floating on moonbeams? It is my dead mother! It is my mother's ghost!' a cousin creeps up behind Fanny, making her scream. This awakens their parents and brings Oscar rushing in. The magic lantern story is clearly a reference to later events (Oscar's death and Emilie's remarriage) though the reversed gender helps to link both Fanny and Alexander with the vision they will both see.

10. Jof is the travelling performer in *The Seventh Seal*.
11. *Images*, p. 238.
12. Bergman, *The Magic Lantern: An Autobiography*, translated by Joan Tate (London: Hamish Hamilton, 1988) p. 21.
13. The magic lantern refers to Bergman's cinematograph that he obtained from his brother one Christmas in exchange for his 100 tin soldiers. Cf. *The Magic Lantern*, pp. 15–6.
14. Marilyn Johns Blackwell, *Gender and Representation in the Films of Ingmar Bergman* (Columbia: Camden House, 1997) p. 209.
15. Egil Törnqvist, *Between Stage and Screen: Ingmar Bergman Directs* (Amsterdam: Amsterdam University Press, 1995) p. 174. Törnqvist also makes an important point (p. 175) that the application of Fanny's name first in the film's title, despite being younger, is not 'conventional etiquette': 'It is a discreet indication of the women's prominent role in the television series – in contrast to male society's "Adam and Eve"'.
16. Blackwell, p. 209.
17. Note also the prominence of Johan in *The Silence* and the unnamed boy in *Persona*.
18. Blackwell, p. 209.
19. Ibid., p. 211.
20. *Images*, p. 381.
21. Gabriel Pearson and Eric Rhode, 'Cinema of Appearance', 1961, *Sight and Sound: A Fiftieth Anniversary Selection*, ed. by David Wilson (London: Faber and Faber, 1982) p. 144.
22. Ibid., p. 147.
23. Ibid., p. 151.
24. Ibid., p. 150.
25. Ibid., p. 151.
26. J.L. Austin, *How to Do Things with Words*, ed. by Marina Sbisa and J.O. Urmson (Oxford University Press, second edn, 1976). These developments are clearly summarized in Andrew Parker and Eve Kosofsky Sedgwick, eds, *Performativity and Performance* (New York and London: Routledge, 1995) pp. 3–4.
27. Performatives are speech acts or utterances that accomplish, in their very enunciation, an action that generates effects, for example, 'I do' (take this man to be my lawfully wedded husband'). Cf. Parker and Kosofsky Sedgwick, p. 3.
28. Austin, p. 22. Cited in Parker and Kosofsky Sedgwick, p. 3. As Parker and Kosofsky Sedgwick assert, the excluded theatrical leads back to associations of art with the perverted, artificial, unnatural, abnormal, decadent and the diseased depicted in the gay 1890s of Oscar Wilde. Ibid., p. 4.
29. Jacques Derrida, *Margins of Philosophy*, translated by Alan Bass (Chicago: University of Chicago Press, 1982). See, for example, p. 325.
30. Parker and Kosofsky Sedgwick, p. 4.

31. *The Magic Lantern*, p. 61.
32. He also wrote the screenplays for *The Best Intentions* (Bille August, 1991), *Sunday's Children* (Daniel Bergman, 1992), *Private Confessions* (Liv Ullmann, 1996) and *Faithless* (Liv Ullmann, 2000/2001). His work continues in the theatre.
33. Peter Cowie, *Ingmar Bergman: A Critical Biography* (London: Martin Secker and Warburg, 1992) p. 338.
34. Frank Gado, *The Passion of Ingmar Bergman* (Durham, North Carolina: Duke University Press, 1986) p. 496. Bergman left Sweden in voluntary exile in April 1976. The scope of this thesis does not afford a focus on films made in West Germany during this interim period such as *The Serpent's Egg* (1977), *Autumn Sonata* (1978) and *From the Life of the Marionettes* (1980). However, certain elements such as their concerns with dream and the human psyche together with their more illusionist style, suggest that they might offer interesting points of comparison with films discussed in the previous chapter.
35. Cf. Cowie, p. 338 and Gado, p. 495.
36. Cf. Cowie, p. 338.
37. The film is shot only a couple of city blocks from Bergman's grandmother's apartment. The servants resemble those from Bergman's father's parsonage in Stockholm, and Bergman also had a 'lame nursemaid' named Maj. *The Magic Lantern*, p. 20. Bergman (*The Magic Lantern*) describes the grandmother's apartment as a replica of his own grandmother's: the magic lantern (p. 15), iron stove in the hallway (p. 19), uncle Carl (p. 26) and the Esmeralda story (p. 11) are all from Bergman's past.
38. Cf. Gado, p. 497.
39. Robert E. Lauder, *God, Death, Art and Love: The Philosophical Vision of Ingmar Bergman* (New Jersey: Paulist Press, 1989) p. 77.
40. Peter Harcourt, 'Journey into Silence: An aspect of the late films of Ingmar Bergman', *Scandinavian–Canadian Studies*, Vol. 5 (1992) p. 22.
41. The earlier films do not fit so comfortably into these categories, for example, *It Rains on Our Love* (1946), *A Ship Bound for India* (1947), *Prison* (1949), *Waiting Women* (1952) and *Summer with Monika* (1952).
42. Harcourt, p. 20. Kalin (p. 165) also asserts: '*Fanny and Alexander* can be seen as an attempt to restore the filmic vision of the 1950s and finally to overcome the discouragement, and even despair, of the 1960s and 1970s.'
43. Charles B. Ketcham, *The Influence of Existentialism on Ingmar Bergman: An Analysis of the Theological Ideas Shaping a Filmmaker's Art*. Studies in Art and Religious Interpretation, Vol. 6 (Queenston, Ontario/Lewiston, New York: The Edwin Mellen Press, 1986) p. 358.
44. Pauline Kael, 'Wrapping It Up', *The New Yorker*, 13 June 1983, p. 117.
45. Ibid., p. 117.
46. Gado, p. 495.
47. Ibid., p. 496.
48. Ibid., p. 496.
49. Ibid., p. 499.
50. Ibid., p. 500.
51. Ibid., p. 498.
52. Ibid., p. 505.
53. Ibid., p. 498.

54. Ibid., p. 498.
55. Ibid., p. 505.
56. Törnqvist, p. 175.
57. As Parker and Kosofsky Sedgwick argue: 'It is the constitution of a community of witness that takes the marriage; the silence of witness (we don't speak now, we forever hold our peace) that permits it; the bare, negative, potent but undiscretionary speech act of our physical presence – may be even *especially* the presence of those people whom the institution of marriage defines itself by excluding – that ratifies and recruits the legitimacy of its privilege', pp. 10–11.
58. As Parker and Sedgwick point out:, 'Dante speaks of refusal – even refusal through cowardice – as something "great".' Ibid., p. 9.
59. As Elin Diamond explains, 'gender critique refers to the words, gestures, appearances, ideas, and behaviour that dominant culture understands as indices of feminine or masculine identity', Elin Diamond, *Unmaking Mimesis: Essays on Feminism and Theatre* (London and New York: Routledge, 1997) p. 45. Judith Butler extends this argument further, arguing that 'the "body" is itself a construction; ... bodies *come into being* in and through the mark(s) of gender'. Judith Butler, *Gender Trouble: Feminism and the Subversion of Identity* (London, New York: Routledge, 1990) p. 8.
60. Joan Mellen, *Women and Their Sexuality in the New Film* (New York: Horizon Press, 1973) p. 107.
61. Constance Penley, '*Cries and Whispers*', *Movies and Methods*, Vol. 1, ed. by Bill Nichols (Berkley, Los Angeles, London: University of California Press, 1976) p. 206.
62. Ibid., p. 208.
63. Varda Burstyn, '*Cries and Whispers* Reconsidered', *CineAction!*, Double Issue Nos. 3/4 (January 1986) p. 33.
64. Presumably Emilie would play Indra's daughter who sees the world with all its illusions stripped bare.
65. *Fanny and Alexander* is set around 1910 and *A Dream Play* was first published in 1902. Michael Meyer notes that it was not until 17 April 1907 that *A Dream Play* was first performed. Bergman was to stage the play many times, and in 1970 he staged it as a successful chamber play, disposing of elaborate stage directions and exercising considerable cutting. August Strindberg, *Plays Two (The Dance of Death, A Dream Play, The Stronger)*, translated and introduced by Michael Meyer (London: Methuen Drama, 1995) p. 172.
66. The name Gustav Adolf may refer to the eccentric Gustaf IV Adolf (1792–1809), whose anti-Napoleonic policies led Sweden to the brink of ruin and the final loss of Finland (1809).
67. Törnqvist, p. 185.
68. Strindberg, p. 169.
69. Blackwell, p. 37.
70. Cf. for example, C.G. Jung, *Jung on Synchronicity and the Paranormal*, introduced by Roderick Main (London: Routledge, 1997).
71. Erik Hedling, 'Bergman and the Welfare State', in *Film International*, Issue 19, Vol. 4, No. 1 (2006) p. 57.
72. Elizabeth Grosz, *Volatile Bodies: Toward a Corporeal Feminism* (Bloomington and Indianapolis: Indiana University Press, 1994) p. 128.

Bibliography

Adams, Ivan, 'Other Bergman', *Star*, 23 October 1958.

Allen, Richard, *Projecting Illusion: Film Spectatorship and the Impression of Reality* (Cambridge University Press, 1995).

Alpert, Hollis, 'The Other Bergman', *Saturday Review*, 21 March 1959.

Alpert, Hollis, 'Style is the Director', *Saturday Review*, 23 December 1961.

Armes, Roy, *Film and Reality: A Historical Survey* (Middlesex, Maryland, Ontario, Victoria: Pelican Books, 1974).

Austin, Britten, *The Swedes: How they Live and Work* (Devon: David and Charles, 1970).

Austin, J.L., *How to Do Things with Words: The William James Lectures at Harvard University in 1955*, ed. by Marina Sbisa and J.O. Urmson (Oxford University Press, second edn, 1976).

Bakhtin, Mikhail, *Rabelais and His World*, translated by H. Iswolsky (Bloomington: Indiana University Press, 1984).

Bassnett-McGuire, Susan, *Luigi Pirandello: Macmillan Modern Dramatists* (London and Basingstoke: The Macmillan Press, 1983).

Baudry, Jean-Louis, 'The Apparatus', translated by Jean Andrews and Bertrand Augst, *Camera Obscura*, Vol. 1 (Fall 1976) pp. 107–13.

Bazin, André, *What is Cinema?*, Vol. 1, translated by Hugh Gray (Berkeley, Los Angeles & London: University of California Press, 1967).

Benjamin, Jessica, *The Bonds of Love* (New York: Pantheon, 1988).

Benshof, Harry M., *Monsters in the Closet: Homosexuality and the Horror Film* (Manchester University Press, 1997).

Bergan, Ronald and Karney, Robyn, *Foreign Film Guide* (London: Bloomsbury, 1992).

Bergman, Ingmar, *Four Screenplays of Ingmar Bergman*, translated by Lars Malmström and David Kushner (New York: Simon and Schuster, 1960).

Bergman, Ingmar, *Wood Painting: A Morality Play*, translated by Randolph Goodman and Leif Sjöberg. Reprinted in Steene, Birgitta, ed., *Focus on 'The Seventh Seal'* (Englewood Cliffs, NJ: Prentice–Hall, 1972) pp. 159–73.

Bergman, Ingmar, *A Film Trilogy* (London: Calder and Boyars, 1967). Originally published as *En Filmtrilogy* (Stockholm: P. A. Norstedt and Söners Förlag, 1963).

Bergman, Ingmar, *Persona* and *Shame*, translated by Keith Bradfield (New York: Grossman, 1972).

Bergman, Ingmar, *Four Stories by Ingmar Bergman: The Touch, Cries and Whispers, Hour of the Wolf, A Passion*, translated by Alan Blair (London: Marion Boyars, 1977).

Bergman, Ingmar, *Fanny and Alexander*, translated by Alan Blair (London: Penguin, 1982).

Bergman, Ingmar, *The Magic Lantern: An Autobiography*, translated by Joan Tate (London: Hamish Hamilton, 1988). Originally published as *Laterna Magica* (Stockholm: Norstedts Förlag, 1987).

Bergman, Ingmar, *Images: My Life in Film*, translated by Marianne Ruuth (London: Faber and Faber, 1995). Originally published as *Bilder* (Stockholm: Norstedts Förlag, 1990).

Bergom-Larsson, Maria, *Film in Sweden: Ingmar Bergman and Society* (London: The Tantivity Press, 1978).

Binh, N.T., *Ingmar Bergman: le magicien du Nord* (Paris: Gallimard, 1993).

Björkman, Stig, Manns, Torsten and Sima, Jonas, *Bergman on Bergman: Interviews with Ingmar Bergman*, translated by Paul Britten Austin (New York: Da Capo Press, 1993). Originally published in 1970. First translated into English by Paul Britten Austin, New York: Simon & Schuster, 1973.

Bliss, Michael, *Dreams within a Dream: The Films of Peter Weir* (Southern Illinois University Press, 2000).

Bondanella, Peter, *Italian Cinema from Neo-Realism to the Present* (New York: Frederick Ungar Publishing Company, 1983).

Bordwell, David, *Narration in the Fiction Film* (University of Wisconsin Press, 1985).

Bordwell, David and Thompson, Kristin, *Film Art: An Introduction*, fifth edn (New York: McGraw-Hill, 1997).

Boyd, David, *Film and the Interpretative Process: A Study of* Blow Up, Rashomon, Citizen Kane, 8½, Vertigo, Persona (New York: Peter Lang Publishing, 1989).

Bragg, Melvyn, *The Seventh Seal*, BFI Film Classics (London: British Film Institute, 1993).

Brecht, Bertolt, *Brecht on Theatre*, edited and translated by John Willet (London: Methuen Drama, 1964).

Browne, Nick and McPherson, Bruce, 'Dream and Photography in a Psychoanalytic Film: *Secrets of a Soul*', *Dreamworks*, Vol. 1, No. 1 (Spring 1980) pp. 35–40.

Burstyn, Varda, '*Cries and Whispers* Reconsidered', *CineAction!*, Double Issue Nos ¾ (January 1986) pp. 33–45.

Butler, Judith, *Gender Trouble: Feminism and the Subversion of Identity* (London, New York: Routledge, 1990).

Butler, Judith, *Bodies that Matter: On the Discursive Limits of Sex* (New York and London: Routledge, 1993).

Carroll, Noël, 'Nightmare and the Horror Film: The Symbolic Biology of Fantastic Beings', *Film Quarterly*, Vol. XXXIV, No. 3 (Spring 1981) pp. 16–22.

Cohen, J.M. ed., *Tales from E.T.A. Hoffmann*, illustrated by Gavarni (London: The Bodley Head, 1951).

Coleman, John, 'Bergman Minus', *New Statesman*, 16 November 1962.

Collins, Jim, Radner, Hilary and Preacher, Ava, eds, *Film Theory goes to the Movies* (London: Routledge, 1993).

Cowie, Peter, *Ingmar Bergman: A Motion Monograph* (Loughton, Essex: Motion, December 1961).

Cowie, Peter, *Ingmar Bergman: A Critical Biography* (London: Martin Secker and Warburg, 1992).

Crowther, Bosley, Review of *Wild Strawberries*, *New York Times*, 2 June 1959.

'Darkly', Review of *Through a Glass Darkly*, *The Times*, 16 November 1962.

Derrida, Jacques, *Margins of Philosophy*, translated by Alan Bass (Chicago: University of Chicago Press, 1982).

Diamond, Elin, *Unmaking Mimesis: Essays on Feminism and Theatre* (London and New York: Routledge, 1997).

Donald, James, ed., *Fantasy and the Cinema* (London: BFI, 1989).

Donner, Jörn, *The Personal Vision of Ingmar Bergman*, translated by Holger Lundbergh (Bloomington & London: Indiana University Press, 1966).

'Dream Sequences in Swedish Film', *Glasgow Herald*, 25 August 1958.

Dyer, Richard, *Stars* (London: British Film Institute, 1979).

Eberwein, Robert T., 'The Filmic Dream and Point of View', *Literature/Film Quarterly*, Vol. 8, No. 3 (1980) pp. 197–203.

Eberwein, Robert T., *Film and the Dream Screen: A Sleep and a Forgetting* (Princeton University Press, 1984).

Elsaesser, Thomas, 'Reflection and Reality: Narrative Cinema in the Concave Mirror', *Monogram*, Vol. 2 (Summer 1971) pp. 2–9.

Fischer, Lucy, 'The Lives of Performers: The Actress as Signifier', *Shot/Countershot: Film Tradition and Women's Cinema* (Basingstoke & London: MacMillan Education, 1989).

Foucault, Michel, *The Order of Things* (London: Tavistock, 1970).

Foucault, Michel, *The History of Sexuality: An Introduction*, translated by R. Hurly (London: Penguin, 1975).

French, Tony, 'Suffering into Ideology': *Through a Glass Darkly*, *CineAction*, Vol. 34 (June 1994) pp. 68–72.

French, Philip and Kersti, *Wild Strawberries* (London: BFI, 1995).

Freud, Sigmund, *Art and Literature*, Pelican Freud Library, Vol. 14 (Harmondsworth: Penguin, 1985).

Freud, Sigmund, *On Sexuality: Three Essays on the Theory of Sexuality and Other Works*, ed. by James Strachey and Angela Richards, translated by James Strachey (Harmondsworth: Penguin, 1985).

Freud, Sigmund, *The Essentials of Psychoanalysis: The Definitive Collection of Sigmund Freud's Writing* (Middlesex: Penguin Books, 1986).

Freud, Sigmund, *The Interpretation of Dreams*, ed. by Angela Richards, translated by James Strachey (London: Penguin, 1991, previously published by Pelican, 1976, ed. by James Strachey).

Gado, Frank, *The Passion of Ingmar Bergman* (Durham: Duke University Press, 1986).

Gervais, Marc, *Ingmar Bergman: Magician and Prophet* (Montreal and Kingston: McGill-Queen's University Press, 2000).

Gibson, Arthur, *The Silence of God: Creative Response to the Films of Ingmar Bergman* (New York, London: Harper and Row Publishers, 1964).

Gilliat, Penelope, Review of *The Virgin Spring*, *Observer*, 4 June 1961.

Godard, Jean-Luc, 'Bergmanorama', *Cahiers du Cinema*, Vol. 85 (July 1958) pp. 75–80.

Goodman, Lizbeth, with Jane de Gay, eds, *The Routledge Reader in Gender and Performance* (London and New York: Routledge, 1998).

Gross, Larry, 'Too Late the Hero: Stanley Kubrick 1928–99' or '"Eyes Wide Shut": In your dreams', *Sight and Sound*, Vol. 9, Issue 9 (September 1999) pp. 20–3.

Grosz, Elizabeth, *Volatile Bodies: Toward a Corporeal Feminism* (Bloomington and Indianapolis: Indiana University Press, 1994).

Hall, Stuart, ed., *Cultural Representations and Signifying Practices* (London: Sage, 1997).

Hammond, Paul, ed., *The Shadow and its Shadow: Surrealist Writing on the Cinema* (London: Polygon, 1991).

Harcourt, Peter, 'Ingmar Bergman's "Cries and Whispers": A Discussion', *Queen's Quarterly*, Vol. LXXXI, No. 2 (Summer 1974) pp. 247–57.

Harcourt, Peter, *Six European Directors: Eisenstein, Renoir, Buñuel, Bergman, Fellini, Godard* (Middlesex: Penguin Books, 1974).

Harcourt, Peter, 'Journey into Silence: An aspect of the late films of Ingmar Bergman', *Scandinavian–Canadian Studies*, Vol. 5 (1992) pp. 20–8.

Harman, Jympson, 'A New Kind of Film', *Evening News*, 23 October 1958.

Harris, Geraldine, *Staging Femininities: Performance and Performativity* (Manchester and New York: Manchester University Press, 1999).

Hedling, Erik, 'Bergman and the Welfare State', *Film International*, Issue 19, Vol. 4, No. 1 (2006) pp. 50–9.

Helpitt, D. Kidd and Osborne, R., eds, *Crime in the Media* (London: Pluto, 1995).

Hibbin, Nina, 'Ingmar Bergman's *The Seventh Seal* – Y for Shocking', *Daily Worker*, 8 March 1958.

Hillier, Jim, ed., *Cahiers du Cinema, The 1950s: Neo-Realism, Hollywood, New Wave* (London: Routledge, 1985).

Houston, Penelope, 'It's That Bergman Again', *Spectator*, 29 September 1967.

Hübner, Laura, 'Her Defiant Stare: Dreams of Another World in *Summer with Monika*', *Studies in European Cinema*, Vol. 2: Issue 2 (2005) pp. 103–13.

Ibsen, Henrik, *Hedda Gabler and Other Plays* (London: Penguin Books, 1950).

Jarman, Derek, *Chroma* (London: Century Random House, 1994).

Johns Blackwell, Marilyn, *Persona: The Transcendent Image* (Urbana & Chicago: University of Illinois Press, 1986).

Johns Blackwell, Marilyn, *Gender and Representation in the Films of Ingmar Bergman* (Columbia: Camden House, 1997).

Johnstone, Keith, *Impro: Improvisation and the Theatre* (London & Boston: Faber and Faber, 1979).

Jones, G. William, ed., *Talking with Ingmar Bergman* (Dallas: Southern Methodist University Press, 1983).

Jung, C.G., 'The Relations between the Ego and the Unconscious' and 'Two Essays in Analytical Psychology', *The Collected Works of C.G. Jung*, Vol. 77 (Princeton, NJ: Princeton University Press, 1953 and 1966).

Jung, C.G., *Jung on Synchronicity and the Paranormal*, introduced by Roderick Main (London: Routledge, 1997).

Kael, Pauline, 'Wrapping It Up', *New Yorker*, 13 June 1983, p. 117.

Kalin, Jesse, *The Films of Ingmar Bergman* (Cambridge University Press, 2003).

Kaminsky, Stuart M. (with Joseph F. Hill), eds, *Ingmar Bergman: Essays in Criticism* (London, Oxford & New York: Oxford University Press, 1975).

Kennedy, Harlan, 'Whatever happened to Ingmar Bergman', *Film Comment*, Vol. 34, No. 4 (July–August 1998) pp. 64–70.

Ketcham, Charles B., *The Influence of Existentialism on Ingmar Bergman* (Lewiston, Queenston: The Edwin Mellen Press, 1986).

Kinder, Marsha, 'The Adaptation of Cinematic Dream', *Dreamworks*, Vol. 1, No. 1, (Spring 1980) pp. 62–3.

Kinder, Marsha, '*From the Life of the Marionettes* to *The Devil's Wanton*: Bergman's Creative Transformation of a Recurring Nightmare', *Film Quarterly*, Vol. XXXIV, No. 3, (Spring 1981) pp. 23–32.

Knight, Arthur, Review of *Through a Glass Darkly*, in *Saturday Review*, 17 March 1962.

Koskinen, Maaret, *Spel och speglingar. En studie i Ingmar Bergmans filmiska estetik* (Stockholm: Norstedts, 1993).

Koskinen, Maaret, *Ingmar Bergman: "Allting föreställer, ingenting är".* *Filmen och teatern – en tvärestetisk studie* (Stockholm: Nya Doxa, 2001).

Lacan, Jacques, *Écrits: A Selection,* translated by A. Sheridan (London: Tavistock, 1977).

Laing, R.D., *The Divided Self* (Baltimore: Penguin, 1959).

Lauder, Robert E., *God, Death, Art and Love: The Philosophical Vision of Ingmar Bergman* (New Jersey: Paulist Press, 1989).

Lejeune, Anthony, ed., *The C.A. Lejeune Film Reader* (Manchester: Carcanet, 1991).

Lemprière's Classical Dictionary (London, Boston, Melbourne and Henley: Routledge & Kegan Paul, 1984).

Leslie, Mallory, 'The Man who Must Make Films', *Evening Standard,* 5 February 1958.

Livingston, Paisley, *Ingmar Bergman and the Rituals of Art* (Ithaca and London: Cornell University Press, 1982).

Mack, John, ed., *Masks: The Art of Expression* (London: British Museum Press, 1994).

Manera, Claudia, 'Carnivalesque Disruptions and Political Theatre: Plays by Dario Fo, Franca Rame and Caryl Churchill' (unpublished doctoral thesis, University of Reading, 1999).

Maslow, Abraham H., *The Farther Reaches of Human Nature* (New York: Viking, 1971).

McConnell, Frank D., *The Spoken Seen: Film and the Romantic Imagination* (Baltimore: John Hopkins University Press, 1975).

McIlroy, Brian, *World Cinema 2: Sweden* (London: Flick Books, 1986).

'Melancholy Swedish Journey', *Scotsman,* 25 August 1958.

Mellen, Joan, *Women and Their Sexuality in the New Film* (New York: Horizon Press, 1973).

Metz, Christian, 'The Fiction Film and its Spectators: A Metaphysical Study', translated by Alfred Guzzetti, *New Literary History,* Vol. 8 (August 1976) p. 85.

Michaels, Lloyd, *The Phantom of the Cinema in Modern Film* (State University of New York Press, 1998).

Michaels, Lloyd, ed., *Ingmar Bergman's 'Persona'* (Cambridge & New York: Cambridge University Press, 2000).

Milne, Tom, Review of *The Virgin Spring,* in *Time & Tide,* 15 January 1961.

Milne, Tom, Review of *The Hour of the Wolf, Monthly Film Bulletin* (BFI) Vol. 35, No. 415 (August 1968) p. 151.

Monte, Christopher F., *Beneath the Mask: An Introduction to Theories of Personality* (Saunders College, USA: The Dryden Press, fourth edn, 1991).

Mosley, Philip, *Ingmar Bergman: The Cinema as Mistress* (London, Boston: Marion Boyars, 1981).

Mulvey, Laura, 'Visual Pleasure and Narrative Cinema' (originally published in *Screen,* Vol. 16, No. 3, 1975) and 'Afterthoughts on "Visual Pleasure and Narrative Cinema", inspired by King Vidor's *Duel in the Sun* (1946)', *Visual and Other Pleasures* (Bloomington: Indiana University Press, 1989).

Napier, A. David, *Transformation and Paradox* (London & California: University of California Press, 1986).

Nicholls, Bill, ed., *Movies and Methods* (Berkeley: University of California Press, 1976).

Nilsson, Lennart, 'The Screen: I am a Conjuror – Visions at the Box Office', *Time,* 14 March 1960.

Nowell-Smith, Geoffrey, *Visconti* (New York: The Viking Press, 1973; originally published London: Secker and Warburg, 1967).

Odell, Colin and Le Blanc, Michelle, *Horror Films* (Harpenden, Herts: Pocket Essentials, 2001).

Orr, John, 'The Screen as Split Subject 1: *Persona*'s Legacy', *Contemporary Cinema* (Edinburgh University Press, 1998).

Ovid, *Metamorphoses* (London: Penguin Books, 1955).

Palm, Göran and Bäckström, Lars, *Sweden Writes* (Stockholm: The Swedish Institute, 1965).

Parker, Andrew and Kosofsky Sedgwick, Eve, eds, *Performativity and Performance* (New York and London: Routledge, 1995).

Partridge, Burgo, 'Cold Comfort on the Farm', *Time & Tide*, 8 June 1961.

Pearson, Gabriel and Rhode, Eric, 'Cinema of Appearance', 1961, *Sight and Sound: A Fiftieth Anniversary Selection*, ed. by David Wilson (London: Faber and Faber, 1982).

Penley, Constance, *Cries and Whispers*, in *Movies and Methods*, Vol. 1, ed. by Bill Nichols (Berkley, Los Angeles, London: University of California Press, 1976) pp. 204–8.

Persson, Göran, 'Bergman's *Persona*: Rites of Spring as a Chamber Play', *CineAction*, Vol. 40 (1996) pp. 22–31.

Petric, Vlada, ed., *Film and Dreams: An Approach to Bergman* (New York: Redgrave Press, 1981).

Pirandello, Luigi, *Diana and Tuda*, translated by Marta Abba (London: Samuel French, 1950).

Powell, Dilys, '*The Seventh Seal*' Review, *Sunday Times*, 9 March 1958.

Pye, Douglas, 'Movies and Point of View', *Movie*, Vol. 36 (2000).

Quigly, Isabel, 'Cardboard Pastoral', *Spectator*, 14 March 1958.

Quigly, Isabel, '*The Seventh Seal*' Review, *Daily Mail*, 24 October 1958.

Quigly, Isabel, 'The Light that Never was', *Spectator*, 9 June 1961.

Review of *The Four Screenplays of Ingmar Bergman*, in *Saturday Review*, 23 December 1961.

Review of *Through a Glass Darkly*, *Time*, 16 November 1962.

Robinson, David, *Das Cabinet Des Dr. Caligari* (London: British Film Institute, 1997).

Sartre, Jean-Paul, *Existentialism and Humanism* (London: Methuen, 2000).

Sitney, P. Adams, 'Color and Myth in *Cries and Whispers*', *Film Criticism*, Vol. 13, No. 3 (Spring 1989) pp. 37–41.

Sjöman, Vilgot, *Dagbok med Ingmar Bergman* (Stockholm: Norstedts, 1963).

Smelik, Anneke, *And the Mirror Cracked: Feminist Cinema and Film Theory* (Basingstoke & New York: Palgrave, 2001, first edn, 1998).

Smith, Murray, *Engaging Characters: Fiction, Emotion and the Cinema* (Oxford & New York: Oxford University Press, 1995).

Sontag, Susan, *Styles of Radical Will* (London: Secker & Warburg, 1969).

Stacey, Jackie, 'Desperately Seeking Difference', in *The Sexual Subject: A Screen Reader in Sexuality* (London: Routledge, 1992).

Steene, Birgitta, *Ingmar Bergman* (New York: Twayne Publishers, 1968).

Steene, Birgitta, ed., *Focus on 'The Seventh Seal'* (Englewood Cliffs, NJ: Prentice-Hall, 1972).

Steene, Birgitta, *Ingmar Bergman: A Reference Guide* (Amsterdam University Press, 2005).

Strindberg, August, *Strindberg Plays: One*, translated by Michael Meyer (London: Methuen Drama, 1987). These translations first published in Great Britain in 1964 by Secker & Warburg. First published as a Methuen paperback in this revised edition in 1976 by Eyre Methuen.

Strindberg, August, *Strindberg Plays: Two*, translated by Michael Meyer (London: Methuen Drama, 1995). These translations first published in Great Britain in 1964 by Secker & Warburg. This collection first published as a paperback original in Great Britain in 1982 by Methuen London, reprinted in this corrected edition in 1991 (twice) by Methuen Drama.

'Sweden Making American publicity', in *Variety*, 16 March 1960.

Telotte, J.P., *Dreams of Darkness: Fantasy and the Films of Val Lewton* (Urbana and Chicago: University of Illinois Press, 1985).

'The Heart of the Matter – in Medieval Dress – Finest Film Sweden has Ever Made', *Manchester Guardian*, 8 March 1958.

Thomas, Deborah Rose, 'The Color Films of Ingmar Bergman' (unpublished master's thesis, University of Warwick, 1978).

Thomson, David, *A Biographical Dictionary of Film* (London: André Deutsch, 1995). Originally published as *A Biographical Dictionary of the Cinema* (Martin Secker and Warburg, 1975).

Todorov, Tzvetan, *The Fantastic: A Structural Approach to a Literary Genre*, translated by Richard Howard (Ithaca and New York: Cornell University Press, 1975). Originally published in French, *Introduction à la littérature fantastique* (Editions du Seuil, 1970).

Törnqvist, Egil, *Between Stage and Screen: Ingmar Bergman Directs* (Amsterdam University Press, 1995).

Turim, Maureen, *Flashbacks in Film* (New York and London: Routledge, 1989).

Turkle, Sherry, *Life on the Screen: Identity in the Age of the Internet* (London: Phoenix, 1997; originally published New York: Simon and Schuster, 1995).

Turner, Victor, *From Ritual to Theatre* (New York: Performing Arts Journal Publications, 1982).

Walsh, Martin, *The Brechtian Aspect of Radical Cinema*, ed. by Keith M. Griffiths (London: BFI, 1981).

Weatherby, W.J., 'Ingmar Bergman's Mirror', *Guardian*, 12 January 1961.

Whitebait, William, Review of *The Seventh Seal*, *New Statesman*, 8 March 1958.

Wilson, David, Review of *Persona*, in *Guardian*, 20 September 1967.

Wollen, Peter, 'Godard and Counter Cinema: *Vent d'Est*', *Afterimage*, Vol. 4 (Autumn, 1972).

Wood, Robin, *Ingmar Bergman* (London: Studio Vista, 1969).

Wood, Robin, '*Persona* Revisited', *CineAction*, Vol. 34 (1994) pp. 59–67.

Zucker, Carole, '"Sweetest Tongue has Sharpest Tooth" the dangers of dreaming in Neil Jordan's *The Company of Wolves*', *Literature/Film Quarterly*, Vol. 28, No. 1 (2000) pp. 66–70.

Other Sources

Coppélia (1994) performed by the Lyon Opera Ballet, choreographed by Maguy Marin, directed and produced by Thomas Grimm, music by Léo Delibes, 'Summer Dance' Series, BBC 2, RM Arts.

Ingmar Bergman Complete: *Bergman and the Cinema, Bergman and the Theatre, Bergman and Fårö Island* (2004) produced and directed by Marie Nyreröd, Sveriges Television and Svensk Filmindustri.

Ingmar Bergman Face to Face (www.ingmarbergman.se).

Ingmar Bergman – The Director (1988) produced by Alan Horrox, directed by Michael Winterbottom, a Thames Television Production for Channel Four in association with Swedish Television 2, Svensk Filmindustri, Die Zeit TV GMBH, TPI Trebitsh Produktion International GMBH.

Ingmar Bergman – The Magic Lantern (1988) produced by Mark Lucas, directed and edited by Jane Thorburn, *An After Image Production*, Channel Four Television.

Masterclass: Cries and Whispers (1990) produced and directed by Mamoun Hassan, presented by Terence Davies with students of the National Film and Television School, A Third Eye Production for Channel Four.

Filmography

Two film titles are given when different titles were used for American and British releases. The British title appears first, followed by a slash. In a few instances, when the film was never formally released in the United States, the first title is ostensibly more common in both territories and the second (preceded by an 'or') is an American alternative.

Directed by Ingmar Bergman unless otherwise stated:

1944
Frenzy/Torment (Hets)
Director: Alf Sjöberg, Assistant Director: Ingmar Bergman. Screenplay: Ingmar Bergman and Alf Sjöberg.

1945
Crisis (Kris)
Screenplay: Ingmar Bergman, adapted from Leck Fischer's play *Moderdyret* (*A Mother's Heart*).

1946
It Rains on Our Love or *Man with an Umbrella (Det regnar på vår kärlek)*
Screenplay: Ingmar Bergman and Herbert Grevenius, adapted from Oscar Braathen's play *Bra mennesker (Good People)*.

1947
Woman without a Face (Kvinna utan ansikte)
Director: Gustaf Molander. Screenplay: Ingmar Bergman and Gustaf Molander.

1947
A Ship Bound for India or *The Land of Desire (Skepp til Indialand)*
Screenplay: Ingmar Bergman, based on Martin Söderhjelm's play.

1947
Music in Darkness/Night is my Future (Musik I mörker)
Screenplay: Dagmar Edqvist, based on her novel.

1948

Port of Call (Hamnstad)
Screenplay: Ingmar Bergman and Olle Länsberg, based on Länsberg's story *The Gold and the Walls*.

1948

Eva
Director: Gustaf Molander. Screenplay: Ingmar Bergman and Gustaf Molander, based on Bergman's short film *The Trumpet Player and Our Lord*.

1948

Prison/The Devil's Wanton (Fänglese)
Screenplay: Ingmar Bergman.

1949

Thirst/Three Strange Loves/(Törst)
Screenplay: Herbert Grevenius, based on a collection of short stories by Birgit Tengroth.

1949

To Joy (Till glädje)
Screenplay: Ingmar Bergman.

1950

Summer Interlude/Illicit Interlude (Sommarlek)
Screenplay: Ingmar Bergman and Herbert Grevenius, based on Bergman's story *Mari*.

1950

This can't Happen Here or *High Tension (Sånt händer inte här)*
Screenplay: Herbert Grevenius, based on the novel *During Twelve Hours* by Peter Valentin (Waldemar Brøgger).

1950

Divorced (Frånskild)
Director: Gustaf Molander. Screenplay: Ingmar Bergman and Herbert Grevenius.

1952

Waiting Women/Secrets of Women (Kvinnors väntan)
Screenplay: Ingmar Bergman.

1952

Summer with Monika/Monika (Sommaren med Monika)
Screenplay: Ingmar Bergman and Per Anders Fogelström, based on Fogelström's novel.

1953

Sawdust and Tinsel/The Naked Night (Gycklarna afton)
Screenplay: Ingmar Bergman.

1953

A Lesson in Love (En lektion i kärlek)
Screenplay: Ingmar Bergman.

1954/55

Journey into Autumn/Dreams (Kvinnodröm)
Screenplay: Ingmar Bergman.

1955

Smiles of a Summer Night (Sommernattens leende)
Screenplay: Ingmar Bergman.

1956

Last Couple Out (Sista Paret Ut)
Screenplay: Ingmar Bergman.

1956

The Seventh Seal (Det sjunde inseglet)
Screenplay: Ingmar Bergman, based on his play *Wood Painting*.

1957

Wild Strawberries (Smultronstället)
Screenplay: Ingmar Bergman.

1957

So Close to Life/Brink of Life (Nära livet)
Screenplay: Ulla Isaksson, based on her short stories *The Friendly and Dignified* and *The Immovable*.

1958

The Face/The Magician (Ansiktet)
Screenplay: Ingmar Bergman.

1959

The Virgin Spring (Jungfrukällan)
Screenplay: Ulla Isaksson, based on the ballad Töre's Daughter in Wänge.

1959/60

The Devil's Eye (Djävulens öga)
Screenplay: Ingmar Bergman, based on Oluf Bang's radio play *Don Juan Returns*.

1960

Through a Glass Darkly (*Såsom I en spegel*)
Screenplay: Ingmar Bergman.

1961

The Pleasure Garden (Lustgården)
Director: Alf Kjellin. Screenplay: 'Buntel Eriksson' (Ingmar Bergman and Erland Josephson).

1961/62

Winter Light (Nattvardsgästerna)
Screenplay: Ingmar Bergman.

1963

The Silence (Tystnaden)
Screenplay: Ingmar Bergman.

1963

All These Women/Now about These Women (För att inte tala om alla dessa kvinnor)
Screenplay: Ingmar Bergman and Erland Josephson.

1963/65

Daniel
An episode in the collective film *Stimulantia*. Screenplay, cinematography: Ingmar Bergman.

1965

Persona
Screenplay: Ingmar Bergman.

1966

Hour of the Wolf (Vargtimmen)
Screenplay: Ingmar Bergman.

1967

The Shame/Shame (Skammen)
Screenplay: Ingmar Bergman.

1967

The Rite/The Ritual (Riten)
Screenplay: Ingmar Bergman. TV: March 25, 1969.

1968

A Passion/The Passion of Anna (En passion)
Screenplay: Ingmar Bergman.

1969

The Fårö Document 1969 (Fårödokument 1969)
Reporter: Ingmar Bergman. TV: January 1, 1970.

1969/70

The Reservation (Reservatet)
Director: Jan Molander. Screenplay: Ingmar Bergman.

1970

The Touch (Beröringen)
Screenplay: Ingmar Bergman.

1971

Cries and Whispers (Viskningar och rop)
Screenplay: Ingmar Bergman.

1972

Scenes from a Marriage (Scener ur err äktenskap)
Screenplay: Ingmar Bergman. TV series/Feature film.

1974

The Magic Flute (Tröllfojten)
Screenplay: Ingmar Bergman, based on Mozart's opera *Die Zauberflöte*.

1975

Face to Face (Ansikte mot ansikte)
Screenplay: Ingmar Bergman.

1976

The Serpent's Egg (Ormens ägg; Das Schlagenei)
Screenplay: Ingmar Bergman.

1977

Autumn Sonata (Höstsonaten; Herbstsonate)
Screenplay: Ingmar Bergman.

1977/79

The Fårö Document 1979 (Fårödokument 1979)
TV: December 24, 1979.

1979/80

From the Life of the Marionettes (Ur Marionetternas liv; Aus dem Leben der Marionetten)
Screenplay: Ingmar Bergman.

1981/82

Fanny and Alexander (Fanny och Alexander)
Screenplay: Ingmar Bergman. Theatrical: 17 December 1983, at Astoria, 197 minutes; and TV in four parts: 17 December 1983 at Grand 2, 312 minutes.

1984

After the Rehearsal (Efter repetitionen)
Screenplay: Ingmar Bergman. TV Movie.

1986

The Blessed Ones (De två saliga)
Screenplay: Ulla Isaksson. TV Movie.

Karin's Face (Karins ansikte)
Screenplay: Ingmar Bergman.

1991

The Best Intentions (Den goda viljan)
Director: Bille August. Screenplay: Ingmar Bergman. TV series/Feature film.

1992

Sunday's Children (Söndagsbarn)
Director: Daniel Bergman. Screenplay: Ingmar Bergman.

1996

Private Confessions (Enskilda samtal)
Director: Liv Ullmann. Screenplay: Ingmar Bergman. TV Movie.

1997

In the Presence of a Clown (Larmar och gör sig till)
Screenplay: Ingmar Bergman. TV Movie.

2000

Faithless (Trolösa)
Director: Liv Ullmann. Screenplay: Ingmar Bergman. TV Movie.

2003

Saraband
Screenplay: Ingmar Bergman. TV Movie.

Index